HESS

Jointly written by the same authors:

DOCTOR GOEBBELS (1959)
HERMANN GORING (1962)
THE JULY PLOT (1964)
HEINRICH HIMMLER (1965)
THE INCOMPARABLE CRIME (1967)
THE CANARIS CONSPIRACY (1969)
THE GERMAN CINEMA (1971)

Roger Manvell and Heinrich Fraenkel

HESS

A BIOGRAPHY

Drake Publishers Inc   New York

B
N586m

ISBN 0–87749–428–2
LCCCN 72–10506

Published in 1973 by
Drake Publishers Inc
381 Park Avenue South
New York, N.Y., 10016

Printed in Great Britain

CONTENTS

ILLUSTRATIONS

Between pages 128 *and* 129

SOURCES

1, 2, 3, 4, 6, 8, 11—Wolf Rüdiger Hess. 5—Fox Photos Ltd. 7, 9—*Radio Times* Hulton Picture Library. 10, 12, 13—United Press International (UK) Ltd. 14—Press Association Ltd.

ACKNOWLEDGEMENTS

The authors would like to acknowledge especially the information they have received during the preparation of this book from Wolf Rüdiger Hess, son of Rudolf Hess, with whom they had frequent meetings both in London and in Germany, and Frau Ilse Hess, whom Heinrich Fraenkel visited in Hindelang in the Allgäu. We are indebted to them for permission to quote from Hess's letters written from England, Nuremberg and Spandau.

Others who have helped (either in interview, or by correspondence, or both) include Dr Gerhard Klopfer, Under-Secretary of State in the Hess Ministry, Heinrich Heim, one of Hess's senior officials, and Hildegard Fath, Hess's former secretary; also Dr Helmut Sündermann, Alfred Leitgen, Hans Streck, Dr Ernst Hanfstaengl, Adolf Galland, Karl Bodenschatz, and Dr Heinz Haushofer. Since their release, Albert Speer and Baldur von Schirach have kindly helped us to reconstruct the life of Hess, as well as their own, in Spandau. Prof. Bürger-Prinz, the eminent psychiatrist who has made a special study of Hess, and Dr Alfred Seidl, Hess's advocate, have also answered our questions.

In Britain, we are specially grateful to his Grace the Duke of Hamilton for information connected with Hess's flight to Britain and the subsequent interviews he had with him.

As in our previous books, we owe much to the help we have received from the officers of the archives which specialize in the history of the Nazi period, and express our debt in particular to Dr H. Hoch of the Institut für Zeitgeschichte at Munich, Dr H. Boberach and Frl Kinder of the Bundesarchiv in Koblenz, and to the librarians of the Wiener Library in London. We are grateful to Dr A. J. P. Taylor for providing us with the material from the Beaverbrook Library which appears in Appendix 3.

We should like to thank the copyright owners for permission to reprint passages from the following copyright material: Konrad Heiden, *Der Führer* (Gollancz); Adolf Hitler, *Mein Kampf* (Jarrolds); Kurt Lüdecke, *I Knew Hitler* (Jarrolds); J. R. Rees, *The Case of Rudolf Hess* (Heinemann); Fritz Thyssen, *I Paid Hitler* (Hodder & Stoughton); Otto Dietrich, *The Hitler I Knew* (Methuen); Ernst

9

ACKNOWLEDGEMENTS

Hanfstaengl, *Hitler - the Missing Years* (Eyre & Spottiswoode); William Shirer, *Berlin Diary* (Knopf, New York); Sir Nevile Henderson, *Failure of a Mission* (Hodder & Stoughton); James Leasor, *The Uninvited Envoy* (Allen & Unwin); William Dodd, *Ambassador Dodd's Diary* (Gollancz); Felix Kersten, *The Kersten Memoirs* (Hutchinson); Sir Ivone Kirkpatrick, *The Inner Circle* (Macmillan); Paul Schmidt, *Hitler's Interpreter* (Heinemann); Winston Churchill, *The Grand Alliance;* Hans Frank, *Im Angesicht des Galgens* (Beck Verlag, Munich); Rudolf Semmler, *Goebbels, The Man Next to Hitler* (Westhouse); G. M. Gilbert, *Nuremberg Diary* (Eyre & Spottiswoode); *Ciano's Diary 1939-43*, ed. Malcolm Muggeridge (Heinemann).

R.M. and H.F.

INTRODUCTION

It has been our aim in this biography to be as objective as possible about Rudolf Hess and his close ties with Hitler and with Nazi policy and practice. We believe that an objective approach is the only proper one in endeavouring to understand and interpret the characters of the Nazi leaders twenty-five years after the terrible events they precipitated in Europe.

It is quite useless, and even dangerous, to dismiss them as monsters and perverts, as if we, who consider ourselves 'normal', could never have been involved had we been there at the time. We need to understand why intelligent human beings came to believe and act in the way the Nazis led the Germans to do. We have written previously about Goebbels, Göring and Himmler, subjecting them to the same kind of scrutiny as we here apply to Hess.

The case of Hess is deeply linked with the Russian hold on Berlin. This unusually spacious prison designed to hold over six hundred captives in strict security now holds this one, aged prisoner. He is guarded by the same contingent of international warders and the same relays of soldiers as if all the group of high-ranking Nazi prisoners were still there. But, one by one, they have been released – Neurath in 1954 after serving seven years of his fifteen-year sentence; Raeder in 1955, his life sentence remitted when he reached seventy-nine years of age; Doenitz in 1956; Funk in 1957, his life sentence remitted; Speer and Schirach in 1966, their twenty-year sentences completed. Some of them have testified that Hess, proud and withdrawn, has for long been completely subdued to his life of confinement. Yet they, many of them no less guilty than he, and perhaps in certain cases more so because of what they actually did, have served their various terms of imprisonment and have been released. Hess, the only one among them to have made a bold and serious bid for peace with Britain in the midst of war, remains a prisoner.

We are well aware that there are solid reasons for this. Hess's bid for peace with Britain was made in full knowledge that there was soon to be war between Germany and the Soviet Union. If he could not make Britain an active ally of Germany in this onslaught (a hope always at the back of the minds of the Nazi leadership), then at least he thought he could neutralize her, and so save his country the burden of conducting a war on two fronts. None of the Nazi leaders, from Hitler outwards, had wanted war with Britain; they had wanted her peaceful acquiescence, along with that of France, while they consolidated their powers in the areas they held to be their legitimate sphere of interest to the east of the German borders as determined by the Treaty of Versailles. As they saw it, Britain was quite unwarrantably intruding into areas outside her rightful regional interests when she finally went to war over the German invasion of Poland. What concern of either Britain or France, they thought, were these eastern areas of Europe?

All this Hess accepted without question as he planned his flight to Britain. And it is precisely this which determines his absolute guilt in the eyes of the Soviet Union. For her, his mission was a powerful, anti-Soviet move. That he signed decrees which helped to initiate the persecution of the Jewish and Polish peoples matters little enough to the Russians. It was his violent anti-Russian attitude which condemned him in their eyes, as it still does today. They wanted his execution at the Nuremberg trial, but their pressure was resisted, and they were overruled. Hess was condemned to life imprisonment, and life imprisonment is what the Russians are determined he shall endure. In this they have for long been opposed by the American, British and French authorities; these would have agreed to the release of Hess during the 1960s.

Spandau prison lies in the British zone of Berlin, and is in a sense like diplomatic territory to which each of the occupying powers has right of entry in its turn. No peace has yet been signed with Germany, though the war ended over a quarter of a century ago. The status of Berlin, deep in the territory of East Germany, the German Democratic Republic, remains a matter of dispute, of occasional blockade, and of passionate national and political feeling. It is unthinkable in the circumstances for the Russians to relinquish their foothold in the prison, unless some very great and permanent advantage could be negotiated in return. But even they would find it difficult to justify mounting guard on a prison entirely devoid of prisoners. So long as Hess remains inside, there is no occasion to face the need for changes of this kind. Anyway, they have stated that after Hess's death they would still insist on Spandau prison being maintained as a symbol of the Berlin Four Power Statute.

It has been suggested Hess should be released while one or other of the Western Powers have charge of him in Spandau, and the matter was still further pressed during the brief period he was brought from prison to a British military hospital at Christmas in 1969. But to take unilateral action in this manner would be to precipitate a major crises in what continues to be a difficult and delicate situation of great importance to the continued peace of Europe, and none of the Powers would risk such an action for the sake of this sick old man who whiles away his time with books, gramophone records, and cups of instant coffee. Too old any longer to work in the prison garden, he is sitting out his time until one day death, if not the Russian authorities, releases him.

His only hope for release lies in some wholesale, negotiated deal between the Russians, their Western partners, and the Germans. The fate of Hess ranks as the merest detail in these far greater considerations, at least from the Russian point of view. However it may turn out, Hess remains a solitary and always dramatic figure. There is no need to waste unnecessary sentiment upon him. He would be the last to want this. But the feelings of both his wife and his son should surely be kept in mind, and they are doing all that they legitimately can to secure his release so that the family can be reunited.

There can be little doubt Hess still believes in the régime to which he devoted his entire active life, and in the Leader whom he venerated, and no doubt still venerates, though he is not permitted to speak of him so long as he remains in prison. There is even doubt that he himself wants to be released. He has never said so. But his wife, now aged seventy, and his only son campaign ceaselessly to have his liberty restored, while people of good-will everywhere, both inside and outside Germany, feel he should spend his last years with his family, for their sake if not for his.

As for Spandau, enough is now enough. The time for mere hot-blooded vengeance has long passed, and that for simple, human justice came long ago. Hess should be released.

R.M. and H.F.

HESS

1

HITLER'S SHADOW

IT IS one of the more interesting sidelights on Hitler's personality that his power over men and women transcended all the barriers and prejudices of class. Among the principal leaders of the Nazi Party Goebbels was an intellectual of working-class origin from the Ruhr; Göring, it might be claimed, was a 'gentleman'—his father had been in the colonial service, with the status of Consul General. Himmler came from a most respectable bourgeois family; his father, Professor Gebhard Himmler, had been tutor to Prince Heinrich of Bavaria before becoming, during Himmler's youth, the headmaster of a school in Bavaria.

Rudolf Hess, a close follower of Hitler in the early days, was another of Hitler's gentlemen. His father, Friedrich Hess, was living in Alexandria at the time of his son's birth on 26 April 1894; Friedrich Hess's father had emigrated from Germany to Egypt, where he had established a business as a wholesaler and exporter. The family on the father's side came from Bavaria,[1] and in 1892 Friedrich Hess had married Clara Muench, the daughter of an industrialist from Hof, by whom he had three children. Alfred Hess, the younger son (born 1897), became initially a businessman like his father; the third child of the family, a daughter called Margarete, was not born until 1908, and was therefore fifteen years younger than her elder brother, Rudolf.[2]

Rudolf Hess's education began in 1900 at a German school in Alexandria, but in 1908 it was decided to send him, at the age of fourteen, as a boarder to the Evangelisches Paedagogium at Godesberg-am-Rhein. In both schools he proved a responsive and intelligent pupil, showing a keen interest in German history, as well in engineering, mathematics, physics and astronomy. His father was a stern disciplinarian, at least while his children were young; meals were served at exact hours, the boys did not speak unless their father first addressed them; bedtime was fixed and unalterable; the food was chosen entirely to suit the taste of the head of the household. 'I am not a goat,' he said once when served a salad, and no salad ever appeared again. Frau Hess was more lenient, her tastes were artistic, and she was interested in music.

The family lived in a large house with a fine garden. In the letters Hess wrote to his mother when, after the second World War, he was confined in Spandau, he recalls the impression the Egyptian setting made on him as a child:

> . . . the garden of Ibrahimieh, with its flowers and its scents, and all the indescribable, imponderable influences of the place: the fiercely hot 'Hamsin', the cool sea air laden with salty fragrance, the winter storms, when the sea was filled with the white crests of waves far out to the horizon, the cry of gulls, the dull rhythm of rolling waves which could haunt us with its melody until we dropped off to sleep. And then there were the mild soft nights of moonshine with the ceaseless howling of the dogs out in the desert—which served only to emphasize the quietness. How many times must you have sat with us children upon some bench beneath the shining star-lit night of Egypt, while you explained to us the great brilliant stars, giving names to all of them . . . what a paradise it was in our garden on the edge of the desert. Do you remember how we would gather violets together and how glorious they smelled; every day we picked another big bunch with enormous flowers . . . And how lovely it was on the sands in those days, before the quays were made, and where one was surrounded entirely by glorious nature where sea and desert met. For the most part an idyllic calm lay upon the water, and we could wade out to the crab-rocks.[3]

Around 1900 Hess's father bought an estate in Reicholdsgrün in the Fichtelgebirge region of Bavaria, and built himself a country house where the family could enjoy holidays in the summer. In another letter to his mother sent from Spandau, Hess remembers leaving Egypt to attend school in Germany:

> In 1908 we travelled home; the Egyptian coast, with the pillars of Pompey, the lighthouse and a few palms as the last visible signs, slowly sank away behind us. My father turned to me and said: 'Take a good look at this country; it may be several years before you see it again.' I went to a boarding school at Godesberg. No one then dreamed how *many* years would pass by—and that we might never see this land again.[4]

At school in Germany Hess is said to have suffered to some extent because his fellow pupils regarded him as a foreigner. This only served to sharpen his patriotism, and the history teacher at Godesberg also had a marked influence upon him.

His schooldays finished, Hess bowed to his father's wish that he should enter the family business, and his hopes of becoming a university student reading science and mathematics had to be set aside so that he could study commerce—first at the Ecole Supérieur du Commerce at Neuchâtel in Switzerland, while after this in 1912 he served an apprenticeship in an export business in Hamburg. His father promised him he should eventually be allowed to go to Oxford University, but the first World War intervened. Among his interests at this time, in addition to reading, was the study of seafaring and German naval history.

At the outbreak of war, the family were in fact assembled at their house in Germany. Rudolf Hess was among the first to volunteer; he had little taste for business, and was glad to leave it at the age of twenty to join the First Bavarian Infantry Regiment.[5] In December 1916 he was wounded in action, and the following year he was seriously injured in the lung. After his convalescence he was commissioned with the rank of lieutenant, serving in the ill-fated List Regiment, which was celebrated for the number of intellectuals who died while serving in it during the earlier years of the war. It was also the regiment in which Hitler served as an officer's runner, though Hess and his future Führer never consciously came into contact with each other at this time.[6] After his convalescence, Hess volunteered in 1918 to join the Imperial Flying Corps. He completed his training as an Officer Pilot in October 1918, but he only served for ten days in November before the armistice, completing a few operational flights. He was demobilized on 13 December.

In 1918, at the age of twenty-three, he decided to abandon any kind of career in business, though he refers many years later to 'the amusing period of my attempts at building and decorating'—the period he spent with the Münchener Wohnungskunst A.G. The family business in Alexandria had been expropriated, and their financial circumstances reduced. The social and political upheaval in post-war Germany affected him much as it affected Hitler and Göring and other ex-Army men with fiercely-held, right-wing views. They felt betrayed and disgraced by their leaders; they faced a Germany they did not recognize subject to mob-rule. The hastily established civil Government signed the armistice after the Kaiser, Wilhelm II, had fled to Holland and the Army High Command had disintegrated. The civilians in the streets were openly hostile to anyone in officer's uniform, and for a while it seemed certain regions in Germany might turn communist, reflecting the revolution already taking place in Russia. Though the socialist revolution openly proclaimed in many German cities, including Berlin, was never more than a momentary political skirmish, it determined many officers and men with right-wing views to establish the so-called volunteer Free Corps to oppose the development of any regional activities by the Left. The Free Corps (Freikorps) were to play a leading part in the German political balance of power until in 1921 the Allies insisted that they be disarmed.

Hess had wanted at first to serve as a pilot, but both his experience and the opportunities open to him were too small. Like Goebbels, whose poor physique and crippled foot had prevented him joining the Army, and Himmler, who had just completed training as an officer-cadet when the war ended, Hess decided to further his education during this period of turmoil. Goebbels was already a student, studying in a succession of universities while Himmler in 1919 entered the Technical High School in Munich to study agriculture. Hess became a student at Munich University the following year, reading history, economics,[7] and geopolitics, coming as we shall see under the influence of Professor Karl Haushofer, who joined the university staff in 1921. Hess, like Himmler, served in the Free Corps during the period of political unrest in Munich in 1919-20.[8]

During the spring of 1919, Bavaria had had for a while a communist state government, and Hess had taken full part in the street fighting which led to its overthrow. On 1 May he was wounded again, this time in one leg. He had also joined a nationalist group with anti-Semitic views,[9] and became a demonstrator and speaker in the streets. The rioting of the political factions often led to violence, bloodshed and murder. While the confederation of states which made up Germany at this time were in varying degrees of upheaval, the German mark began to decline in value—the first phases of its later, catastrophic collapse during the years 1921-23. The mark, which in 1918 was rated at 4 to the US dollar, stood by January 1922 at 186, and by January 1923 at 7,260, dropping the following months to astronomical figures enumerated in billions. This economic debacle, more than anything else following the suppression of the embryonic communist-socialist governments in Germany, spurred those with right-wing views to take violent action against any form of government which did not re-establish the kind of authoritarian rule they desired. For Hitler, the collapse of Germany in 1918 was a godsend. As Hess wrote later: 'For Adolf Hitler the revolt of 1918 was a necessity of Fate, for, despite its criminal leadership, it swept away many survivals of a time that was outlived, survivals that would have created obstacles to the National Socialist revolution.'[10]

The story of Hitler's emergence as a right-wing agitator during this period has been told frequently. Munich was to be the centre for his activities, and indeed during the early 1920s this city was to be more of a centre for political struggle than Berlin. In any case, the central Weimar government in Berlin was too weak to exercise effective control over the activities of the regional governments of the autonomous states, and especially so in Bavaria, which was traditionally alien from Prussia and the north. The government in Munich came increasingly under the blackmailing influence of the right-wing partisans, who were opposed to the Republican constitution upheld in the north. The Free Corps found its natural habitation in Munich, a hot-bed for extremists and lovers of the uniform.

Hitler lived in Munich from 1919, where he acted as a 'political instructor' for the Army. It was in Munich that he became the seventh member of the minuscule German Workers' Party, taking charge of its propaganda from January 1920. In April he left the Army, and in effect seized power in the Party, which he had renamed in February the National Socialist German Workers' Party. From now on he was to build the Party's strength by incessant public meetings and speeches. It is now that we begin to see the formation of the future leadership of the Party, starting on various levels—Captain Ernst Roehm, of the Army District Command, for instance, began at the top, actually preceding Hitler in his Party membership. Hess joined the Party in a very junior capacity in April 1920; his membership number was 16.[11] Göring, newly returned from his self-imposed exile in Sweden, heard Hitler speak and immediately joined the Party in the autumn of 1922. He was twenty-nine, and Hitler gave this former air ace command of the storm-troopers, who acted as body-guards at the Party's public meetings. Himmler, six years younger than Hess and an ardent admirer of Roehm, did not join formally until August 1923, three months before Hitler's abortive Munich Putsch, which was to put himself, Roehm and Hess into custody, and send Göring out of Germany for a second term of exile. Hess was active in the Party's interests at the university right up to the Putsch. A letter of 15 February 1923 to a fellow student, Friedrich Stöckle, is preserved in the Koblenz archives; Hess says that he wants to meet him, and that he will be easily recognizable because he will be wearing his Party badge.

After the second World War, at the International Military Tribunal at Nuremberg, Göring was to describe the effect Hitler's speeches made upon him at this time, an effect very much the same as they would have had upon Hess, who, five years younger than the Leader, was already a Party speaker, and as fully prepared as Göring to accept Hitler's authority:

> I inquired and found that . . . he held a meeting every Monday evening. I went there, and Hitler spoke about that demonstration, about Versailles . . . and the repudiation of the Treaty. He said that . . . a protest is successful only if backed by power to give it weight. As long as Germany had not become strong, this kind of thing was to no purpose.
>
> The conviction was spoken word for word as if from my own soul. On one of the following days I went to the business office of the NSDAP . . .
>
> I just wanted to speak to him at first to see if I could assist him in any way. He received me at once and after I had introduced myself he said it was an extraordinary turn of fate that we should meet. We spoke at once about the things which were close to our hearts—the defeat of our Fatherland . . . Versailles. I told him that I myself to the fullest extent, and all I was and possessed, were completely at his disposal for this, in my opinion, most essential and decisive matter: the fight against the Treaty of Versailles.[12]

Ilse Pröhl, whose family lived in Berlin, first met her future husband in the spring of 1920 in Munich, where she had been sent to complete her qualifying examinations (Abiturium) for the university. She and Hess were fellow boarders in a villa in Schwabing, the 'Latin quarter' of Munich. She was attracted by this 'young man in field-grey uniform, the orange lion of the Free Corps on his sleeve.' Hess, unlike the rest living at the villa, was already wrapped up in politics. Later in life she wrote, 'he rarely smiled, did not smoke, despised alcohol, and had no patience with young people enjoying dancing and social life after a war had been lost.' When she had first met him on a staircase of the villa, he had clicked his heels, but had given her a 'none too friendly glance from under his bushy eyebrows'. She remembers that he first showed real excitement after attending a meeting, accompanied by Haushofer, at which Hitler spoke. Ilse went with him to another meeting, and was introduced to Hitler.

According to Hitler's biographer Heiden, a wealthy German living in Spain had established a prize at the University of Munich for a thesis on the nature of the man who could lead Germany back to her former glory. This subject attracted Hess, who wrote down his own portrait of this future leader. He won the prize by writing such paragraphs as these:

> For the sake of national salvation the dictator does not shun to use the weapons of his enemy, demagogy, slogans, street parades, etc. Where all authority has vanished, only a man of the people can establish authority. This was shown in the case of Mussolini. The deeper the dictator was originally rooted in the broad masses, the better he understands how to treat them psychologically, the less the workers will distrust him, the more supporters he will win among these most energetic ranks of the people. He himself has nothing in common with the mass; like every great man, he is all personality . . . When necessity commands, he does not shrink before bloodshed. Great questions are always decided by blood and iron. And the question at stake is: Shall we rise or be destroyed?
>
> Parliament may go babbling, or not—the man acts. It transpires that despite his many speeches, he knows how to keep silent. Perhaps his own supporters are the most keenly disappointed . . . In order to reach his goal, he is prepared to trample on his closest friends . . . For the sake of the great ultimate goal, he must even be willing temporarily to appear a traitor against the nation in the eyes of the majority. The law-giver proceeds with terrible hardness . . . He knows the people and their influential individuals. As the need arises, he can trample them with the boots of a grenadier, or with cautious and sensitive fingers spin threads reaching as far as the Pacific Ocean . . . In either case the treaties of enslavement will fall. One day we shall have our new, Greater Germany, embracing all those who are of German blood . . .
>
> The work must not be cut to the towering dimensions of its builder, or the whole will totter at his decease like the State of Frederick and Bismarck. New independent personalities, to guide the steed of Germania remounted in the future, do not thrive under the dictator. Therefore, he performs his last great deed: instead of drinking his power to the dregs, he sets it down and stands aside as a loyal adviser.[13]

Heiden also asserts that Hess at Hitler's request began to keep a confidential card index for future reference listing the faults and weaknesses of Party supporters.

Hess, in fact, was by 1921 drawing very close to Hitler, who recognized in this personable and well educated young man the kind of disciplined follower who could be most useful to him both as a confidant and as a sounding-board for his ideas. The extent to which he was in Hitler's confidence is revealed by the fact that it was he, not Hitler, who wrote on the Party Leader's behalf to the Bavarian Premier, Gustav von Kahr, after he had accompanied Hitler on a visit to the Prime Minister. The letter is dated 17 May 1921:

> Hitler is convinced that revival is only feasible if it is possible to lead the masses, particularly the working class, back to nationalism. But this can only be done in conjunction with some reasonable, honest socialism . . . Actually, a good many former Communists and USP men [Independent Socialists] have joined the NSDAP. In the Circus Krone, after Hitler's rousing speech, 2000 ex-Communists stood up to sing 'Deutschland über Alles'; class differences have been bridged, and at our meetings the manual worker gossips and argues with officers and students. For me, an Auslandsdeutscher [German from abroad] who loathes all party-wrangling, this movement means 'the party above parties' which is destined for a great future. As for Herr Hitler, I know him very well, since I speak to him almost daily and have a close personal relationship with him . . . To add some weight to my words, I would ask your Excellency to obtain a reference about me from General Prof. Dr Haushofer, with whom I am on terms of close friendship.[14]

Göring was very happy to take charge of the SA (Sturm-Abteilungen), an organisation disguised for legal purposes as an athletics group, but in fact the strong-arm forces of the Party, used to protect the speakers at meetings and rallies, throw out opponents and create deliberate disturbances in the halls or streets when Hitler wanted them to help bring the Party to prominence. As well as speaking for the Party, Hess was an active leader in the ranks of the SA. On 4 November 1921 he took the lead in a brawl with the Social Democrats and Communists which resulted in his fourth injury in battle—this time a gash on his head which left a permanent scar. Hess saw a beer-mug being aimed at Hitler, and stood in its path to protect his leader. Hess was to arrange a special body of students to act as SA men. Hitler claimed in *Mein Kampf* that it was this experience which led to the formation of the SA. His exaggerated language is typical of the feverish atmosphere of those meetings:

> In a few moments the hall was filled with a yelling and shrieking

mob. Numerous beer-mugs flew like howitzers above their heads. Amid this uproar one heard the crash of chair legs, the crashing of mugs, groans and yells and screams.

It was a mad spectacle. I stood where I was and could observe my boys doing their duty, every one of them.

There I had the chance of seeing what a bourgeois meeting could be.

The dance had hardly begun when my Storm Troops, as they were called from that day onwards, launched their attack. Like wolves they threw themselves on the enemy again and again, in parties of eight or ten, and began steadily to thrash them out of the hall. After five minutes I could see hardly one of them that was not streaming with blood. Then I realized what kind of men many of them were, above all my brave Maurice, Hess, who is my private secretary today, and many others who, even though seriously wounded, attacked again and again, as long as they could stand on their feet. Twenty minutes long the pandemonium continued. Then the opponents, who had numbered seven or eight hundred, had been driven from the hall or hurled out headlong by my men, who had not numbered fifty. Only in the left corner a big crowd still stood out against our men and put up a bitter fight. The two pistol shots rang out from the entrance to the hall in the direction of the platform and now a wild din of shooting broke out from all sides. One's heart almost rejoiced at this spectacle which recalled memories of the War.[15]

Kurt Lüdecke, who joined the Party at this time, explained:

The brawl led to the development of a specialized and highly effective 'hall-fight technique', in which the Nazis employed every conceivable tactic for defeating even the most unequal assaults upon their meetings. This day was notable also for the formation of the 'SA', the 'Sturm-Abteilung', usually called 'Storm Troopers'. At first their function was to protect Nazi rallies and serve as Party police, but in time they became the real political soldiers of the Party, Hitler's praetorian guard.[16]

Hess was to play a prominent part in the notorious Munich Putsch of 8 November 1923. Hitler was impatient to try his strength at revolution on a regional level, and mount an out-and-out assault on the weak Bavarian government, led by Gustav von Kahr. Tension had been increased by the French occupation of the Ruhr in January. The SA were

drilled in a military style at more or less secret sessions held in the
woods outside Munich, while everything was done to persuade other
individuals and organisations with nationalistic leanings to make
common cause with the National Socialists. The model was Mussolini's
march on Rome the previous October. Hitler was planning a preliminary
march on Munich to be followed by a 'defensive' march on Berlin. He
failed to draw in the local Army Commandant, General Otto von
Lossow, but he was successful in winning General Ludendorff to the
cause. The proclamation of martial law on 27 September by Gustav
Stresemann, the new Chancellor, brought matters to a head; Stresemann's object was to draw closer to the Allies. Inflation was roaring up
the German streets; the mark was falling now disastrously. Von Kahr
called a public meeting for 8 November in the auditorium of the
Bürgerbräukeller, which held 3,000; on this date the mark in fact
reached its nadir in devaluation; 4.2 billion to the dollar. Hitler, fearing
that von Kahr might forestall him by issuing his own challenge to the
federal government in Berlin, determined to take over this meeting and
lead a march on the State government buildings in Munich.

The storm-troopers were assembled to support their leaders. Hitler,
closely followed by Göring and Hess, burst in on the packed hall,
firing his revolver at the ceiling.[17] Von Kahr, who was speaking, fell
silent in astonishment; beside him were the Premier of Bavaria, von
Lossow, and other ministers. The audience put down their beer-mugs
and stared at the intruders; they saw that a machine-gun had been
mounted at the entrance. Hitler, incongruously dressed in a morning
coat which did not fit, was standing on a table with his pistol pointed at
the ceiling. 'No one can leave the hall,' he said. 'The National Revolution
has begun.' The hall was surrounded by armed storm-troopers.

Leaving Göring in charge of the assembly, Hitler and Hess hustled
the ministers from the platform into a side-room reeking with beer-
fumes, and there, at gunpoint, endeavoured to bluff them into forming a
coalition government under Ludendorff, who, said Hitler, was expected
to arrive at any moment. He threatened to kill himself if his revolution
failed. The ministers did not know what to do, and while they hovered
in uncertainty Hitler, in a state of wild excitement and with the expression of a madman, ran back to the assembly and proclaimed that a new
government was in process of being formed, and that he himself was to
be in charge of the National Government. He demanded a march on
Berlin. Hitler called for beer once he was back in the side-room. The
conspirators were joined by Ludendorff, who was angry because he had

been hurried to the meeting and given no advance warning that such an action had been imminent. Bluffing the ministers still further, Hitler obtained their grudging consent to his proposals, and they all filed back to the platform, where the audience learned of the 'accord' which had been reached. The assembly shouted with enthusiasm and then began to leave for home. While Hitler was called away to settle a brawl between some Bavarian soldiers and the storm-troopers, the three ministers were permitted by Ludendorff to leave. Once Lossow reached his office, he put the Army in readiness, although he had given his word of honour to Ludendorff not to frustrate the coup.

Hess too was active. He sent storm-troopers to round up opponents of the Party and bring them to the Bürgerbräukeller to be held as hostages. Two of them, both ministers, Hess bundled into a car and took under guard into the mountains to a hide-out where they could be kept in custody. Others were forced by Göring to take part in the march on the government centre, which began at eleven o'clock on the following morning, 9 November. The march was led by Ludendorff and Hitler.

By half past twelve, the column of some 3,000 men led by Hitler had reached the centre of Munich, where Roehm was besieged in the old War Ministry. The procession was opposed by armed police in a narrow street, and firing commenced, breaking up the marchers. Hitler was apparently pulled to the ground by a comrade. Göring was badly injured in the groin. Others lay around, dead or wounded. Ludendorff alone marched on unscathed with all the obstinacy of age and rank. The rest fled; Hitler, who had dislocated his shoulder, was taken away by car. He was arrested two days later at the house of his friend, Ernst Hanfstaengl. Roehm and his men surrendered.

Hess was still driving with his hostages through the mountains. When news of the collapse of the coup in Munich reached them, the small party in the car disintegrated like leaves in the wind. The armed guards fled; the driver was only solicitous to get the ministers back to Munich. Utterly disillusioned, Hess took to a mountain trail which would enable him to cross the border into Austria. Göring, his wounds festering, was also taken over the border by his wife.

Hess did not stand trial alongside Hitler, who with Ludendorff, Roehm and seven other men prominent in the march, was finally brought to trial on 26 February 1924. Göring and Hess were still in exile. The trial was a veiled affair, mostly held behind closed doors to exclude the press and the public, and to shield the tarnished reputation of Kahr and Lossow. The charge was high treason, and the president of the hearing was Franz Guertner, Bavarian Minister of Justice, who was later to be Minister of Justice in Hitler's Cabinet. In spite of the seriousness of the charge, and the blood that had been spilt, Ludendorff was found 'not guilty' when the verdict was given on 1 April, while Hitler received a sentence of five years 'fortress-detention', with the proviso that if he behaved well, he might be set free on probation after serving only six months. In fact, he served only a further eight and a half months, and was released on 20 December 1924. At the hearing he was astute enough to take the offensive, claiming all the credit of the abortive coup d'état for himself, and so achieving a spectacular martyrdom. He had no qualms about 'fortress-detention', a form of 'honorary' custody designed for political offenders and keeping the prisoners in the minimum of restraint.

He returned to Landsberg castle, an obsolete fortress with civilian guards in the little baroque town of Landsberg in the valley of the Lech. He had been held there in custody since his arrest on 11 November 1923. He lived well as did the other National Socialists who were to join him in the castle, including Hess. Hitler had a large, first-floor room which caught the summer sunshine and he could wander at will in the garden. According to Alan Bullock, on his thirty-fifth birthday just after the trial, he was loaded with presents and flowers. He could receive as many visitors as he wished.

When he learned the outcome of Hitler's trial, Hess, still in exile, had decided he should return and take his proper place beside his Leader. At a further trial, held later in April he, along with some 40 others, received a mild sentence of 18 months. So Hess joined Hitler in Landsberg. He was given a good room on the first floor, the sign of a privileged prisoner. Life in confinement proved easy and pleasant for him—prolonged conversations with Hitler, reading connected with his university studies, and visits from his friends, including Professor Haushofer and Ilse Pröhl, the girl he was eventually to marry who visited him every week. He looked after his health, practising physical training and the high-jump in the garden of the fortress.[18]

A picture of Hitler enjoying his confinement is given by one of his supporters of the period, Kurt Lüdecke, who later left the Party and went to live in the United States. He visited Hitler at Landsberg:

An hour by train brought me to the ancient fortress of Landsberg, a charming little city, dreaming in baroque on the River Lech. The whole atmosphere of the place, even when I reached the gates, was inviting. A genial guard took me in tow, chatting pleasantly about Herr Hitler as he led me toward the wing where the 'prisoner of honour' was housed. It seemed as if man, stone, and nature had mellowed with warmth and respect for the famous malefactor.

Somewhere beyond the window of the waiting-room, the warder told me, lay an open-air gymnasium for the prisoners. While I was peering out for a glimpse of them, the door behind me opened. I turned. There stood Hitler.

He was wearing leather shorts and a Tyrolean jacket, his shirt open at the throat. His cheeks glowed with healthy red, and his eyes shone; the fire-eater had not been quenched by his time-serving. On the contrary, he looked better physically, and seemed happier than I had ever seen him. Landsberg had done him a world of good!

He greeted me with the hearty air of a host receiving a guest. Gone from his manner was the nervous intensity which formerly had been his most unpleasant characteristic. He appeared calmer and more certain of himself.

A warder accompanied him, a jolly fellow with friendly eyes. When we sat down at the table to talk, the keeper sat also, to comply with the rules; but he chose a chair almost out of earshot and kept beaming indulgently on his favourite prisoner, looking more Santa Claus than Cerberus . . . The prisoners arose at six, breakfasted at seven, and walked in the garden from eight until ten. Lunch with his fellow-prisoners [some additional twenty members of the unsuccessful coup], with Hitler presiding, sounded more like a social affair. In the afternoon one prisoner served tea to the others in their rooms. Before and after the six o'clock supper, which was also served in their cells, they were again free to exercise in the garden for an hour or so. Lights-out sounded at ten for all prisoners except Hitler. He was permitted to read or work until midnight or longer. Considering the hectic tempo of the life he had been leading, this sojourn in prison was exactly what Hitler needed. It gave him time to rest, to think and to plan.[19]

The compilation of *Mein Kampf*, on which Hitler had been brooding before he went to prison, took place during the pleasant months spent in Landsberg.[20] Hitler is said to have dictated the book, which may account for its turgid and unreadable style. That a man who was a master of propaganda through the spoken word should have failed so miserably when it came to the written word, may seem at first incomprehensible.

But Hitler's effect was always achieved through the exercise of his personality; once his hypnotic power was removed, what he said or wrote almost always appears prolix and utterly without style or regard for his audience. He is said to have dictated the chapters first of all to Emile Maurice, who accompanied him to prison and acted as his batman, and, when he was joined later in April by Hess, to have accepted his services as an aide and secretary in order to complete the book, first at Landsberg and, after his release, in Berchtesgaden. Hitler in fact initially typed out the manuscript with two fingers on the Governor's type-writer, which was kindly loaned him for the purpose. Hess's collaboration was largely advisory, helping Hitler to formulate his ideas on paper and assisting with the proofs. He certainly took no dictation, nor did he type any of the manuscript.[21]

Dr J. R. Rees, one of the psychiatrists in charge of Hess's case after his landing in Britain, says of the compilation of *Mein Kampf*: 'Hess himself regards this as a definite collaboration, and it seems to me probable that as a student of Karl Haushofer some of the ideas and concepts he had acquired of geo-politics found their way into the writing of the Nazi Bible.'[22] Hanfstaengl, who used to visit Hess at Landsberg, confirms this impression:

> This was by no means the taste of Hess, who only grudgingly left Hitler's side while I was talking to him. This was the period of his greatest and lasting influence, helping Hitler to collect his ideas for *Mein Kampf*. Hess was another whistler, like Rosenberg, to which he added the exasperating habit of fooling around with the chair he was sitting on. He would sit on it the wrong way round, pass it through his legs, sit on the back, twirl it on one leg, like an amateur acrobat trying to show off. He could not bear to see Hitler exposed to any views other than his own and was always trying to distract attention. All Hess could do was talk in catch-phrases. 'We must learn to be much more brutal in our methods. That is the only way to deal with our enemies,' he would chant. 'A little more of that and the Bürger-bräu affair would have ended differently.' He loved the word 'brutal', which in German is pronounced with a rolling 'r' and equal stress on both syllables, and Hitler also seemed to take pleasure in the sound of it. You could almost feel him quicken as he roared out the word at Hess's prompting. There was a very close bond between the two at this period, and for the first time I heard them speak to each other on 'thou' terms, although later in public they

did not . . . Roehm used to try it on, but he never got thou'd back . . . for all that, I was extremely worried about the narrowing of his prejudices in Hess's company in gaol.

A letter survives written by Hess on 16 July while he was in Landsberg to a university friend, H. H. Heim.[23] The letter has a special interest for later explanation of Hitler's attitude to leadership of the Party while he was confined, as well its expression of Hess's own views:

I have been hoping to send you an answer by Herr Hitler to your friend's letter, along with my thanks for kindly lending me the two volumes 'Das Deutsche Volkstum'. But just now Herr H will have nothing to do with political day-to-day problems. A final attempt this morning was also in vain. He will not change his mind for, after all, he has publicly stepped down from leadership. His reason is that he cannot accept responsibility for what happens outside without his knowledge and possibly against his better judgment. Nor is he in a position to sort out and to resolve internal bickering—not from here at any rate. He considers it useless to be bothered with all these petty troubles.

On the other hand he is quite convinced—and so am I now more than ever—that he will impress people from above [von oben her] with his own spirit, and so destroy all distortions of the truth.

The kind of hooliganism and idiocies perpetrated by some of the Völkische are no reflection on Hitler himself. And this will be even clearer when, in the autumn, Hitler's book appears. This will give people a true picture of Hitler, the man, no less than Hitler, the politician.

My apologies again for returning the letter only now, also for underlining certain words. I did this in order to draw Hitler's attention to these passages. And thanks again for the two volumes which, I suppose, I can keep for some time. I was particularly interested in the passage about German surroundings, and as a geopolitician, I was pleased to see that such influences as geographical position, soil, and so on were not forgotten.

The brochure about conscription for labour [Arbeitsdienstpflicht] is the best I have so far read about the subject. What matters is to combine all forces for the struggle against communism which, more dangerous than ever, is preparing for its big coup.

All the more deplorable is the unpleasant situation within the völkische movement described in your friend's letter, and I am very well aware of it. I think that very soon now in the desperate struggle against the seductive communist pest everybody will line up behind Hitler. Let's hope that he regains his freedom of action soon enough.

But even if communism doesn't force us into unity, I don't think we should take the distortions within the folk movement all that tragically. After all, Hitler's personality and the effects and side-effects of his tremendous oratory will set us right.

Professor Karl Haushofer, who was to be an important influence upon Nazi thinking and strategy, was a regular visitor to Landsberg. After Hess's release on New Year's Eve Haushofer offered him the post of his assistant at the Deutsche Akademie at the University, but Hess turned this down in February in favour of becoming Hitler's secretary, a position he was to hold until 1932. One of the first important engagements he had was to attend a major conference in Munich on 27 February 1925, at which Hitler reformed the Party, making of it a nationalist rallying-point to which eventually other would-be nationalist leaders slowly gravitated—including Roehm and Hitler's most serious rival as the Party leader, Gregor Strasser. In May 1926 a General Meeting of the Party acknowledged Hitler as their supreme leader. Membership was growing; by the end of 1925 it was 27,000, and by the end of 1927, 72,000.

Karl Haushofer, a former military attaché in the German embassy in Tokyo, who became a general during the First World War, had been since 1921 a Professor in Geo-politics at the University of Munich at the time Hess was attending as a student.[24] He was in his early fifties, and given to psychic premonitions, one of his gifts which first impressed the impressionable young man. At heart Haushofer was a right-wing monarchist, but with the departure of the Kaiser, his dream of a greater Germany expanding its territorial claims and taking a lead in the world resulted in his becoming one of the intellectual influences, or 'prophets', of the Nazi movement. He was, unlike Hitler and the Nazi hierarchy, widely travelled in Europe and Asia, and he believed fervently in the establishment of a *Herrenvolk*, or superior race composed of the Anglo-Saxon peoples, uniting the British with the Germans in world domination or leadership. He was, accordingly, pro-British right up to the time of the second World War.

Haushofer was the principal exponent in Germany of geo-politics, which sought to explain the political development of nations in terms of geographical factors. Hess lost no time in introducing Haushofer to Hitler, and he became, in effect, Hitler's advisor during the crucial period when the Nazi leader was gestating his political testament, which was soon to find expression in *Mein Kampf*. As we have seen, he was a frequent visitor to Landsberg when the book was finally being written. Konrad Heiden, writing in the 1940s during the war, described Haushofer's interpretation of the geo-political forces at work during the first half of the century as follows:

Hitler's learned friend, General and Professor Karl Haushofer, had developed a new type of military science based on a division of the world into great land and sea masses. Previously the Power dominating the sea had dominated the world; today, however, Haushofer, himself a pupil of Rudolf Kjellen, the Swedish geographer, taught that this condition had been reversed. Immediately after the World War he had been of the opinion that the great battle fleets would gradually be transformed into 'scrap iron' by growing swarms of U boats and airplanes. Both planes and submarines depended for their power on land bases from which they could not stay away for any protracted period. But this is not the chief reason for the rising importance of the mainland in world politics. Through the development of the continental trade economy, the great inner spaces have become 'less dependent on the coast'; in modern world politics, domination of the production centres is decisive, no longer domination of the trade routes.

Haushofer took for granted the decline of the British Empire, based on English domination of trade routes; all territorial relations, based only on trade and especially maritime relations, would soon be broken. This would first happen in Asia with its great land blocks of China and Russia, and Japan would not necessarily be the winner in the 'Eurasian space catastrophe'. For Japan is also a Power based on sea lanes; but today we stand, as Haushofer puts it, 'at the great turning point in the favourable position of the island empires'. Against the coming catastrophe he saw but one help, the early union of continental Europe. As late as 1932 he could conceive of this, though reluctantly, only under the leadership of French democracy, with at least the approval of the British: 'Either democracy and pacifism create a sort of United States of Europe by 1950 at the latest, or the Eurasian space catastrophe will inevitably occur—probably in the form of a retrogressive small-spaced dismemberment even of the so-called colonial Powers'. The great land mass, not control of the sea, is today the aim of high politics.[25]

The mathematics of *Lebensraum* (living-space) were simple as far as Hitler was concerned. Germany, cramped for living-space which did not permit the population to grow (62.5 million people in 436,000 square kilometres) must become one of the new land-empires which were to replace such sea-empires as Britain represented, with the white population of her Empire (some 70 millions) dominating a quarter of the inhabited Earth. The greatest land empire was that of the Soviet Union, Germany's alien neighbour, which always appeared in Hitler's eyes the giant Germany must ultimately overcome and whose land she should covet. Germany's expansion lay in the East. Haushofer was also convinced of the importance of Japan, which seemed to him Germany's equivalent in the Far East, needing *Lebensraum* even more obviously. He regarded the Japanese as the Prussians of Asia because of their expertise, their efficiency, and their tireless patriotism.

Although Hess had, he thought, more important things to do in 1925 at the age of thirty than graduate at Munich University, he became a close friend of the Haushofers, whose younger son, Albrecht, a poet and musician (born 1903, and so nine years junior to Hess) was also to be a Professor of Geography and Geo-politics in Berlin during the 1930s. According to Heiden, it was Hess who introduced to Hitler another intellectual with experience abroad—Walter Darré, who had been born in the Argentine in 1895 and who held a position as a civil servant in the Prussian Ministry of Agriculture until 1929, the year in which he published his influential book, *Blood and Soil*. *Blood and Soil*, together with Alfred Rosenberg's *The Myth of the Twentieth Century* (1930), were to provide for the Nazis a further stimulus with a strangely racialist bias. Darré, later to become Himmler's friend and adviser, extolled the essential nobility of the Nordic peasants in his book; it was, he claimed, the good blood of their stock which combined with the good earth they tilled to create the health and strength of central Europe. Darré's thinking finally convinced Hitler and Himmler that the Jewish and Slav peoples, in particular, had to be purged from the Germanic lands which the Nazi régime came to dominate between 1938 and 1944. They saw no solution as they moved east but genocide of those whom they regarded as racially inferior or degenerate. It was Alfred Rosenberg who supplied the necessary 'philosophy' of toughness; he preached against the humane ideas, such as they were, of Christianised Europe, and advocated a religion of blood—the strength of the rulers to rule. Christianity, he declared, was a soft and decadent religion imported from the Orient, a religion quite unsuited to Nordic Man.[26]

Hitler took what suited him from Haushofer's relatively academic approach to world problems, and grafted it onto the totally unacademic and unscientific ramblings of Rosenberg and Darré. Darré's racialism had been sharpened by the travels he had undertaken for his Ministry in Latvia and Estonia, ostensibly to study farming methods. His primary concern, however, was to report on the conditions in which the racial Germans of the area lived, and the degree to which they preserved the Germanic culture they represented under alien domination. These reports were sent to Haushofer's *Deutsche Akademie* in Munich, where research into the culture of Germans abroad was undertaken. Hess became specially interested in the work of the Academy, the springboard for his later specialization in the control of Germans living abroad once the régime was established.

As Hitler's secretary and close associate from 1925 to 1932, his activities were to become inseparable from those of Hitler himself. He was paid initially 300 marks a month. He was at the administrative heart of the conspiracy for power during this seven year period which was to culminate in Hitler's seizure of power in 1933. Hitler is said to have told Hess, 'I shall need seven years before the movement is on top again.'[27] It was during this period that Hess developed himself into the alter ego of the leader, but always at the slight distance of a devoted follower, not an intimate friend. Hess, unlike Roehm, seldom addressed Hitler with the familiar '*du*'. He was, it must be remembered, seven years younger than his leader. For him, Hitler was always to be 'The Chief' or 'Mein Führer'. According to Hanfstaengl, it was Hess who originated the title in imitation of Mussolini's 'Duce'. The 'Heil Hitler' greeting began at this time—'Heil' followed by a person's name was not an unusual term of address in Austria.

Konrad Heiden has a strange passage which is perhaps coloured by melodrama. It implies an almost mystical link between the two men:[28]

Suddenly, in the midst of a conversation, Hitler's face grows tense as with an inner vision; these are the moments in which the humanly repulsive falls away from him and the unfathomable is intensified until it becomes truly terrible. His eyes peer into the distance, as though he were reading or gazing at something which no one else sees; and if the observer follows the direction of his gaze, sometimes, it has been claimed, Rudolf Hess can be seen in the far corner, with his eyes glued to his Führer, apparently speaking to him with closed lips. It may be that the strange atmosphere of such scenes confused the observer, making him see more than was there. But it is certain that in the decisive years of his career Hitler used his younger friend as a necessary complement to his own personality; as a stage director or spiritual ballet master who helped him shape his own powerful but formless and uncertain nature into whatever image he momentarily wanted.

When preparing a speech, he declaimed large sections of it to his friend Hess; he practised gestures and facial expressions at the mirror. He practised other things too. There was an important visitor to be received; the reception was previously rehearsed with Hess. Hess had to meet the stranger in advance, take a good look at him and report. Then there would be an interview like the following:

Hitler: Fire away, Hess! Can he be used or not?

Hess: He can be used. But he's the silent type.

Hitler (suspiciously): Critical?

Hess: No, embarrassed. Would be terribly glad to admire, but he's embarrassed.

Hitler: They are all prepared. For ten years they have heard of me, for the last year they have heard of nothing else but me. What does he expect?

Hess: Authority, of course. You can speak at length. Your will is unshakable. You give laws to the age.

Hitler: Then I'll speak with the firm voice, without yelling?

Hess: Of course.

Hitler utters a few sentences. Hess, the human tuning-fork, listens: '. . . No, not like that, quiet—no passion, commanding. You want nothing of him. It is Destiny that speaks . . .' At length the adviser falls silent. Hitler is in the swing.

According to Heiden, Hess continued to compile secret evidence recording the individual actions not only of the Party's enemies, but also revealing facts about the Party members themselves.

Ernst ('Putzi') Hanfstaengl, the wealthy young member of Munich society with a leaning towards culture who had adopted Hitler before the Putsch and to whose home Hitler went immediately on leaving Landsberg, describes Hess at this period as 'a moody introvert, jealously suspicious of anyone who approached Hitler too closely . . . He was as morose and aloof with me as with everybody else.' However, Hanf-staengl recognized that Hess was at least an officer and a gentleman who, in contrast to most of Hitler's entourage, should have shared with him the task he had set himself of teaching Hitler 'the norms and ideas of civilized existence'. But Haushofer and Hess, he considered, were bad influences on Hitler because of their 'narrow foot-slogging mis-conceptions of global politics'.

Because he was so near the heart of Hitler's activities, Hess slips into anonymity during this period. Unlike Goebbels, Hitler's Gauleiter in Berlin from 1926 and his head of Party Propaganda from 1928 and a Deputy in the Reichstag, he does not have a distinct career in his fight for the Party's cause. There is not a single reference to him in Goebbels' flamboyant, egotistical account of these years, *My Part in Germany's Fight*. But the strength of his position at the Brown House in Munich, Hitler's headquarters until 1933, must not be underestimated. Rosen-berg grumbled to Lüdecke in 1932, 'It is unfortunate, for Hess is con-stantly around Hitler, and his influence with him is growing.' He played a considerable part in the organisation of the annual Party rallies held at Nuremberg.[29]

What was perhaps uppermost in Hess's personal viewpoint and dominated his outlook throughout his political career was detestation of Communism. This emerges, for example, in a letter preserved at Koblenz and addressed on 18 October 1930 to Albrecht Haushofer, then aged twenty-seven, who was about to visit England. Hess tells him to stress in England that aspect of the Party which makes it a bulwark against Bolshevism. He says, very revealingly, that 'if our voters did not have us to vote for, they would go to the extreme left.' He adds that Haushofer should stress this not for the Party's sake, but for the sake of Germany itself.[30]

In 1927 Hess married Ilse Pröhl, one of the first women members of the Nazi Party and close enough to Hitler to be in the old Mercedes which his supporters hired in order to meet him when he had been released from Landsberg fortress on 20 December, ten days before Hess, who was not freed until New Year's Eve. Once they were married, Hess forbade his wife to take any further direct part in political activities. His son, Wolf Rüdiger, was not born until ten years later, in 1937. It has even been suggested that the marriage was first suggested to Ilse by Hitler himself. Whether this is true or not, the witnesses at the wedding were Hitler and Haushofer.

On 20 November, a month before the wedding, Hess wrote a letter to his parents, which reveals something of the nature of his past association with Ilse.[31] It is, to say the least, a strange statement to make, and reveals his odd sense of humour:

> I'm telling you about a wedding and a honeymoon when, perhaps you aren't even aware of your elder son intending matrimony. Or don't I have to tell you anyway? Maybe you took it for granted that one day I'd ask that good comrade of so many years, the partner of so many mountaineering and skiing excursions, the loyal friend in both good and bad days, the constant visitor to the fortress, the one who thinks and feels alike with me—that one day I would ask Ilse Pröhl to sail with me into the haven of matrimony. Fortunately I don't have to give you a detailed description of her, for after all, you know her. I don't have to assure you, like a good son, that she is an angel, and why she is an angel. Or, to use a metaphor employed by Schopenhauer in a letter, I don't have to explain to you why I am convinced I have fished out of a sack full of snakes the one eel that had strayed into it. Knowing your opinions on marital age, dear father, I am sure you are glad that the eel is six years younger than me. Moreover, the two of us, the eel and I, do not expect a heaven on earth, for ever and ever; I dare say we're too mature for such optimism. But then, we know each other and we are fond of each other, and what we look forward to on our joint path may well be better than 'heaven' in the conventional sense. Anyway, we haven't much to do with heaven in the conventional sense, nor with the conventional confessions of the Churches—maybe just because we really are too deeply religious. We don't know any pastor compatible, hence we have decided to make our own deal with God Almighty and to do without any Church formalities.

His mother replied in rather the same vein:

> We remember how at the beginning of the war you wrote to us, 'Share my joy. I'm in the infantry!' Frankly we weren't all that pleased, but we didn't want to spoil your fun. And now once again you end, 'Share my joy'. This time, I can assure you, we do so most sincerely and heartily.

Hess is mentioned as being present on a number of occasions, both important and unimportant. He is always Hitler's shadow. A series of amusing glimpses occurs in *The Early Goebbels Diaries*,[32] the narcissistic scribblings of the youthful agitator during the years when Hitler was deciding to win him over to his wing of the Party in Munich, away from his Party rival, Gregor Strasser, in the north. Goebbels, overwhelmed by the sudden attentions being paid him by the romantic figure of Hitler, is ecstatic in his response to the beauties of Bavaria after the grinding, dreary rounds he has had to fulfil as Party agitator in the Ruhr. Everything was light and luxury. He arrived in Munich as Hitler's guest on 13 April 1926. 'To the Reichsadler,' he exclaims to himself in the school notebooks in which he used to record his diary, 'Concert! Hitler is with me all the time.' Then he adds, 'Streicher, May, Hess, Gengler, all of them here.' He found Franz Gengler (a news editor on Hitler's newspaper, *Völkische Beobachter*) a slimy customer, while Otto May, Hitler's then propaganda chief (the position Goebbels wanted but was not to have until November 1928), 'unpleasant'. But Hess was quite different—'Alone with Hess,' he writes. 'Talk. He is a kind fellow.' He also met and liked Himmler—'a good fellow and very intelligent'. Goebbels had only three days in Munich, and made the most of them, pleasing Hitler by giving him flowers and, he says, impressing him with his personal brilliance and scintillation as a platform speaker. On the day he left it was raining, but Hitler and Hess came for him in the car. It was an enthusiastic leave-taking. 'Adolf Hitler, I love you, because you are both great and simple. A genius . . . Farewell! He waves,' records Goebbels, still in ecstasy.

Goebbels met Hess again the following July in Berchtesgaden— 'Serious discussions. Hess is quite enthusiastic.' And, a week later, Hitler arrives and the car awaits him with Hess and others—'Hitler talks and romanticises. He is a dear and pure—a child.' Goebbels was entranced by the lake and mountain scenery which had such a life-long attraction for the Führer. He spoke for Hitler at Augsburg, and again Hess was there watching. Hitler gave Goebbels a bunch of roses. He needed to; this wooing and the luxury of Berchtesgaden was in prepara- tion for offering him the hardest of all tasks—to become Party Gauleiter (which at this stage meant campaign and propaganda organiser) in Berlin.

Up to 1928, Hess, the ex-officer and gentleman, was useful to Hitler for contacting representatives of the upper and wealthy classes.[33] Hitler in the early years was always unsure of himself in polite society, and preferred to send a delegate to negotiate with such people as the aristocrats or the industrialists than to enter their offices or drawing- rooms himself. It is for this reason that men such as Göring and Hess were useful—when they wanted to, they knew how to behave. Göring did not regain Hitler's favour until the spring of 1928, when he returned to Germany to seek some employment after undergoing successive temporary cures for the drug-addiction which he had first acquired while being treated for his gangrenous wounds after the 1923 Putsch. Before Göring took over as Hitler's chief ambassador with the industrialists who were to finance the Party, it was Hess who in 1928 approached the banker Fritz Thyssen on Hitler's behalf, as Thyssen himself has stated:[34]

> Rudolf Hess was instrumental in bringing about a closer personal association between the Nazis and myself. He came to me sometime during 1928, on the initiative of old Kirdorf, for many years the director general of the Rhenish-Westphalian Coal Syndicate, with whom I was on friendly terms. Hess explained to me that the Nazis had bought the Brown House in Munich and had great difficulty in paying for it. I placed Hess in possession of the required funds on conditions which, however, he has never fulfilled. For by no means did I want to make the Nazis a present; I merely arranged a foreign loan for the National Socialist party through the banks. At that time Hess received the money, which he was obligated to pay back. But he returned only a small part of it; for the rest I myself simply had to 'acknowledge receipt'. Kirdorf had been a member of the National Socialist party long before me.

Hess was also present at Hitler's conference in Berlin on 21–22 May with Otto Strasser, the brother of Gregor. The Strassers represented the left-wing of the Party, and were in favour of the nationalisation of industry. The result of these disputes was that Otto Strasser broke away from Hitler, or more precisely, was driven out of the Party. He founded his own, private Party, the Black Front, which came to nothing. Hitler's instinct enabled him to judge the conditions prerequisite both for gaining and preserving power—he had a sixth sense in this matter. His final struggle with Gregor Strasser was not to come until later; Gregor preferred at this stage not to go along with his brother.

According to Hans Frank in his memoirs written while a prisoner at Nuremberg, Hitler was deeply depressed following the suicide of his young niece, Geli Raubal, at his flat on 17 September 1931. Frank, at that time a young lawyer who was in favour with the Party because he had conducted several cases for them, was visited by Hess, who told him Hitler was very concerned at the ugly rumours circulating about his relations with his niece, and was even thinking of retiring from public life. Frank told Hess to reassure Hitler, and offered his legal help in dealing with these 'calumnies'.[35]

In 1931, it was Hess who introduced the journalist Otto Dietrich into Hitler's circle. Dietrich was to become Reich-Press chief from 1933–45, a Party office separate from Goebbels' Propaganda Ministry. Hess foresaw his usefulness, and the memoirs Dietrich was to write in prison camp after the war are among the most useful personal records of contact with Hitler. An interesting letter written by Hess to Gregor Strasser on 9 September 1932 survives.[36] It informs Strasser that Hitler wants the Party's Press Department, involving both Dietrich and Hanfstaengl, to be under his (Hess's) supervision, and not under R. A. Reinhard. Reinhard was assistant to Max Amann, who ran the Party's publishing house, the Eher-Verlag.

By 1932 Hitler, who always had a strong feeling of loyalty towards his oldest supporters, realized it was time to reward Hess for his long service. On 15 December he put him in charge of a Central Party Commission to supervise the policy of the Party in the regions through-out Germany; he became, in fact, controller of the political activities of the Party, with the special charge of crushing the kind of opposition which Gregor Strasser, in particular, represented. It was known that General von Schleicher had approached Strasser with a view to bringing him into the Cabinet as Vice-Chancellor and by so doing splitting the Nazi Party into two, as well as securing the co-operation of the Trade Unions. When this had failed, Hitler had accused Strasser of disloyalty, and he had resigned a week before Hitler set up the Central Party Commission to control the Party. For Hess, this was the beginning of his rise to high office. He was no longer a nonentity, Hitler's shadow, but a Party leader in his own right. Thyssen, who, it will be remembered, had been among the first of the big industrialists to donate or loan Hitler money, provides an interesting comment on the Hitler-Strasser relationship at this time:

> Strasser and I maintained outwardly pleasant relations, but he did not like me very much. Within his party he sided with the extreme Left, and he suspected me on account of my past connection with the German National party. Consequently, I got no direct news of his conversations with the other owners of heavy industry. As to his numerous conversations with General von Schleicher, all I knew of them was through the National Socialist party. The party was

very suspicious of these interviews. They were considered to be treacherous toward Adolf Hitler, and I openly shared this opinion.

Whether General von Schleicher might eventually have succeeded in forming a cabinet chiefly by German Labour—this question can no longer be answered. His negotiations with Strasser appear to have been very successful. I was even told that Schleicher counted on the support of a part of the Social Democratic labour unions. His aim apparently was to separate the unions from the parties, which in the case of the National Socialist party would have had the natural consequence of splitting the party in two.

At that time I sent Rudolf Hess a copy of the letter I had addressed to the secretary of a Rhenish industrial enterprise and in which I expressed the opinion that the manner in which Strasser worked against Hitler was contemptible. Hess answered me in a very cordial letter.[37]

By now the Nazi Party was in a strong, though not dominant position. In 1928 their small vote of 810,000 for the Reichstag elections had given them only 12 deputies—the Communist vote had been 3,265,000 and that of the Social Democrats 9,150,000. Two years later their vote had increased (largely through the unemployed voters) to 6,409,600, and they had 107 deputies in the house; Party membership stood at around 180,000. In 1932, the crucial year with two Reichstag elections (the second of which, in November, was the last truly free vote Germany was to enjoy before Hitler's seizure of power), they had at first doubled their votes and secured a 39 per cent hold on the seats in the house, only to slip back by some two million votes at the second poll, losing 34 seats in consequence. In the same year Hitler inevitably lost the contest for the Presidency to Hindenburg, though he had secured at the second Presidential poll almost $13\frac{1}{2}$ million votes against over $19\frac{1}{4}$ million for Hindenburg. Hitler, determined to keep his policy of securing power by using constitutional machinery, had to resort to a hard deal conducted behind the scenes in order to secure some place in government from which he could manoeuvre himself into a position of absolute power. The opportunity came through the determination of Vice-Chancellor von Papen to oust Schleicher from the Chancellorship, which he had previously held himself, by coming to what he hoped could be realistic terms with Hitler.

Hess appears once again as present on an important historic occasion

—the celebrated secret meeting mutually sought between Hitler and Papen at the house of the Cologne banker, Kurt von Schröder, on 4 January 1933.[38] This meeting paved the way for Hitler's Chancellorship in 1933 by discussing the form of coalition between Papen's Nationalists and Hitler's Party to replace the present Schleicher Cabinet. Hitler learned the extent to which Hindenburg, the aged President, was under pressure to yield to the need to give the Nazi Party some degree of office in the government. Papen, in fact, was trying to sell out Schleicher and drive a hard bargain with Hitler. It was soon to emerge, however, that it was Hitler who drove the hard bargain, though when the Cabinet was formed after Hitler had become Chancellor on 30 January its membership was composed of only three Nazis (Hitler, Göring and Frick) against nine members representing the other Nationalist interests. Papen, as Vice-Chancellor, held that he could effectively control Hitler. He was soon to learn otherwise.

Goebbels gives the inside view of how the Party leaders received the news of Hitler's appointment. Although Hess is not mentioned by name, he was there to share in this triumph with the rest:

It seems like a dream. The Wilhelmstrasse is ours. The Leader is already working in the Chancellery. We stand in the window upstairs, watching hundreds and thousands of people march past the aged President of the Reich and the young Chancellor in the flaming torchlight, shouting their joy and gratitude.

At noon we are all at the Kaiserhof, waiting. The Leader is with the President of the Reich. The inward excitement almost takes our breath away. In the street the crowd stands silently waiting between the Kaiserhof and the Chancellery. What is happening there? We are torn between doubt, hope, joy and despair. We have been deceived too often to be able wholeheartedly to believe in the great miracle.

Chief-of-Staff Roehm stands at the window the whole time, watching the door of the Chancellery from which the Leader must emerge. We shall be able to judge by his face if the interview was happy.

Torturing hours of waiting! At last a car draws up in front of the entrance. The crowd cheers. They seem to feel that a great change is taking place or has already begun.

The Leader is coming.

A few moments later he is with us. He says nothing, and we all remain silent also. His eyes are full of tears. It has come! The Leader is appointed Chancellor. He has already been sworn in by the President of the Reich. The final decision has been made. Germany is at a turning-point in her history.

All of us are dumb with emotion. Everyone clasps the Leader's hand; it would seem as if our old pact of loyalty were renewed at this moment.[39]

The way was now clear to consolidate the absolute power to which the Chancellorship was the first important step. The period between 30 January—with the crowds in the city streets singing the Horst Wessel anthem and *Deutschland, Deutschland über Alles* while Hitler held his first Cabinet—and 24 March, when the Enabling Law gave Hitler his dictatorship, were weeks of feverish activity. Hitler's position was insecure; his government was only held together by virtue of a highly unstable coalition, and the Reichstag, in which he did not command a majority vote, could at any time dismiss his Cabinet. Hitler was determined on two lines of action—to stage another speedy election, which would be openly within the law and the constitution, and secondly to ensure by means which were highly illegal that his representation in the next house would be such that he could command a majority for whatever legislation he might devise.

On his side were a few powerful factors: the image of his own success, the ruthless energies of Goebbels, who was determined to use strong-arm methods to swing the election by the use of intimidation, and the rapid machinations of Göring who, having secured the office of Minister of the Interior in the all-powerful state of Prussia, proceeded without delay to reform the civil service and police force so that it would be obedient to Nazi discipline. The key to control of the Reichstag, of which Göring was President, was to render the Communist vote impotent. To secure this, a great incident had to be staged which could be represented as an abortive attempt by the Communists to secure power by a coup d'état. The Reichstag fire of 27 February came at so convenient an hour only because it was directly engineered by the Nazis. Göring stepped in overnight and ordered mass arrests of the Communists, including many Reichstag deputies. The police, fully reinforced in advance by the SA and the SS, were poised ready to do their duty before the flames were brought under control.

Faced with the intimidation of many voters in the streets and at the polls, the last multi-party election could scarcely be called an altogether free one. The Communists had been prevented from holding any public meetings early in February, and their journals had been suppressed. Even the Social Democrats had not been immune from having their political meetings and rallies broken up. The streets were filled with marching men, while radio loudspeakers roared out the Nazi message. Yet Hitler still only mustered 44 per cent of the poll on 3 March. But with the Communist deputies prevented from voting in the Reichstag, Hitler's Enabling Act was passed on 24 March by the combined vote of all the right-wing parties against the single opposition of the Social Democrats.

The Enabling Act was passed within three days of the opening of the newly elected House; the vote took place under the intimidating gaze of Göring as Reichstag President. Hitler was master of Germany.

2

'CONSCIENCE OF THE PARTY'

DURING the eight years between Hitler's accession to power and Hess's quixotic flight to Britain, the Führer's dedicated adjutant was to have innumerable, high-sounding offices heaped upon him. Hitler's two instinctive drives—to surround himself with men with whom he had over the years become familiar, and to secure his own position by adopting a 'divide and rule' policy in the distribution of his appointments—made it certain that anyone as outstandingly loyal as Hess would achieve a wide range of powers, many of them overlapping, however, with powers conferred on others. The nature of the appointments conferred on Hess were often left vague, but there can be no question that his position became extremely powerful, if diffuse.

After the election held in March 1933, Hess became a member of the Reichstag. Then, on 21 April 1933, a few days before his thirty-ninth birthday, he was created Deputy (*Stellvertreter*) to the Führer, an office technically relating only to matters internal to the National Socialist Party.[1] However, this office was to be defined in the widest terms in the Party Year Book:

> By decree of the Führer of 21 April, 1933, the Deputy of the Führer received full power to decide in the name of the Führer all matters concerning Party leadership. Thus, the Deputy of the Führer is the representative of the Führer, with full power over the entire leadership of the National Socialist German Workers' Party. The office of the Deputy of the Führer is therefore an office of the Führer. In essence, it is the duty of the Deputy of the Führer to direct the basic policies of Party work, to give directives, and take care that all Party work be done according to National Socialist principles. All the threads of the Party work are gathered together by the Deputy of the Führer. He gives the final Party word on all intra-Party plans and all questions vital for the existence of the German people. The Deputy of the Führer gives the directives required for all the Party work,

in order to maintain the unity, determination and striking power of the National Socialist German Workers' Party as the bearer of the National Socialist philosophy. In addition to the duties of Party leadership, the Deputy of the Führer has far-reaching powers in the field of the State. These are:

One, participation in national and State legislation, including the preparation of Führer's orders. The Deputy of the Führer in this way validates the conception of the Party as the guardian of National Socialist philosophy.

Two, approval of the Deputy of the Führer of proposed appointments for officials and labour service leaders.

Three, securing the influence of the Party over the self-government of the municipal units.[2]

Since from 1933 the Nazi Party and the State became increasingly integrated, the Party organisations under Hess concerned with, for example, foreign policy, racial policy, technological development and education were to be correspondingly the centres of guidance to those offices of State which remained nominally at least in existence. Since Hitler was to govern largely by decree, Hess was to become the author and co-signatory of many of Hitler's legal pronouncements.

On 1 December 1933, Hess became Reich Minister without Portfolio, and a member of Hitler's Cabinet, along with Roehm, who was shortly to be assassinated; his specific task was to guarantee close co-operation between the Party and the SA, on the one hand, and the public authorities on the other. Much later, on 4 February 1938 he was appointed to Hitler's Secret Cabinet Council, which was concerned with the planning which led directly to Hitler's acts of aggression, 1939–41. On 30 August 1939 Hitler appointed him to the Council of Ministers for Defence of the Reich. Once the invasion of Poland had started, on 1 September 1939, Hitler in his speech before the Reichstag that morning declared Göring his successor, and Hess the second in line to his throne.[3] Had Hess possessed as lively an aesthetic as he had a political sense in direct agreement with his master, who knows that he might not have been Hitler's first deputy. Otto Dietrich, the Party's Press Chief, wrote after the War:

Culture and art, of which Munich was to be the shining symbol visible throughout Germany, were to Hitler a particularly important factor in the life of the nation. In 1934, after returning from a visit to Hess's newly decorated home in the Isar Valley near Munich, he mentioned that he could not make Hess his successor as Führer because the latter's house betrayed such a lack of feeling for art and culture. Göring, whom he respected for his broad grasp of the political significance of art, was shortly afterwards appointed Hitler's successor.[4]

Hess and his office became the channel through which all legislation or decrees of the Reich had to pass, except matters concerned with the Armed Forces, the Police and the Foreign Office. In fact, Hess issued his own decree to that effect in October 1934. He declared that he had been given the right to participate in legislation by the Führer, and that any department of authority promoting legislation should submit the draft in good time for him to approve or amend it. Hess thoroughly approved of this arbitrary system of achieving legislation without benefit of discussion in Parliament. In a speech made on 16 January 1937, he said:

> National Socialism has seen to it that vital necessities of our nation can today no longer be talked to pieces by a Reichstag and made the object of haggling between Parties. You have seen that in the new Germany decisions of historic scope are made by the Führer and his Cabinet—decisions which in other countries must be preceded by parliamentary debates lasting days and weeks.[5]

Shortly before the flight to Britain, Hess's range of duties were the subject of comment in the *National Zeitung* (27 April 1941):

> Rudolf Hess was once called the 'Conscience of the Party'. If we ask why the Führer's Deputy was given this undoubtedly honourable title, the reason for this is plain to see. There is no phenomenon of our public life which is not the concern of the Führer's Deputy. So enormously many-sided and diverse is his work and sphere of duty that it cannot be outlined in a few words; and it lies in the nature of the obligation laid on the Führer's Deputy that wide publicity hears little of the activity of Rudolf Hess. Few know that many Government measures taken, especially in the sphere of war economy and the Party, which meet with such hearty approbation when they are notified publicly, can be traced back to the direct initiation of the Führer's Deputy.[6]

To list the decrees the wording of which Hess either supervised or approved prior to signing them on Hitler's behalf would be to trace the whole day-by-day history of the institution of Nazi tyranny down to the smallest details. Some of the more important laws in which he participated, such as those initiating the persecution of the German Jews, will be discussed later. But the vast traffic of business through his headquarters in Munich was two-way: decrees, regulations, instructions and memoranda poured out, while in equal profusion enquiries, problems and complaints poured in from the Party administration throughout the country. Hess's office became a sorting-house for all those with problems to solve which affected Party policy or procedure. As Otto Dietrich points out, when Hitler became less and less interested in the parochial details of the Party now he was in power and had the State at his command, 'decisions on Party matters were handed down by him through Hess.' Hanfstaengl describes this, light-heartedly:

Hess, in his ill-defined capacity as head of the Party liaison staff, tried to act as Hitler's middleman. His actions were disowned by Hitler so often that in the end he never took a decision, but put people off with vague promises of looking into the matter. Exasperated regional leaders coined a phrase to describe his attitude: 'Come unto me all ye that are weary and heavy laden, and I will do nothing.' Hess was already becoming highly peculiar and went in for vegetarianism, nature cures, and other weird beliefs. It got to the point where he would not go to bed without testing with a divining-rod whether there were any subterranean watercourses which conflicted with the direction of his couch. His wife used to complain: 'I have as much experience out of our marriage as a candidate for confirmation.' Bormann was still Hess's assistant. He was tidy, modest and thrifty, and, I thought, a good influence, as he and Hess waged a continuous campaign against corruption in the Party, and Bormann tried to keep orderly accounts. Hess gradually became a nobody, a flag without a pole. Even Hitler once said to me of his capacity as Party deputy: 'I only hope he never has to take over from me. I would not know who to be more sorry for, Hess or the Party.'

The only thing they all had in common were their petty rivalries and jealousies. Göring and Goebbels hated each other in their competition to make the biggest splash in Berlin; Göring and Roehm hated each other in their fight to curry favour with the Army. Even the personally mild Himmler had his knife into Goebbels, who had tried to turn Hitler's mind against the SS cavalry unit, which he described as smacking of class privilege. It was the apple of the old veterinary student's eye. Göring hated Hess, whom he called a *Piesel*—a sort of half-gentleman, for having failed to turn up without excuse at a birthday party given by the Crown Prince.[7]

The truth is that Hess became more and more dilatory in handling the endless stream of complaints, so many of which were either stupid or parochial. He let the files lie unanswered, or passed them over to subordinates. He was a man who liked action, and desk work did not, in the end, appeal to him.

As Hanfstaengl reveals, in July 1933 an important addition had been made to Hess's entourage. Martin Bormann had become his Chief of Staff, with the rank of Reichsleiter, the highest in the Party hierarchy.[8] Six years younger than Hess, he had trained as a gunner during the last month of the war, but had not seen action. He had served in the Free Corps Rossbach in 1922, when it was an illegal formation, and had been concerned in the notorious murder of another recruit, Walter Kadow, who was suspected of being a communist agent. Bormann was among those subsequently arrested and tried for murder, along with Rudolf Hoess, the future commandant of Auschwitz. Hoess was sentenced to ten years imprisonment as the ring-leader; Bormann was sentenced to one year as an accomplice, and served his full term, after which he returned to his normal work in farm management. He joined the Nazi Party in 1927, and after various staff jobs in the Party office and the SA in his area, became in 1930 Chief of the Aid Fund of the Nazi Party (*Leiter der Hilfskasse*). Although poorly educated he was good at figures and honest with money. His responsibility was to look after the families of men killed or wounded during action on behalf of the Party. His rise from obscurity was aided by his marriage in 1929 to Gerda Buch, daughter of the chairman of the Nazi Party Court, which maintained Party discipline. Gerda was another of those staunch young German women who, like their menfolk, responded readily to Hitler's uncompromising form of patriotism; Hitler was a witness at their wedding. Hess had gained for himself a stocky, powerfully built young assistant, thick-necked, with hard brown eyes. They were to form a relentless, hardworking and dedicated team, with a relationship not dissimilar to that of Heydrich and Himmler—that is, one in which a growing sense of rivalry developed. Each of these able young assistants, Heydrich and Bormann, was an obsessive power-seeker; they sought increasingly to command the attention of Hitler independently of their superiors. Both were to succeed, though Heydrich's independent career was to be cut short when he was assassinated in Prague in 1942. Bormann, as we shall see, had his own method of gaining direct access to the Führer. Like Hess, Bormann held honorary rank in the SS, Lieutenant-General (SS-Gruppenführer) from 30 January 1937, and General (Obergruppenführer) from 21 July 1940. Bormann's pursuit of power, however, was conducted entirely behind the scenes. He hated the limelight. He had a rasping unpleasant voice, which did not fit him for public speaking.

Hess and Bormann, as we have seen, were either the signatories or co-signatories on behalf of their Party headquarters of a vast flood of decrees, orders and memoranda of instruction or advice, some for immediate publication, some secret or confidential. The recipients were Party and State officials at various levels, according to the nature of what was sent, but the normal procedure was to make Gauleiters responsible for ensuring that their subordinates knew and acted upon the regulations which piled up upon the desk. The regulations which could be made public were published in a succession of volumes entitled *Decrees of the Deputy of the Führer*. Following the Enabling Act of March 1933, Hitler's Law to secure the Unity of Party and State (which included Hess's appointment to the Reich Cabinet) in effect did away with the need to pass further legislation through the Reichstag, which remained only as a nominal body which could be assembled from time to time to hear Hitler's more important speeches. Government by decree was the order of the time, and since Hitler detested documentation and despised any form of detailed administrative work, it remained for Hess and his officials to put into formal language many of the arbitrary, never-ceasing demands of the Führer as the net tightened in every department of civil life. He was even instructed to interfere with the due course of the law, reviewing sentences passed on those deemed in the courts enemies of the Party, the Führer or the State, and increasing these if he saw fit; indeed he was instructed to take 'merciless action' against them.

Most of this work was conducted from the Brown House, the Party headquarters in Munich.[9] Nevertheless, Hess had to visit Berlin constantly, and it was here that Lüdecke describes an interview with him in March 1933 at the Berlin office of his Ministry of the Verbindungsstab (Liaison Staff) in the Wilhelmstrasse; Lüdecke was anxiously advising the disbandment of the Nazi units in the United States:

There sat a man not easy to read. Luxurious, dark hair crowned a strong angular face; he had grey-green eyes under heavy, bushy brows; a fleshy nose, a firm mouth, and a square determined jaw. Slender and lean-limbed, he was goodlooking and rather Irish in appearance. There was a restrained fanaticism in his eyes, but his manner was collected and quiet. I recall him as a commanding presence, a compliment one can pay to only a few of the higher Nazi chiefs.

Hess did not put me at my ease. I couldn't make him out, and he didn't help me a bit. He was polite, too polite, very cool, and I couldn't get at him, couldn't draw anything out of him. When I told him that it was imperative to dissolve the American organization, at least the Nazi units depending on Munich, he was evasive. 'I'll think it over,' he said. 'It seldom pays to destroy something if there's nothing to put in its place.' It was almost to the word what Hitler had said.

'But I have something to put in its place. Much better, much more effective, to have influence in a rising native American organiza- tion than to try to impose any Nazi organization on Americans. It won't work!'

But it was useless. I was unable to kindle his humour. He re- mained non-committal, elusive, not once looking straight into my eyes, which I held fixed on him. After a shifting, manœuvring talk of fifteen or twenty minutes I left him dissatisfied.[10]

The Brown House in Munich, however, was to be the centre for Hess's activities in his capacity as Stellvertreter, the Führer's Party deputy. Both Dr Gerhard Klopfer, Hess's Under-Secretary of State, and Heinrich Heim, appointed Hess's legal adviser in 1934 and based in Berlin, have emphasized that Hess's prime task was to filter legislation— not only issuing decrees of his own but advising and vetting legislation affecting such matters as agriculture, health and education.[11] A close liaison, therefore, had to be kept with other Ministries at the Berlin office.

In spite of the new circumstances which separated them, Hess was to remain close to Hitler throughout the period of his office. He was his frequent guest at the Chancellery in Berlin or at Berchtesgaden. Hess was one of the few men Hitler felt he could really trust. But Hess did nothing to counteract the Führer's growing regard for Bormann, who took over the detailed administration of the *Adolf-Hitler-Spende der Deutschen Industrie*, the fund which the grateful industrialists maintained as a gift of gratitude to Hitler for saving Germany from Communism.[12] This fund was not accountable and could be spent as Hitler wished, and Bormann made it his business to use the fund in a way most likely to please the Führer. One of the first developments was the rebuilding of the Villa Wachenfeld in the Obersalzberg above Berchtesgaden, the house which Hitler had first of all rented in 1928 and then bought after he became Chancellor. The new house, the celebrated Berghof, was opened in 1936, and the whole surrounding territory expropriated and developed to give Hitler a magnificent mountain estate. In addition, he built the Kehlsteinhaus, the Tea House, on a peak high above the Berghof reached by an elevator inside the mountain. At the same time, Bormann, who lived in Munich, built himself a villa within easy reach of the Berghof. Bormann also interested himself later in Hitler's great projects for Linz, the Führer's birthplace in Austria, and which he wanted to make the repository for the most lavish art collection in the world. For this an organisation of art experts was eventually set up in June 1939, the *Sonderauftrag Linz* (Special Linz Mission) under Dr Hans Posse, director of the Dresden Art Gallery, in order to acquire works of art on a massive scale from the plundered collections of occupied Europe. Bormann arranged to be the administrator for this project as well.

According to evidence given after the war at the International Military Tribunal at Nuremberg, a circular letter sent by Hess to a number of large German industries was found in the Krupp files asking for donations to this fund. Hess wrote:

The fund rests upon an agreement between the Reich management of the NSDAP and leading representatives of German industry, to put at the disposal of the Reich leadership the funds required for the unified execution of the tasks which fall to the lot of the SA, SS, and other political organisations.[13]

According to Dietrich:

In 1934 I heard that 'business' had voluntarily donated to Hitler— in gratitude, so to speak, for the boost he had given to the economy —a fund of several million marks annually which was to be at his personal disposal, to use as he saw fit. Hitler himself in no way requested these funds and so far as I know never himself directed the spending of them. Under the name of Adolf Hitler Industrial Fund the sum was administered by Rudolf Hess, then chief of staff, and later Party Secretary, and Martin Bormann. Bormann, acting as trustee, used the money for Hitler's personal projects . . .

Using the millions of the Industrial Fund to enlarge Hitler's private holdings around the Berghof, Bormann skilfully wheedled his way into Hitler's favour. He established himself so securely that Hitler more and more came to consider him indispensable. As a result the brainless Bormann won more and more political influence. Hitler trusted him right down to the end, recognizing in Bormann a blindly obedient instrument who would pass on and execute his commands without the slightest deviation. In Hitler's will, which bears Bormann's signature as witness, Hitler recommended him to posterity as his 'most loyal Party comrade'.

In 1936 Bormann came to Berchtesgaden armed with money from the Industrial Fund. He bought parcel after parcel of land around Hitler's house and began literally to bore holes into the mountain. Hitler watched these proceedings with some initial doubts, but after a while he let Bormann have his head. He would often pun on the name saying Bormann was certainly a man for boring.[14]

Hess's involvement in the establishment and consolidation of the regime took three main forms—the supervision (and signing) of decrees, the control of Ernst Bohle's work among Germans based abroad (to be described later), and direct intervention on Hitler's behalf in certain negotiations, especially in Austria and the Sudeten territory in Czechoslovakia.

A selection of the decrees signed either by Hess or Bormann, acting as his deputy, decrees ranging from the highly important to the merely characteristic, is on pages 227-32. A glance through these will show that Hess was equally concerned in subjecting the nation to Nazi discipline through the SS and Gestapo, in maintaining Party control in the appointment of civil servants, in establishing the Nazi race laws and in depriving the Jews of their place in society and their rights in property, in stamping out any Christian influence remaining in the Party. He also signed such major pieces of legislation as the incorporation of Austria into the Reich (March 1938), and the incorporation of Danzig and certain Polish territory into Greater Germany (September and October 1939). He was involved, too, in the decrees subjecting the Poles to the harsh discipline of Nazi occupation.

In education he established departments to control both teachers and students in the universities; for example, on 18 July 1934 the Nazi League of German students came under his control. In May he founded the Rassenpolitische Amt of the Party 'to represent the Party in all legislative measures in racial policy.' He was a signatory to the decrees establishing compulsory military service in March 1935. In September 1935 he ordered all Party agencies to report to the Gestapo any person who criticized the Nazi Party or its institutions. In the same month the notorious Law for the Protection of Blood and Honour was published; this prohibited marriage and extra-marital intercourse between Jews and citizens of 'German or related blood'. In 1936 began a whole series of decrees aimed against the influence of the churches. In May 1938 he signed a decree depriving Jews of the right to vote or hold any office in the state; in July of the same year clergy were forbidden to hold any Party office. In July he withdrew the licences to practice from Jewish physicians, though they were allowed to continue to treat fellow-Jews. On 12 November 1938 he published the notorious decree excluding Jews from the economic life of Germany; this followed the pogrom of 8 November. In a confidential instruction of 14 December he reiterated the need for Party officials to co-operate with the Gestapo. Further decrees in 1939 removed the rights of Jews to make claims in cases arising from the pogroms of the previous November, and permitting their eviction by German landlords.

But these were the years in which Hess's advisory supervision of legislation was in full operation. A week after the seizure of power he made an initial, clumsy attempt to intervene in economic affairs by submitting to Hitler a scheme to call on the Reichsbank to reveal to the Government the affairs of its larger debtors—in particular he wanted to find out the credits held by certain newspapers. He believed, erroneously as it turned out, that the Bank had an obligation to do this if required by the Government. This suggestion led to a great deal of agitated correspondence, culminating in an angry letter in April from Hjalmar Schacht, who had resumed office as President of the Bank in March at Hitler's invitation, demanding that no decision should be taken concerning policy until his return from the United States, for which he was about to sail. A leading official at the Bank then made it clear that the Bank had to treat individual clients' accounts as strictly confidential. All the regulations required was that the Bank should keep the Government informed on the general state of currency and public finance. Schacht sent his letter to Heinrich Lammers, the Secretary of State in the Reich Chancellery, on 26 April. This led to internal correspondence not only with Hess's department but also the Finance Ministry, and Lammers stressed that any unlegalised interference in public and private banking must be avoided, and that any Party members taking such liberties would be dealt with severely. Hess had merely stirred up trouble in these early, unstable days of the regime. It was an error of judgement due to inexperience.

Hess was better equipped for action than large-scale administration. He was closely involved in the climax to the prolonged struggle between Ernst Roehm, Commandant of the SA on whose strength in the streets and meeting-halls Hitler had so greatly depended to bring him to power, and the Chancellor who by 1934 found the existence of this large body of restive, unruly men—between two and three million in numbers— an embarrassment now that he had achieved his objective. Roehm represented, like Gregor Strasser before him in the political field, a disruptive force in the Cabinet. His ambition was to merge the SA with the professional Army, a much smaller body than the SA, but with all the tradition and strategic knowledge of the German Army behind it. Roehm wanted to become Minister for Defence, with charge of all armed forces. He regarded himself as a professional soldier, though he had resigned his commission in 1923 and favoured the undisciplined life of the Free Corps or of the mercenary to a career in the German Army, with whose High Command Hitler had been most careful to come to terms during these difficult, early years of the regime. The Army, on the other hand, had nothing but contempt for the SA. In spite of his unwillingness to jettison old comrades, Hitler was finally persuaded to rid himself of Roehm. Characteristically, he did so in as melodramatic a manner as possible. At dawn on 30 June 1934 the growing tension finally broke in the form of a summary act of violence; Hitler, with his supporting cavalcade of cars, swept into the lakeside resort of the Tegernsee where Roehm was on sick-leave with his young, homosexual companions, and the arrests and shootings began, simultaneously in the roadside by the sanatorium, and in Munich, Berlin and elsewhere.[15] Roehm, Hitler was later to claim, was planning a coup d'état, and this was made an opportunity to kill anyone who had proved or might prove an embarrassment to his authority, and, indeed, to settle old scores. Among the hundreds assassinated on 30 June and during the days following were not only Roehm himself (who was not killed until 6 July), but the former Chancellor Schleicher, with whom Roehm was said to be plotting, and Gregor Strasser. Formal congratulations were sent to Hitler by President Hindenburg and General von Blomberg, the Minister of Defence.

Undoubtedly the men who had brought most pressure to bear on Hitler to rid himself of Roehm were Göring and Himmler, the young man (aged only 34 in 1934) who was rapidly acquiring supreme power over the political police (the Gestapo, established by Göring in Prussia during 1933) as well as the SS, the so-called élite force, which had provided the shock-troops in the sudden action against the SA. Since all records of this Night of the Long Knives were destroyed—other than the subsequent descriptions of such eye-witnesses as Gisevius and Papen (himself almost done to death)—it is difficult to trace exactly the part played by individual Nazi leaders in this violent purge. Himmler and his able assistant Heydrich are said to have provided the principal dossier of charges against Roehm which were to be heaped upon him by Hitler in his order of the day after Roehm's execution and in his speech to the Reichstag on 13 July giving his own version of the purge. He charged Roehm with luxurious living, the misuse of money, sexual perversion and corruption. Bormann, who had served in the SA, undoubtedly contributed to this dossier—more especially as his father-in-law, Walter Buch, was Chairman of the Nazi Party Court and so responsible for the maintenance of discipline within the Party. Hess, it will be remembered, had kept his own secret files on the behaviour of prominent Party members, and the sexual behaviour of men such as Roehm would be as repugnant to him as it was to Himmler. It was part of the functions of Hess's Verbindungsstab in Berlin to keep these secret records.

Hess's part in the purge cannot be determined exactly.[16] He did, however, issue a stern warning to any political rebels in a broadcast on 25 June, mention of which is made by Lüdecke:

In a radio speech over a nation-wide hook-up, Hitler's deputy voiced the Chancellor's view, hitting directly both at the reactionaries and at the *provocateurs* who under the guise of the 'Second Revolution' were aiming to start a rebellion against the National Socialist revolution. 'Some day,' said Hess, 'Hitler might deem it necessary to drive developments ahead through revolutionary methods, but the Revolution must be steered by him alone. Hitler is the great strategist of the Revolution; he knows the limits of what can be attained at a particular time, with the means at hand and under existing circumstances. He acts after close and ice-cold appraisal of the situation, often seeming only to serve the moment, yet always pursuing the ultimate aims of the Revolution . . . Woe to him who breaks faith, and thinks to serve the Revolution through rebellion! Woe to him who clumsily tramples the Führer's strategic plans in the hope of quicker results.'[17]

Another record of his function is made by Hans Frank, later to become the Governor-General of Poland. Frank, aged thirty-four, was Party adviser on law and Hitler's Minister of Justice in Bavaria, and he was alarmed from the legal point of view at the long list of SA leaders whom Hitler required should be executed at the Stadelheim prison in Munich. He was supposed to have, he says, a hundred SA men at his disposal to act as an execution squad. He protested on the telephone to the Brown House, where Hitler had retired after his foray to Tegernsee. Hitler showed his anger—'I and the Reich decide about them, not Bavaria,' he said. Frank decided to take the matter up with Hess. Hess was, says Frank, 'much calmer, more matter-of-fact, and somehow more of the gentleman than Hitler'.[18] Finally a compromise was reached, and only nineteen men, who were held to be already 'incriminated' were handed over for execution, while legal proceedings were started against other men held in custody.

Hess also intervened in the notorious case of Dr Willi Schmid, a distinguished music critic who was taken from his home in Munich by four SS men on the evening of 30 June. He had been mistaken for Willi Schmidt, a local SA leader. His body was returned to his wife sealed in a coffin which she was forbidden by the Gestapo to open. Frau Schmid, who was later to become an American citizen, swore an affidavit in 1945 that Hess came and visited her, expressed his sorrow for the mistake that had been made, and arranged for her to receive a pension. She described the background to this visit:

On 7 July an official of the Gestapo, one Regierungsrat Brunner, came to my residence. He said that he had come to express his sorrow for the 'regrettable accident'. I asked him what was the reason for having arrested my husband, and many other questions. He refused to answer any question I asked him.

During the following weeks the Gestapo twice tried to offer me money, and messengers were sent to my house with this money. They never stated why the money was being offered, and did not want a receipt or any other formal acknowledgement of it. I refused this money each time. The first time the messenger brought it back with him, but the second time he insisted on leaving it at my apartment. I took the money to the Braunhaus, NSDAP headquarters in Munich where I told an official what had happened and that I refused to accept the money. A Captain Fritz Wiedemann who was a member of Rudolf Hess's staff overheard my conversation and he offered me his assistance. He told me that I could leave the money there and that he would endeavour a legal pension of some kind for me. He also said that he would try to obtain a statement for me that my husband was entirely innocent of any wrong. Shortly thereafter I received a phone call, a voice on the other end of the line saying to me that Heinrich Himmler desired to speak to me. A very arrogant voice then came on the line and told me that I had better accept the money which had been offered me and keep quiet about the matter. I repeated my refusal and hung up. I immediately contacted Captain Wiedemann and told him about the phone call from Himmler. Not long thereafter, on 31 July, Rudolf Hess came personally to visit me accompanied by an adjutant. He said that he had come to express his sympathy, and to assure me that the guilty ones would be punished. I told him not to punish the young boys who had taken my husband away that night but to punish the really guilty ones who were responsible for their acts. He told me that I should think of my husband's death as the death of a martyr for a great cause. He promised me that he would personally concern himself with the case.

This visit was followed by a letter from Rudolf Hess, dated September 24, 1934, in which Hess referred to his visit and in which he stated that my husband was not in 'any way' shot because of any connection with the Roehm Revolt or because of any guilt on his part. A copy of this letter, attested by a Munich notary, Dr Kleinmann, is attached hereto. I had this copy made in case the Gestapo should find the original and take it from me. Unfortunately I have since lost the original of this letter. However, my present husband has seen the original of this letter, and his affidavit to this effect is attached hereto. Both my brothers-in-law have also seen the original of this letter, and their names and addresses are given below.

Upon the request of Mr Hess the Nazi party paid me a monthly pension of one thousand marks which was the approximate salary my husband earned before his death.[19]

Hess was to be a prominent figure at all the annual Nazi rallies held in Nuremberg. He appears in the film *Triumph of the Will*, which Leni Riefenstahl made in September 1934, less than three months after the Roehm purge. Hess in his opening speech alluded to it, as he stood in the Congress Hall filled with a great mass of people with lights flooding down on their heads and on the decor of the symbolic eagles of the Third Reich. He spoke of the Nazi dead who must be remembered at such a time. 'The Führer is Germany,' he said, 'when he judges the nation judges', a reference to Roehm. He referred also to the revival of the Army under Hitler, and the greatness of the future—'only then will the Führer be appreciated as he should be.' He ended by claiming that 'Germany is home for Germans all over the world.' Leni Riefenstahl rehearsed Hess, along with other Party leaders, for the film, making them speak in the empty hall. Speer in his autobiography noted how effective Hess was as he spoke the words, 'Mein Führer, I salute you in the name of the Party Congress. The Congress now proceeds. *Es spricht der Führer!*' Speer comments: 'He seemed so convincing that afterwards I wasn't quite sure of the genuineness of his feelings.'[20] Early in 1934, Speer had been appointed head of the department of architecture in Hess's Ministry. However, he could excite little aesthetic response in him. When the previous July he had shown Hess his designs for the Party Congress decorations, Hess had barely looked at them. 'Only the Führer can decide all this,' he had said, and made arrangements for Speer to see Hitler.

It became customary for Hess to open the proceedings, and introduce Hitler to the vast assembly. William Shirer, the American journalist, was present at the 1934 rally:

This morning's opening meeting in the Luitpold Hall on the outskirts of Nuremberg was more than a gorgeous show; it also had something of the mysticism and religious fervour of an Easter or Christmas Mass in a great Gothic cathedral. The hall was a sea of brightly coloured flags. Even Hitler's arrival was made dramatic. The band stopped playing. There was a hush over the thirty thousand people packed in the hall. Then the band struck up the Badenweiler March, a very catchy tune, and used only, I'm told, when Hitler makes his big entries. Hitler appeared in the back of the auditorium, and followed by his aides, Göring, Goebbels, Hess, Himmler, and others, he strode slowly down the long centre aisle while thirty thousand hands were raised in salute. It is a ritual, the old-timers say, which is always followed. Then an immense symphony orchestra played Beethoven's Egmont Overture. Great Kleig lights played on the stage, where Hitler sat surrounded by a hundred Party officials and officers of the army and navy. Behind them the 'blood flag', the one carried down the streets of Munich in the ill-fated Putsch.

Behind this, four or five hundred SA standards. When the music was over, Rudolf Hess, Hitler's closest confidant, rose and slowly read the names of the Nazi 'martyrs'—brown-shirts who have been killed in the struggle for power—a roll-call of the dead, and the thirty thousand seemed very moved.[21]

Sir Nevile Henderson, who as British Ambassador in Germany was only authorized to attend one of these rallies officially in 1937, describes the great assembly as follows:

The displays themselves were most impressive. That of the Party leaders [or heads of the Party organisations in the towns and villages throughout the country] took place in the evening at eight pm, in the stadium or Zeppelinfeld. Dressed in their brown shirts, these 140,000 men were drawn up in six great columns, with passages between them, mostly in the stadium itself, but filling also all the tiers of seats surrounding the stadium and facing the elevated platform reserved for the Chancellor, his Ministers and his guards, the massed bands, official guests, and other spectators. Hitler himself arrived at the far entrance of the stadium, some 400 yards from the platform, and, accompanied by several hundred of his followers, marched on foot up the central passage to his appointed place. His arrival was theatrically notified by the sudden turning into the air of the 300 or more searchlights with which the stadium was surrounded. The blue-tinged light from these met thousands of feet up in the sky at the top to make a kind of square roof, to which a chance cloud gave added realism. The effect, which was both solemn and beautiful, was like being inside a cathedral of ice. At the word of command the standard-bearers then advanced from out of sight at the far end, up the main lane, and over the further tiers and up the four side lanes. A certain proportion of these standards had electric lights on their shafts, and the spectacle of these five rivers of red and gold rippling forward under the dome of blue light, in complete silence, through the massed formations of brown-shirts, was indescribably picturesque. I had spent six years in St Petersburg before the War in the best days of the old Russian ballet, but for grandiose beauty I have never seen a ballet to compare with it. The German, who has a highly developed herd instinct, is perfectly happy when he is wearing a uniform, marching in step, and singing in chorus, and the Nazi revolution has certainly known how to appeal to these instincts in his nature. As a display

of aggregate strength it was ominous; as a triumph of mass organisation combined with beauty it was superb.

The review of the Hitler youth was no less an object lesson from
an observer's point of view. Standards, music, and singing again
played a big part in the performance, and the fervour of youth was
much in evidence. The speeches on that occasion were made by
Hitler, Hess and Baldur von Schirach, the leader of the Hitler
youth.[22]

He also describes Hess, whom he met on a number of occasions:

Rudolf Hess was the Führer's deputy, appointed to represent him
when or wherever he could not himself attend any function. In a
sense he seemed to me to be a sort of adopted son to Hitler, and on
the outbreak of war he was named as second after Göring in the
order of succession to the leadership of the German nation. In less
troublous times he might well have been named first, but his
authority with the army would scarcely have been great enough in
war-time to hold the balance between the soldiers and the Nazi
Party.

Tall and dark, with beetling eyebrows, a famous smile and in-
gratiating manners, Hess was perhaps the most attractive-looking
of the leading Nazis. He was not inclined to be talkative, and in
conversation did not convey the impression of great ability. But
people who knew him best would have agreed that first impressions—
and I never got further with him than that—were deceptive, and he
certainly wielded in Germany more influence than people generally
believed. I would have summed him up as aloof and inscrutable,
with a strong fanatical streak which would be produced whenever
the occasion required it.

Hess, like most of the leading personalities in the Party, was constantly in demand as a speaker, both on the platform and before the
microphone, mostly he spoke at rallies and congresses organized in
Germany, and his speeches were frequently published—a collection
of them appeared in 1938.[23] The occasion for the speeches might be a
Congress for German Chambers of Commerce Abroad, a regional (or
Gau) Party rally, the opening (in September 1934) of the Seventh
International Congress of Roadbuilders in Munich (traffic experts
from some fifty nations), a factory gathering of workers engaged in the
rearmament programme, an international youth congress, a gathering
on Reich-Peasant Day, addresses to students or youth leaders or civil

servants. Always it was the same collection of themes—the greatness of Hitler, the need for absolute loyalty to him and the Party, the resurrection of the German Army, the danger from Bolshevism and Jewry. There were many national occasions which called for speeches and broadcasts—such as the re-occupation of the Rhineland, or the period just before and after the Night of the Long Knives. And there were special occasions, such as his address in Stockholm to the German-Swedish Society in May 1935, or his address (recorded on sound-film in March 1937) sent to American women attending a congress in Chicago—'Believe me,' he said from the screen, 'we do not want another war; we want to save mankind from such calamity.' It should be noted that it was Hess, not Göring, who coined the phrase 'guns instead of butter' in a speech he made at Hof on 11 October 1936.[24] Hess was also, as we shall see, principal spokesman for the Party at the rallies for Germans abroad.

During the course of his administrative career, Hess entered his forties. Both at home and in his office he was a quiet, reserved, but also very domesticated man. His son, Wolf Rüdiger, was not born until 18 November 1937, and remained an only child to whom his father was devoted. He was deeply fond of his wife, but because he preferred her to keep outside politics she only accompanied him on social occasions, such as going to a concert or the theatre. In his private life Hess was very different from most of the other Nazi leaders, particularly Göring and Goebbels, who acquired great wealth and set up luxurious establishments. Like Himmler, he belonged to the more austere and puritan wing of the Party hierarchy. He lived in relatively modest comfort in a house in the Harthauser Strasse, situated in the fashionable district of Harlaching in Munich. The only luxury he allowed himself was a fine Mercedes sports car, painted brown for easy recognition; this he delighted to drive at speed.

Though he had little time for reading until he began his long period of confinement in 1941, he retained the enthusiasm of a mature student for books of a conventional kind. The one art to which he always responded was music; in the letters he sent his wife after 1941 he makes constant reference to it. He comments on Wagner, for example:

You have to be present in Bayreuth to get the most out of the music. The finest effect—surpassing all the others, I thought—was produced, not by *Meistersinger* but by *Tannhäuser*. Ever since I saw it performed in Bayreuth in 1930—or was it 31—with Toscanini conducting, this has stood out as one of the most wonderful experiences of its kind in my life. Yet at that time I wasn't in the best of receptive moods, not sufficiently relaxed to enjoy the anticipation or succumb to the full influence of the solemn moment when the music starts. For all this can be most impressive at Bayreuth where you get a community of kindred souls and an atmosphere is radiated back and forth between the audience and the performers.[25]

Speer, in his autobiography, says of Hess, 'He was very fond of chamber music, and his circle of acquaintances included some odd, but interesting types.'[26]

Hess's principal secretary, Hildegard Fath, has described him as a most courteous man to work for.[27] He became increasingly easy-going with years in office, and people he had known for a long while were permitted to call him 'Herr Hess' instead of 'Herr Minister'. Bormann was correspondingly detested for his brusqueness and harshness to his subordinates. Hess, on the other hand, has been described to us by both Heim and Klopfer as a quiet, very reserved man, even at times austere and off-putting to strangers. They claim his cultural interests to have been fairly wide, though he was not outstandingly intelligent. He had a distinct if somewhat odd sense of humour, but revealed it only to those who knew him well.

According to Josef Wulf and others, including Speer, he seemed to do little to exploit the omnipotence of his position. He let Bormann virtually supplant him, and refrained from sitting about at Berchtesgaden in order to be ready to listen to Hitler's endless rambling into the small hours of the night. He made Albert Speer, who in 1934 was attached to Hess's Ministry as departmental chief in charge of architecture, promise not to let the housing programme suffer because of Hitler's growing obsession to erect great public monuments. Hess was a vegetarian as well as a teetotaller and non-smoker, and when he went to the Chancellery or the Berghof he was worried about the food. According to Speer:

> About once a fortnight Hess would appear at luncheon, followed by his adjutant carrying a container with his food to be warmed in the Chancellery-kitchen. For a long time Hitler did not notice that Hess used to bring his own vegetarian dishes. When he learned about it, he turned to Hess at the table and said in some annoyance: 'I have an excellent diet-cook here. If your doctor has prescribed something special for you, she could certainly prepare it. You cannot

bring your own food here.' Hess argued stubbornly trying to explain to Hitler that his food should contain certain biologically dynamic ingredients. Whereupon he was told that if that were so he might as well have his meals at home. After this, Hess's appearances at lunch were even rarer.[28]

Hitler was also at this time a vegetarian, a teetotaller and non-smoker.

Hess developed certain eccentricities, which became more marked during the 1930s. Apart from his fastidious attitude to food, he fussed about his health and, like Himmler, resorted to special herbal remedies. As Speer says, 'Hess was very interested in homeopathy, studying many books on the subject.' His health deteriorated, like that of the other Nazi leaders, and eventually, in 1940, it was Himmler who recommended that Felix Kersten, his masseur, should examine Hess. Writing in his diary the following year, in May 1941, Kersten said:

> It was a year ago that Himmler asked me to examine Hess; since then I have treated him too. I established that he was suffering from trouble in the gall-bladder and stomach pains. In Hess I encountered a man who was quiet, friendly and grateful. He frequently spoke of his home in Egypt, for which he longed. He often said too that he would be happiest if he could retire to the loneliness of the Bavarian mountains . . .
>
> Hess was a good and helpful person, very modest in his way of life. He was a vegetarian, surrounded himself with clairvoyants and astrologers and despised official medical views.[29]

The medical reports prepared after his arrival in England provide a detailed account of both his health and his attitude of mind to it:

> He stated when in England that he had at various times suffered from trouble with his gall bladder, from renal trouble, from colitis, and also from a pain in the region of the heart. The fact that he was a teetotaller and non-smoker, coupled with his general personality make-up, may suggest that the old cardiac pains before he came to this country were symptoms of effort syndrome. In 1937 he had had a prostatitis, but the nature of this is unknown . . . We know from the history given by him, and it was confirmed by his late secretary, that he had since 1933 at any rate attacks of abdominal pains. She also said that he was not very good at climbing up steep slopes 'on account of the wound in his lung' . . . He had also had from time to time since 1933 attacks which were said to be due to his gall bladder.

C

We know that he had consulted numerous doctors, running from one to the other and never having the patience to let any one physician carry out treatment. Recently, particularly since 1938, he had turned more and more to unorthodox practitioners, those practising nature-cure, irido-diagnosis, and chiropraxy. His secretary related that the Führer had ridiculed Hess for his running around to all sorts of doctors and quacks. This account of his growing hypochrondria and concern for his health is borne out by the fact that on his arrival in Scotland his pockets were stuffed with homeopathic and nature-cure medicines, and his account of the dietetic restrictions that he had placed upon himself provided further confirmation. He excluded eggs, jams and dried foods, and drank only very weak tea.

Hess's mother is said to have had a marked interest in nature-cure and semi-medical matters, in contrast to his father, who in his later years had grown away from being the rather dour, stern man that he was when Hess was a boy, and had become a normal cheerful old gentleman who liked plenty of amusement. Part of the interest which Hess displayed in the various medical interests was, we believe, caused by a fear of cancer. He was dissatisfied that no cure for cancer had been found, and felt that possibly through unorthodox practice some solution of the problem could be found. Further he had a constant drive to greater efficiency, feeling that if he was tired something must be wrong with him . . . It would seem that Hess's interest in horoscopes and the semi-occult, which has been spoken of in the Press, began about the beginning of the war. He placed great emphasis on the influence of the stars and on the diagrams worked out for him by an elderly woman fortune-teller.[30]

Hess had always loved the open-air and the mountains. After his confinement in 1941, he complained that this was among the keenest of his memories, an experience he missed acutely: 'How closely my life is bound up with mountains! Isn't it extraordinary? I estimate that roughly one half of my life has been spent somewhere near a high mountain range.' In a letter written from Spandau in February 1948 he recollects the climbs and walks on the mountains he used to have with Ilse, and he ends:

The last of these mountain expeditions (for all one knows just now) was in the summer of 1939, the descent from Karli's Berghäusel, behind us bad weather gathering round the ridges of the Wetterstein

—so lovely and so moving to remember, and so strangely symbolic.[31]

There seems to have been some exaggeration about Hess's alleged dependence upon clairvoyants and his obsession with astrology. It became a current joke at the time, though Hess was among the more popular of the Nazi leaders. According to James Leasor:

> Hess was a very superstitious man, and sometimes his super-stitions were misinterpreted. When his wife Ilse was preparing for the birth of her child, Hess was desperately anxious to father a son. He knew the old German belief that a summer which sees an unusual number of wasps also sees a predominance of male babies. One afternoon during that summer, when he and his wife and secretary took tea in the garden of their house in Harthauser Strasse, a number of wasps became stuck in the mouth of the honey jar. Hess carefully picked each one out with his spoon, washed the honey off, and then put them out in the sun to dry. His secretary interpreted this as evidence of his kind heart; it was nothing of the sort, but a sign of the strength of his superstitions.[32]

Hess's interest in astrology, as we shall see, was to have dire consequences in Germany.

Hitler, who had had no direct experience of countries apart from Germany and Austria before becoming Chancellor, worked under the naive assumption that any German who had been born abroad could be regarded as an authority on foreign countries. It was because Hess had been raised in Egypt during his early youth that Hitler decided he should supervise the various organisations concerned with the control of German nationals resident abroad, as well as the investigation of possible links with foreign nationals of German racial extraction.

On 3 October 1933 Hess took over the Party's Ausland (Foreign) Organisation, which had been founded in May 1931 at Hamburg, and in the same year put this department in the charge of Ernst Wilhelm Bohle—a German who had been born in Bradford, England and raised in South Africa, and so had the necessary magic touch of contact with foreign parts. Bohle at thirty-one was at the time the youngest man to hold the rank of Gauleiter, and he enjoyed Hess's close friendship along with Leitgen, Hess's adjutant. In an affidavit sworn by Bohle and quoted at the Nuremberg trial, he defined his office as follows:

> The purpose of the Ausland Organization was, upon the assumption of power, to hold together in an organized way the approximately

3,300 Party members living outside the boundaries of Germany. Beyond that, through them the Germans abroad, who could have only a very vague idea of the political happenings at home, were to be taught the philosophy and the political programme of the new State.

Only native Germans could become members of the Party. The acceptance of foreigners or former Germans who had acquired citizenship in another State was strictly prohibited.[33]

When he took direct charge of the Ausland Organisation, Hess ordered that all German nationals living abroad must make contact with the Party through Bohle's office. At the same time, all Party members going abroad on Party business had to notify Bohle of their activities. On 23 February 1934 Hess issued an instruction at Bohle's request that every Gau bordering on the North Sea or the Baltic was to establish special facilities for German sailors, fishermen and the like, who went abroad regularly. The following May, Bohle was permitted to enlarge his administration, and Hess's younger brother Alfred was appointed Bohle's deputy.[34] In October, over and above his responsibilities for the Ausland Organization, Bohle joined Hess's Ministry to take charge of all problems concerned with Germans living abroad (*Sachbearbeiter für alle auslandsdeutsche Fragen*).[35] He had already the previous December, 1933, obtained from Hess permission to deal directly with the Foreign Office.

In 1934 the Aussenpolitisches Amt (Foreign Political Department) of the Party under A. Schumann became directly subject to Hess, after Schumann had made some objection to Hess's ruling that his news-service had to be co-ordinated with the SS Security-Service. During the mid-1930s there was to be constant bickering between the various departments in the Party and the Foreign Office concerning differences of responsibility and the inevitable overlapping of functions. It was characteristic of organizations under the Nazis to develop a multiplicity of overlapping departments, partly because of the needs of individual administrators to extend their powers into fields normally controlled by others, and partly to check on each other's activities. Hess was constantly invading what was technically the territory of the Foreign Office. For example, correspondence survives from 1936–37 with Lammers of Hitler's Chancellery which led to Bohle being appointed in 1937 Chief of the Auslands Organization of the Foreign Office, ostensibly to enable German Party 'leaders' abroad to be given titles which would enable them to be officially integrated with the German embassies and legations.

A further organisation under Hess's control was the People's League for Germans Abroad, the VDA (*Volksbund für das Deutschtum im Ausland*) which was concerned with racial Germans who were citizens in other countries. Hess's initial instructions to them in 1933 was that they could be all the more effective if 'they kept free from the influence of official Germany, no matter whether Government departments or Party units.' Professor Karl Haushofer became President of the VDA, and maintained a close link with the long-established German Auslandsinstitut, founded in Stuttgart in 1917 for 'scientific research on Germanism in the world, maintaining cultural connections with emigrants, and informing the people at home about Germanism abroad and about foreign countries.' This institute had a large library and had been a centre for information and publications on this subject for many years prior to the Nazi régime.

Karl Haushofer was also put in charge of the Volksdeutscher Rat (VR), Council for Germanization founded by Hess in October 1933. He sent a confidential memorandum to the key departments of State and Party stating that 'the strengthening and unity of universal Germanism (*Gesamtdeutschtum*) and all relevant questions within the Reich were to be taken care of and supervised' by himself. This organization was not to be publicized in order to avoid complications in foreign politics, but through it Hess aimed to create permanent contact with German minorities abroad. At a conference with Neurath, Hitler's Foreign Minister, on 17 November 1933, it was agreed that the VR should be used in an advisory capacity by the Foreign Office. On 13 March 1934 Hess stipulated that the VR should be the centre for dealing with Sudeten-German problems. But the interests of the VR were not to be solely abroad. Through creating so many departments with near-similar functions and interests either inside or alongside the Party and the State, Hess only created troubles for himself which he became either too preoccupied, too disinterested, or too dilatory to resolve. During 1934–35 there were constant differences between the VR and Bohle; on 31 January Karl Haushofer wrote his son Albrecht about a most friendly meeting with Hess in which he assured him he could not dissolve the VDA, in spite of Bohle's public statements that his organization was in charge of all National Socialist activities abroad, and that he would 'reactivate' the VR. The previous September Hess had told Bohle that the AO must not concern itself with Germans abroad of foreign nationality, and the VDA was not to meddle with Germans abroad who retained their German nationality. But the intrusions went on, and Hess left vague instructions with Leitgen to look into these disputes. Later, in 1935, Haushofer was very disturbed because Hess, in order to avoid trouble, failed to send him as a delegate to the VDA Congress in Königsberg. In an impassioned letter ('very confidential, lieber Rudolf, and please destroy after perusal') Haushofer claimed that this made his VR organisation look absurd. Finally in the autumn, Hess yielded to Haushofer's recommendation that the VR should be supplanted by a new (and camouflaged) institution, the members of which were to be trusted Party adherents. Later, however, there was to be trouble with Dr Steinacher, the VR representative in Berlin, and a Sudeten-Deutscher. In 1936 Haushofer insisted he be removed, in spite of his friendship with the Sudeten leader, Konrad Henlein, and this took place a year later.

It is clear, therefore, that Karl Haushofer's influence over his former pupil was still strong. But he, too, had his problems; his wife was a *Mischling*, or part-Jew, since her father, Hofrat Ludwig Mayer-Dors was of Jewish descent. Haushofer's son Albrecht, therefore, had Jewish blood, and this, but for Hess's protection, would have meant difficulty in obtaining work. It was through Hess's influence that he obtained a professorship in political geography in the Berlin Hochschule für Politik in the spring of 1935. Albrecht, aged thirty-two, was already a poet of esoteric distinction, as well as a supporter of his father's theories of geo-politics. Albrecht was to send Hess a letter, dated 7 September 1935, expressing deep gratitude on behalf of himself and his brother:

I know what I now have to thank you for. It is not so much the post—however suitable for what I hope to achieve—it is for having a spiritual and mental load lifted from me, so heavy that I can't really talk about it. Having been spared the ignominy of being considered an inferior German, fit only for the dustheap—being spared this is something my brother and I owe entirely to your intercession. You will understand me when I say that it is very difficult for a proud man to owe so much gratitude, and that he will need to search his heart very deeply before becoming a petitioner. I could not have done it. I could not have accepted so peculiar a blessing—not even for my father's sake—if I did not feel sure that if need be I would be able to do everything for you as a person, as a human being. It may seem far-fetched just now, but for me to say it to you just once, and to say 'Yes' to it, is something truly profound.[36]

In fact, Hess's anti-Semitism may at first have been tempered by other considerations; a memorandum drafted for Hess in the spring of 1934 survives which recommends preferential treatment and full citizenship for Jews resident in Germany for several generations and conspicuous for the merit of their lives and their service to the Father-land. It appears to have been drafted by Albrecht Haushofer. Indeed, the Haushofers were to remain on the closest terms with Hess up to 1941.

However, it was the legislation against the Jews which Hess signed that most troubled the American ambassador in Berlin, William E. Dodd, Junior; he makes a number of references to this in his published diary, for example:

I . . . received a copy of formal instructions to the Nazi Party that they must refuse all associations with Jews, must not, if lawyers, assist Jews in any way, and, if clerks in Jewish stores, must not wear their Party badges. And the 'wicked race' must in no public places be recognized or allowed to associate with the Aryans. These are the instructions that have been before the Party for a year and a half. This copy bore the name of Rudolf Hess, personal adjutant to Hitler, and the date was August 16, 1934 . . .

The wife of a Secretary of a German Legation in the Balkans called this morning to see if it would be possible for me to assist her in a difficulty forced upon her and her husband by Hitler's representative, Rudolf Hess, who has ordered her husband to prove that none of his ancestors or his wife's were Jews. This lady was born here, of American-German parents. If she cannot prove that neither of her grand-parents were Jewish, her husband must resign his position in the German Foreign Service.[37]

Hess was to expand a great part of his eloquence on the platform to German representatives from abroad. It was part of his function at great rallies, as we have seen, to pay special tributes to Hitler, to introduce him or to administer oaths of loyalty to him as Führer. He even exacted a 'mass oath-taking' by radio on 25 February 1934, addressed to a million political, youth and other 'leaders'. 'Adolf Hitler is Germany, and Germany is Adolf Hitler,' he declaimed. 'Whoever gives his oath to Hitler gives it to Germany.' At the Nuremberg rally of 1934, which was attended by many Auslandsdeutsche, including some from China, Japan, and Central and South America who had never yet been 'home', Hess made a resounding speech, and dedicated seventy-three new AO banners. During the night of 10–11 September Hitler received twenty leaders of European and Overseas Party groups. A few months later, on 18 November, Hess made another big speech at Bremerhaven for the German seamen. It was Goebbels who claimed that while diplomats are the envoys of the Reich, seamen are the ambassadors of the nation.

In November 1936 5,000 Amtsleiter (Party District Leaders) from all over the world assembled for the fourth Reich Congress of the AO. Bohle spoke first, stating with the note of aggression sounding, that 'the new Germany was determined to protect every single one of her citizens even beyond the borders of the Reich.' Hess followed this with a speech in which he declaimed that the Germans abroad were no longer unguarded and that 'whenever and wherever they found themselves in trouble powerful new ships, the swastika proudly displayed, would sail in to protect them.' This referred to the Spanish Civil War, and to the fact that in July the German Embassy in Madrid had asked for German warships to safeguard the lives and property of Germans in Spain. The *Deutschland* and the *Admiral Scheer* had evacuated 15,000 Germans—a forceful show of action widely noticed at the time by the so-called Great Powers.

This, indeed, was the period during which Hitler was beginning openly to express his defiance to the rest of the world. He was removing the camouflage with which he had formerly covered his aggressive policy and activities. The elder statesmen in Germany, representatives of aristocratic or bourgeois tradition, were being shelved—Neurath from the Foreign Office, Blomberg and Fritsch from the Army, Schacht from Economic Affairs. Ribbentrop at this stage was merely an 'expert' in foreign politics on Hess's ministerial staff; he was appointed German Ambassador in London on 26 July 1936, the month when Franco sent personal letters to Hitler and Göring asking for Germany's intervention. The two members of the AO who had brought these letters gave them to Bohle; refusing to pass them to the Foreign Office, Bohle gave them to Hess, who immediately sent them by messenger to Hitler in Bayreuth. Hitler at once gave Franco his support, while Hess put the entire AO machinery at Göring's disposal to assist with the delivery of armaments to Spain, while private companies were set up to secure the delivery from Spain of iron ore, olive oil, wool, and other raw materials, many of them important for German rearmament.

At the fifth Reich Congress of the AO, held 29 August to 5 September in Stuttgart (the 'city of the Germans Overseas', as Munich was the city of the Nazi Movement, and Nuremberg the city of the Party Rallies), some 10,000 Germans from abroad poured in to hear addresses by all the Nazi leaders except Hitler—by Göring, Goebbels, Hess, and even Himmler. Hess made the point that German armaments were intended 'to serve the security of Germans abroad as well as that of the Reich,' but he added that National Socialism was not meant for export. The other speakers had stressed the Führer's yearning for peace.

In his dealings with Germans in the United States, Hess was wary. In 1933 he dissolved the National Socialist local groups (*Ortsgruppen*), such as those in New York, Chicago, Detroit or Los Angeles. 'With regard to the Americans, anything which might be held provocative must be avoided,' he said. Bohle was warned by Captain Mensing of the New York Norddeutscher Lloyd Agency in the autumn of 1933 that the activities of the Bund (a self-appointed movement of 'Friends of the New Germany') were threatening German-American relations. Hess immediately ruled that Party members must refrain from party-political activities while in the United States, and take their instructions from Bohle.[38] The Bund, he said, should elect an American citizen for its President, and keep its activities social. He instructed Bohle to appoint a representative in the United States to see these rules were observed. Further than this, in February 1934, Hess decreed that German nationals should resign from the Bund, since it was an American, not German inspired organization; however, this decree was not published in case it might offend the Germans in the United States. In October 1935 a further decree was issued to all German consulates in the United States stating that German citizens should be urged to leave the Bund. A further embarrassment arose through a fascist movement founded by William Dudley Pelley and calling itself the Silver Shirts of America. Its grotesque programme of militant Christianity, anti-Semitism and anti-Communism did not suit Bohle, who wrote to that effect to Hess in February 1934. He was prepared to welcome, however, their anti-Semitism. Hess, indeed, was anxious to restrain the activities of Germans abroad which he could not easily control, and which gave Germany a bad name. Early in 1934, for example, he had to warn the Party groups in Roumania to be less ostentatious in showing their financial dependence on the Reich. The German ambassador, Count von der Schulenburg, went so far as to urge Hess to stop payments to political parties in Roumania, or their individual representatives. In June 1934 Albrecht Haushofer was sent to Poland in an unsuccessful attempt to iron out differences among the German minority groups, but the visit was camouflaged to avoid trouble with the Polish government.

By 1937, Bohle's AO had grown into a department employing some 800 staff, and Hess himself was becoming involved to some extent in Germany's expansionist aims.[39] At the same time, he was becoming increasingly dilatory. In March 1935, Hitler had ordered that Hess be consulted by the Foreign Office about the appointment of all senior officials sent abroad, so that they might have Party approval; an enquiry of 16 December 1935 referring to intended appointments of about a dozen senior diplomats received no answer until 8 April 1936.

The exact degree of active participation by Hess in the Austrian Anschluss is difficult to trace. Dollfuss, the Austrian Chancellor, was murdered on 25 July 1934 in the abortive Putsch by the local Nazis; the Anschluss itself took place in March 1938, and the murder of Dollfuss was regarded by Hitler at the time as disastrous. Seyss-Inquart, the member of the new Chancellor Schuschnigg's Cabinet who became Hitler's agent during the difficult, interim period in the strained relations between Germany and Austria, saw both Göring and Hess in July 1937 in order, he claimed at Nuremberg, to urge on Hitler a policy of restraint so that the Austrian Nazis could achieve their own victory without such dire interference from Germany.[40] Naturally, however, they would no longer take action without Hitler's knowledge and approval, and Hitler preferred the Anschluss to wear at least a mask of legality. Schuschnigg was to be forced into a state of capitulation. Göring, on the eve of the Anschluss, suggested that Hess or Bormann would be the appropriate people to restrain the leaders of the Nazi community within Austria at the time when, working on a top diplomatic level, Göring himself, with Seyss-Inquart, was to bring off the final diplomatic coup in Austria. This would be far better than German intervention after fighting in the streets.

When the German troops eventually marched in peaceful triumph into Austria after Göring's notorious coup d'état by telephone, Hess and Himmler were the first top leaders to enter the country by air. They arrived in Vienna by noon on 12 March 1938, and it was Hess who signed the law on 13 March which declared the union of Austria and Germany. On 24 July Hess made his notorious speech commemorating the unsuccessful Putsch of 1934, during which Dollfuss was murdered. The occasion was described by the American Consul-General in Vienna, and his statement was read out during the International Military Tribunal at Nuremberg:

> The two high points of the celebration were the memorial assembly on the 24th at Klagenfurt, capital of the Province of Carinthia, where in 1934 the Vienna Nazi revolt found its widest response, and the march on the 25th to the former Federal Chancellery in Vienna by the surviving members of the SS Standarte 89, which made the attack on the Chancellery in 1934. The assembled thousands at Klagenfurt were addressed by the Führer's Deputy, Rudolf Hess, in the presence of the families of the thirteen National Socialists who were hanged for their part in the July 'Putsch'. The Klagenfurt Memorial Celebration was also made the occasion for the solemn swearing in of the seven recently appointed Gauleiter of this Ostmark. From the point of view of the outside world, this picture of Reichsminister Hess was chiefly remarkable for the fact that after devoting the first half of his speech as expected, to praise of the sacrifices of the men, women, and youth of Austria in the struggle for greater Germany, he then launched into a defence of the occupation of Austria and an attack on the lying foreign Press and on those who spread the idea of a new war. 'The world was fortunate,' declared Hess, 'that Germany's leader was a man who would not allow himself to be provoked. The Führer does what is necessary for his people in sovereign calm and labours for the peace of Europe, even though mischief makers, completely ignoring the deliberate threat to the peace of certain small States, distinctly claim that he is a menace to the peace of Europe.'[41]

Hess, it is plain, realized that the Sudetenland was now growing ripe for the taking. He had first met Konrad Henlein, the Nazi Sudeten leader, in September 1934 in his home territory of Wunsiedel in Bavaria. It would seem at this comparatively early period Hess advised caution, and then conceded to Henlein and his party, the SHF (*Sudetendeutsche Heimatsfront*) considerable autonomy; in his speech a month later at Böhmisch Leipa (21 October) Henlein went out of his way to confirm the Party's loyalty to the Czechoslovak State, and renounced any kind of violence. He even went so far as to stress his own party's interest in the 'freedom of the individual' in contrast to National Socialism! Germany was to give his party generous financial help in the 1935 elections, with remarkable results, since with 44 seats it became the strongest single party in the country. Hess had further talks with

Henlein in October 1936, since not everyone in Germany, including Bohle, entirely approved of the Sudeten leader. After this, however, Henlein could now afford to draw closer to the Führer, and said so in a memorandum to Hitler of 19 November 1937, in which he stated that his party 'had had to camouflage its faith in National Socialism as an ideology and as a political principle though at heart it was yearning for nothing so deeply as incorporation of the Sudeten territory into the Reich.' Hitler's plan thereafter was for Henlein to step up his demands to the Czech government to such a degree as to create an impasse. While Henlein was presenting these demands to the government, Hitler on 21 April 1938 was discussing with Keitel, his Chief of Staff, the best way to achieve a lightning assault on Czechoslovakia which would be finished before any nation could interfere and sufficiently 'provoked by incidents' to cover the aggression as an inevitable act of retaliation. Keitel wrote to Hess on 27 September 1938 asking for the Party's participation in secret mobilization, the day before Hitler had publicly declared that he had no more territorial demands to make in Europe. The Sudeten territory was entered by German forces on 1 October and six months later Czechoslovakia as a whole was occupied. On 7 November 1938 Hess made a speech on the occasion of the initiation of the Sudeten German Party into the NSDAP:

> 'If we had to defend our rights, then they would have really got to know us, we, the National Socialist Germans. The Führer,' he declared amidst the ringing cheers of the masses, 'learned his lessons. He armed at a speed that no one would have believed possible. When the Führer has gained the power and, especially, since the Führer has awakened the will of the German people to put their strength behind their rights, then Germany's right will be conceded.'[42]

Hess also intervened in Poland, to which, it will be remembered, he had sent Albrecht Haushofer in 1934. On 27 August 1939 he spoke thus of Poland:

> Rudolf Hess, constantly interrupted by vociferous applause from the German citizens living abroad, as well as fellow countrymen from the district of Styria, stressed the unexampled forbearance shown by Germany towards Poland, in the magnanimous offer of the Führer that had ensured peace between Germany and Poland. An offer that Mr Chamberlain seems to have forgotten, for he says

he has heard nothing of Germany's having tried to solve certain acute present-day questions by peaceful discussion. What else was the German offer then, if it was not such an attempt ?[43]

During and after the conquest of Poland, it was he who signed the decree incorporating Danzig into the Reich (1 September 1939),[44] the decree incorporating Polish Territories into the Reich (8 October 1939) and, on 12 October, a decree concerning the use of Polish territory for German lebensraum and economic expansion. That Hess was a party to the extreme measures taken by the Germans in Poland has to be accepted. Two documents at least survive to prove this. The first (Document PS-3245 at the Nuremberg Tribunal) is dated 21 February 1940 and concerns the strengthening of the Waffen SS in Poland because 'through their intensive National Socialist training in racial problems, the Waffen SS must be looked upon as particularly well qualified for employment in the Occupied Eastern Territories.' The second (Document 96-R at the Tribunal) is a letter from the Reich Ministry of Justice to the Chief of the Reich Chancellery, and dated 17 April 1941; this concerns penal laws for Jews and Poles in these occupied territories of Poland, and asserts that Hess's recommendations for specially strict treatment have been taken into account.

> The suggestions of the Deputy Führer have been taken into consideration to a far-reaching extent. Number 1: Paragraph 3: contains a general crime formula on the basis of which any Pole or Jew in the Eastern territory can in future be prosecuted, and any kind of punishment can be inflicted on him for any attitude or action which is considered punishable and is directed against Germans . . .
> In accordance with the opinion of the Deputy of the Führer, I started from the supposition that the Pole is less susceptible to the infliction of ordinary imprisonment . . . Under these new kinds of punishment prisoners are to be lodged outside prisons in camps and are to be forced to do the heaviest and hardest labour.
> The introduction of corporal punishment, which the Deputy of the Führer has brought up for discussion, has not been included in the draft. I cannot agree to this type of punishment because its infliction does not, in my opinion, correspond to the cultural level of the German people.[45]

Throughout the whole period of his administration Hess co-ordinated his multifarious activities on behalf of the régime between his control of the Party's machinery and the control of his Ministry. In particular, as we have seen, he acted as a broker for complaints, difficulties, problems. A significant interchange of correspondence relating to an officer who had protested about SS excesses in Poland can serve as an example.[46] Hess wrote to Brauchitsch from Munich on 20 February 1941 recalling that a year ago he had reported to the Führer that the then Chief of Staff of the First Army, Major General Mieth, had gravely reproached the SS at a confidential meeting of officers. He had stated that the SS had been responsible for mass executions in Poland without proper trial. There had been incidents between the SS and Wehrmacht. '*The SS had sullied the honour of the Wehrmacht*' (Hess used italics). 'Soon after the Führer told me that Major General Mieth had been relieved of his duties. But I have now learned that the Führer was misinformed and that Mieth had, indeed, been promoted Lt-General. Please let me know whether you are prepared to deal with Mieth now since the Führer assumed he had been dealt with a year ago. Or would you rather have me or Fieldmarshal Keitel take the matter up with the Führer again?' The correspondence dragged on into March, with both Brauchitsch and Keitel attempting to shelve the matter, and with Hess complaining that men of the Wehrmacht are forbidden to lodge complaints concerned with 'internal matters'. There the correspondence ended.

Hess took part in the great public occasions—he was with Hitler at the time of the Munich agreement, in Compiégne on 21 June 1940 for the signing of the armistice by the French, wearing according to Shirer in *Berlin Diary*, a grey party uniform. On 11 November, Armistice Day, and three days after the explosion in the Bürgerbräu Keller in Munich after Hitler had spoken for an unusually brief period, it was Hess who broadcast at the State funeral for the victims. 'This *Attentat* has taught us how to hate,' he cried. On 1 May 1940, Labour Day, when Hitler spoke annually—it was Hess who replaced him, speaking from the Krupp munition works in Essen.

On Hess's presence at Compiégne, Ilse Hess has an interesting comment:

It is not generally known that it was my husband who, before the signing of the armistice terms in the historic railway coach at Compiégne, urged upon Hitler in a long and earnest discussion the unwisdom of forcing any terms that might offend the honour of a defeated enemy and thus might tend to bar the way to a lasting understanding between the two ñations. It was only after assurance on this that he withdrew his original refusal to be present at Compiégne.[47]

This should be linked with the comments made by Felix Kersten, Himmler's Finnish masseur, who also attended Hess. Kersten at Bad Godesberg-on-Rhine notes on 24 June 1940 in his secretly-kept diary:

I've been here for more than a week with Rudolf Hess in the Hotel Dresen. Hess is very busy and excited about recent events—the French armistice—and suffering in consequence from severe stomach pains. Meanwhile he was in the Forest of Compiégne and came back yesterday.

During the treatment, still charged with tension, he sketched to me the course of recent events, and spoke of the future, which he envisaged as an era of fruitful Franco-German co-operation.

'You forget England,' I told him. 'Her whole history, the laws of her political life, her very nature will never suffer her to leave things as you imagine. She will be going against her own existence if she does not take appropriate counter-measures. You're also forgetting the toughness of England. The English haven't such a Utopian cast of mind as the Germans.'

Hess replied: 'We'll make peace with England in the same way as with France. Only a few weeks back the Führer again spoke of the great value of the British Empire in the world order. Germany and France must stand together with England against the enemy of Europe, Bolshevism. That was the reason why the Führer allowed the English Army to escape at Dunkirk. He did not want to upset the possibility of an understanding. The English must see that and seize their chance. I can't imagine that cool, calculating England will run her neck into the Soviet noose, instead of saving it by coming to an understanding with us.'[48]

Writing on 15 May 1941, after Hess's flight to Britain, Kersten notes:

He was constantly saying that he could not go on with this existence. He was firmly resolved to stake his life on a great deed in the service of Germany. Once, when headquarters were in Belgium and Hess had to go to an interview with Hitler, he asked me to accompany him. We drove through towns and villages which had been shelled during the recent heavy fighting. Later Hess said to me with tears in his eyes that it was horrible to see these once flourishing areas so laid waste. The war should not last any longer. The world must come to see that Germany was unconquerable. And he, Hess, had to stretch out his hand, to bring about a reconcilation between Germany and the other nations.

Another time he told me that he had to concentrate all his powers and harden himself—he needed all his strength for the deed which would secure the salvation of Germany. When I asked what he meant by this 'salvation', Hess replied that he could not tell me, but he was preparing for an act of historic importance.

Though so unassuming, Hess was always regarded as one of the few men close to the Führer and still (as far as anyone could be) in his confidence.* As Shirer notes on 1 December 1940, he was 'the only man in the world he fully trusted.' This trust was soon to be shattered.

Hess was already disobeying Hitler in one significant respect. He was piloting an aircraft. His love for the air, which had developed during the first world war, lasted throughout the 1920s and 1930s. He was well-known for this, as Sir Nevile Henderson noted of Hess in his memoirs: 'Up to 1935 flying remained his hobby, and he actually won an important civil contest whilst a Cabinet Minister'; this was a trophy awarded him in 1934 for winning a race for sporting aircraft flown round the Zugspitze. However, Henderson adds, 'After that Hitler forbade his risking his life by any further excursions into the air.'

The mission which was to be the great feat of his life was already developing in his mind. And to achieve this, flying an aircraft, and flying it alone, would be essential.

* Shortly before this book went to press, confirming evidence of Hess's close relationship with Hitler in the early 1930s came to our notice. The significant interviews Hitler gave Richard Breiting, editor of the right-wing *Leipziger Neueste Nachrichten*, in 1931, are now published in Edouard Calic's book *Unmasked* (Chatto & Windus, 1971). Hess was present at these interviews and received Breiting at the Brown House, insisting on the confidential nature of the interviews, which were not to be published. Hitler constantly turned to Hess during the interviews, to corroborate what he was saying, and at one such stage Hess said 'Our Fuhrer has always insisted that our most natural ally is England'. Hitler referred to Professor Karl Haushofer as one of his 'experts', while he described Hess as his 'closest adviser' (*Unmasked*, pp. 50 and 73).–R.M. and H.F.

3

QUIXOTIC MISSION

THE REASON for Hess's mission to Britain lay in Hitler's desire for some kind of understanding with the Anglo-Saxons, but an understanding based upon his own terms for the rest of Europe, and in particular, for the East. In the face of the menace represented by the Soviet Union, he could never understand why Britain went to war over Poland, a country lying far outside what he regarded as her proper sphere of interest. After the fall of Poland, he made his notorious speech in the Reichstag in which he spoke of his desire for a peaceful co-existence with France, and then added:

> I have devoted no less effort to the achievement of an Anglo-German understanding, nay, more than that, of an Anglo-German friendship . . . I believe even today that there can only be real peace in Europe and throughout the world if Germany and England come to an understanding . . .
>
> Why should this war in the West be fought ? For the restoration of Poland ? The Poland of the Versailles Treaty will never rise again.

He was no more anxious than his generals to fight a war on two diverse fronts. Once he had decided to invade the Soviet Union, the struggle in the West, confined by 1940 to Britain alone, seemed all the more illogical in Hitler's judgement. He could not understand why Britain should want to defy him; surely by now, he thought, it must be self-evident even to the most prejudiced of those islanders, even to the war-monger Churchill, that the suppression of the Communist régime in the East was as much in Britain's interest as it was in his own. Had he not gone out of his way in August 1939 to offer his personal guarantee to defend the British Empire, in return for Britain's support in his case against Poland and his demand for the return of Germany's former colonies ?

A further attempt to secure peace was made through neutral channels, but this only met with the rebuff of silence. Hitler, still unhappy, made his final plea on 19 July 1940 in another speech to the Reichstag:

> Mr Churchill ought perhaps, for once, to believe me when I prophesy that a great Empire will be destroyed—an Empire which it was never my intention to destroy or even to harm . . . In this hour I feel it to be my duty before my own conscience to appeal once more to reason and common sense in Great Britain as much as elsewhere. I consider myself in a position to make this appeal since I am not the vanquished begging favours, but the victor speaking in the name of reason. I can see no reason why this war must go on.

At the same time he made very full preparations for Operation Sealion, the invasion of Britain, to be preceded by a devastating assault from the air.

It is in the light of this desire that the two Haushofers, Karl and Albrecht, father and son, attempted their own form of intervention. On 31 August 1940 Karl Haushofer had a prolonged conversation with Hess, which included a three-hour walk under the trees of Grünwald; the well-known interchange of letters during September between father and son, on the one hand, and between Hess and the Haushofers on the other, sowed the seed which led to Hess's flight to Britain the following May.[1]

On 3 September Karl Haushofer wrote to his son:

> As you know, everything is so prepared for a very hard and severe attack on the island in question that the highest ranking person only has to press a button to set it off. But before this decision, which is perhaps inevitable, the thought once more occurs as to whether there is really no way of stopping something which would have such infinitely momentous consequences. There is a line of reasoning in connection with this which I must absolutely pass on to you because it was obviously communicated to me with this intention. Do you, too, see no way in which such possibilities could be discussed at a third place with a middle man, possibly the old Ian Hamilton or the other Hamilton?

Ian Hamilton referred to General Sir Iain S. M. Hamilton,[2] then aged eighty-seven, and 'the other Hamilton' to the young Duke of Hamilton, who was a friend of Albrecht, and serving in the RAF. Haushofer then went on to tell his son that he had suggested to Hess it might be possible to send a secret mission to Lisbon to initiate peace negotiations .with Britain, using a Mrs Roberts, an old friend of the family who was in Lisbon, as a point of contact. On 10 September, Hess wrote to Karl Haushofer, following a meeting with Albrecht:

Dear Friend: Albrecht brought me your letter, which, at the beginning, besides containing official information, alluded to our walk together on the last day of August, which I, too, recall with so much pleasure.

Albrecht will have told you about our conversation, which besides *volksdeutsch* matters, above all touched upon the other matter, which is so close to the hearts of us both. I reconsidered the latter carefully once more and have arrived at the following conclusion:

Under no conditions must we disregard the contact or allow it to die aborting. I consider it best that you or Albrecht write to the old lady, who is a friend of your family, suggesting that she try to ask Albrecht's friend whether he would be prepared if necessary to come to the neutral territory in which she resides, or at any rate has an address through which she can be reached, just to talk with Albrecht.

If he could not do this just now, he might, in any case, send word through her where he expects to be in the near future. Possibly a neutral acquaintance, who had some business to attend to over there anyway, might look him up and make some communication to him, using you or Albrecht as reference.

This person probably would not care to have to inquire as to his whereabouts only after he got there or to make futile trips. You thought that knowing about his whereabouts had no military significance at all; if necessary you would also pledge yourselves not to make use of it with regard to any quarter which might profit from it. What the neutral would have to transmit would be of such great importance that his having made known his whereabouts would be by comparison insignificant.

The prerequisite naturally was that the inquiry in question and the reply would not go through official channels, for you would not in any case want to cause your friends over there any trouble.

It would be best to have the letter to the old lady with whom you are acquainted delivered through a confidential agent of the AO to the address that is known to you. For this purpose Albrecht would have to speak either with Bohle or my brother. At the same time the lady would have to be given the address of this agent in

L.—or if the latter does not live there permanently, to which the reply can in turn be delivered.

As for the neutral I have in mind, I would like to speak to you orally about it some time. There is no hurry about that since, in any case, there would first have to be a reply received here from over there.

Meanwhile let's both keep our fingers crossed. Should success be the fate of the enterprise, the oracle given to you with regard to the month of August would yet be fulfilled, since the name of the young friend and the old lady friend of your family occurred to you during our quiet walk on the last day of the month.

With best regards to you and to Martha,

Yours, as ever,
R[UDOLF] H[ESS]

On 15 September Albrecht wrote an official memorandum concerning the meeting he had had with Hess. He headed it, 'Are There Still Possibilities of a German-English Peace?':

On 8 September I was summonded to Bad G [Godesberg] to report to the Deputy of the Führer on the subject discussed in this memorandum. The conversation which the two of us had alone lasted 2 hours. I had the opportunity to speak in all frankness.

I was immediately asked about the possibilities of making known to persons of importance in England Hitler's serious desire for peace. It was quite clear that the continuance of the war was suicidal for the white race. Even with complete success in Europe, Germany was not in a position to take over inheritance of the Empire. The Führer had not wanted to see the Empire destroyed and did not want it even today. Was there not somebody in England who was ready for peace? . . .

I ought not—precisely because of my long experience in attempting to effect a settlement with England in the past and my numerous English friendships—to make it appear that I seriously believe in the possibility of a settlement between Adolf Hitler and England in the present stage of development. I was thereupon asked whether I was not of the opinion that feelers had perhaps not been successful because the right language had not been used . . .

He suggested next certain possible contacts in high positions, and then went on:

As the final possibility I then mentioned that of a personal meeting on neutral soil, with the closest of my English friends: the young Duke of Hamilton, who has access at all times to all important persons in London, even to Churchill and the King.

I stressed in this case the inevitable difficulty of making a contact and again repeated my conviction of the improbability of its succeeding—whatever approach we took.

The upshot of the conversation was H's statement that he would consider the whole matter thoroughly once more and send me word in case I was to take steps. For this extremely ticklish case, and in the event that I might possibly have to make a trip alone—I asked for very precise directives from the highest authority. From the whole conversation I had the strong impression that it was not conducted without the prior knowledge of the Führer, and that I probably would not hear any more about the matter unless a new understanding had been reached between him and his Deputy.

Albrecht remained completely sceptical; he was convinced the English would prefer an alliance with America to one with Germany. Nevertheless, he wrote as Hess had desired him to Mrs Roberts in Lisbon. But he sent a letter to his father on 19 September saying that he thought the whole thing 'a fool's errand', and enclosed a file of the previous letters and the memorandum, together with a copy of the letter he had sent the same day to Hess. This read:

I have in the meantime been thinking of the technical route by which a message from me must travel before it can reach the Duke of H[amilton]. With your help, delivery to Lisbon can of course be assured without difficulty. About the rest of the route we do not know. Foreign control must be taken into account; the letter must therefore in no case be composed in such a way that it will simply be seized and destroyed or that it will directly endanger the woman transmitting it or the ultimate recipient.

In view of my close personal relations and intimate acquaintance with Douglas H[amilton] I can write a few lines to him (which should be enclosed with the letter to Mrs R, without any indication of place and without a full name—an A would suffice for signature) in such a way that he alone will recognize that behind my wish to see him in Lisbon there is something more serious than a personal whim. All the rest, however, seems to be extremely hazardous and detrimental to the success of the letter.

Let us suppose that the case were reversed: an old lady in Germany receives a letter from an unknown source abroad, with the request to forward a message whose recipient is asked to disclose to an unknown foreigner where he will be staying for a certain period—and this recipient were a high officer in the air force (of course I do not know exactly what position H holds at the moment; judging from the past I can conceive of only three things: He is an active air force general, or he directs the air defence of an important part of Scotland, or he has a responsible position in the Air Ministry).

I do not think that you need much imagination to picture to yourself the faces that Canaris or Heydrich would make and the smirk with which they would consider any offer of security or confidence in such a letter if a subordinate should submit such a case to them. They would not merely make faces, you may be certain! The measures would come quite automatically—and neither the old lady nor the air force officer would have an easy time of it! In England it is no different.

Now another thing. Here, too, I would ask you to picture the situation in reverse. Let us assume that I received such a letter from one of my English friends. I would quite naturally report the matter to the highest German authorities I could contact, as soon as I had realized the impact it might have, and would ask for instructions on what I should do myself (at that, I am a civilian and H is an officer).

If it should be decided that I was to comply with the wish for a meeting with my friend, I would then be most anxious to get my instructions if not from the Führer himself, at least from a person who receives them directly and at the same time has the gift of transmitting the finest and lightest nuances—an art which has been mastered by you yourself but not by all Reich Ministers.

In addition, I should very urgently request that my action be fully covered vis-à-vis other high authorities of my own country—uninformed or unfavourable. It is not any different with H. He cannot fly to Lisbon—any more than I can!—unless he is given leave, that is unless at least Air Minister Sinclair and Foreign Minister Halifax know about it. If, however, he receives permission to reply or to go, there is no need of indicating any place in England; if he does not receive it, then any attempt through a neutral mediator would also have little success.

In this case the technical problem of contacting H is the least of the difficulties. A neutral who knows England and can move about in England—presumably there would be little sense in entrusting anyone else with such a mission—will be able to find the first peer of Scotland very quickly as long as conditions in the Isle are still halfway in order.

Through the old friend I will write a letter to H—in a form that will incriminate no one but will be understandable to the recipient—with the proposal for a meeting in Lisbon. If nothing comes of that, it will be possible (if the military situation leaves enough time for it), assuming that a suitable intermediary is available, to make a second attempt through a neutral going to England, who might be given a personal message to take along. With respect to this possibility, I must add, however, that H is extremely reserved—as many English are toward anyone they do not know personally. Since the entire Anglo-German problem after all springs from a most profound crisis in mutual confidence, this would not be immaterial.

I already tried to explain to you not long ago that, for the reasons I gave, the possibilities of successful efforts at a settlement between the Führer and the British upper class seem to me—to my extreme regret—infinitesimally small. Nevertheless I should not want to close this letter without pointing out once more that I still think there would be a somewhat greater chance of success in going through Ambassador Lothian in Washington or Sir Samuel Hoare in Madrid rather than through my friend H.

Would you send me a line or give me a telephone call with final instructions? If necessary, will you also inform your brother in advance? Presumably I will then have to discuss with him the forwarding of the letter to Lisbon and the arrangement for a cover address for the reply in L[isbon].*

A final enclosure was a copy of Albrecht's draft letter to the Duke of Hamilton, which he had sent for Hess's approval:

My dear D . . . , Even if this letter has only a slight chance of reaching you—there is a chance and I want to make use of it.

First of all, to give you a sign of unaltered and unalterable personal

---

* Since this book was prepared for press, James Douglas-Hamilton's *Motive for a Mission* has appeared (See Bibliography). In this the full circumstances of the relationship of Albrecht Haushofer and the Duke are given, including the fact that Haushofer had already written at length to him on 16 July 1939 (see p. 91). The British censor intercepted the second letter sent via Lisbon, and confronted the Duke with it in February 1941 (see p. 146).–R.M. and H.F.

attachment. I do hope you have been spared in all this ordeal and I hope the same is true of your brothers. I heard of your father's deliverance from long suffering; and I heard that your brother-in-law Northumberland lost his life near Dunkerque. I need hardly tell you how I feel about all that . . .

Now there is one thing more. If you remember some of my last communications before the war started you will realize that there is a certain significance in the fact that I am, at present, able to ask you whether there is the slightest chance of our meeting and having a talk somewhere on the outskirts of Europe, perhaps in Portugal. There are some things I could tell you, that might make it worth while for you to try a short trip to Lisbon—if you could make your authorities understand so much that they would give you leave. As to myself—I could reach Lisbon any time (without any kind of difficulty) within a few days after receiving news from you.

If there is an answer to this letter, please address it to . . .

On 23 September Albrecht confirmed to Hess himself that he had written to Mrs Roberts in Lisbon. All this, as Frau Ilse Hess points out, was undertaken with Hitler's knowledge. The most that came of this interchange was that on 28 April Hess sent Albrecht to Geneva to discuss the possibilities of peace with Professor Karl Burckhardt, President of the Swiss Red Cross. Burckhardt, though anxious to help in a strictly anonymous capacity, was also pessimistic about the outcome; Burckhardt added, however, that he brought 'greetings from his English friends'.

The Duke of Hamilton, whose distinction as an aviator had included piloting the first flight over Everest in a light aircraft in 1933, was commanding a fighter squadron based on the airfield at Turnhouse, west of Edinburgh. Hess had had the chance to see him during the 1936 Olympic Games, which were held in Germany. The Everest mission was the kind of flying Hess most admired; he had himself wanted to be the first solo flier from Germany to the United States after the first world war, and a year had been spent preparing for this before the flight was abandoned. In September 1939 Hess had asked Hitler's permission to join the Luftwaffe, which the Führer refused, ordering Hess to abandon flying altogether. Hess gave his word of honour not to fly for a year. When the year was up, in September 1940, he quietly resumed his flying without risking a reminder to Hitler that the duration of the ban was ended so far as he was concerned. He showed great interest in the new Messerschmitt pursuit aircraft. At first he approached Ernst Udet, the air ace, then a general in the Luftwaffe. Udet refused to co-operate without official authorization to do so. Later Hess himself was to describe what happened in a letter written to his wife from captivity, although at the time she knew little or nothing of what he was doing:

> I should add that this was the reason for a certain cooling off in my relations with Udet. He did not want me to fly the ME when I was living near Berlin and wished to practise flying with this machine, ostensibly 'just for fun'. The innocent man made it a condition that I should obtain a special permit from the Führer, whose reluctance to let me fly had meant a ban for a period which had just expired. I might just as well have placed myself voluntarily in protective custody! Yet it was actually quite lucky for me that nothing did come of my desire to fly just then, since to do so anywhere near Berlin could hardly have been kept secret. Sooner or later the Führer would have learned of my activities and the result would have been a new ban on my flying, this time perhaps for longer than a year. And, having pledged my word, it would have been out of the question for me to evade this in any way, my plan would have come to an abrupt end, and I should never have ceased to blame myself for my lack of caution. These little rubs with Udet never went so far as to be really unfriendly. Soon afterwards I chanced to hear of his flying a Storch and landing his machine—nearly if not quite—*inside* one of the hangars in the Berlin Airport—purely for the fun of it! I wrote to him straight away saying that, of course, I understood that juggling of this sort was a necessity for the Quarter-master General of the Air Force, and that he had, as a matter of course, obtained permission from the Führer! He rang me up, as cheerful as you please but implored me, at the same time, on no account to mention the matter in 'the highest circles'. I had to laugh.[3]

Hess turned next for help to Professor Willi Messerschmitt, the celebrated aeronautical engineer.[4] Messerschmitt knew nothing of Hitler's order prohibiting Hess from flying; he had known Hess for many years and their relationship was most friendly. Hess was even more friendly with Theo Croneiss, one of the directors of the Augsburg Messerschmitt Works. It seemed quite natural to Messerschmitt that Hess should take a technical interest in the latest development in his planes, the ME 110, and that he should request the chance to pilot one of these aircraft during the tests, at first with General Hans Baur,

Hitler's personal pilot, and later on his own, after he had refurbished his skills by piloting the ME 108 and 109.[5] As Hess wrote later to his wife:

> I certainly never dreamed at one time how vitally important my technical and mathematical gifts would some day become in my life. Without this knowledge, I could not have achieved the 'flight of my life', nor could I ever have mastered the complicated mechanism of the ME machine or navigated it.[6]

According to Messerschmitt, Hess undertook some twenty flights[7] within a period of six months or so. As soon as he had graduated to piloting the ME 110, he was shrewd enough to ensure that he always flew in the same individual aircraft. Both Messerschmitt and Croneiss were much occupied, and delegated the detailed arrangements to a young pilot at the works, who was placed at Hess's disposal at any time the Deputy Führer could spare a few hours to come to Augsburg for his flights. Hess therefore gradually obtained a certain independence at Augsburg, though at the same time, with his future flight in mind, he began to suggest to Messerschmitt certain modifications so that the aircraft, which was short-range owing to the limited supply of fuel it was equipped to carry, could have its range increased sufficiently to take Hess from Augsburg to Scotland, a flight distance little short of 900 miles. What worried him, Hess said to Messerschmitt over a cup of coffee after one of his flights, were the operational limitations of this splendid fighter aircraft—but then, he added, if additional tanks were fitted it would undoubtedly lose its flexibility. 'Not a bit of it,' said Messerschmitt, and to prove his point had two reserve tanks each holding 700 litres, built into the wings of the ME 110. Hess made a similar challenge concerning radio equipment compatible with the increased operational radius which the additional fuel permitted. 'Of course we can do this,' said Messerschmitt, and put the apparatus into the same craft.[8] By now Hess commanded the confidence of everyone with whom he came into contact at Augsburg; they were flattered to have such intimate conversations with the Deputy Führer, and struck by his interest in the special, modified ME 110 to which he was so devoted. To cover himself, Hess hinted vaguely that his flying was not merely for recreation, and that he might have to undertake a special mission to Norway in this particular craft,[9] which he had managed to get transformed from a two-man to a one-man machine.

Ilse Hess was aware only that her husband was preoccupied with some special plan of his own:

I admit, however, that it was no secret to me and others around him that he was engaged in planning something out of the ordinary. He was extremely busy with all sorts of activities, and his state of tension was visible. Boxes were packed and then unpacked. (At the Messerschmitt works at Augsburg he repeatedly flew with an ME 110, by way (so he said) of 'recreation'.) His silence alone, however, would not have impressed me, for since our marriage in 1927 an unwritten law existed that private and public affairs were to be kept strictly apart. My husband despised men in public office who could not 'keep their mouths shut at home', and it was not my way to ask questions if he said nothing.

But as time passed it became clear to me that his increasingly frequent journeys to Augsburg could hardly be explained as recreation, as mere distraction from the cares of office. One day I was waiting by myself in my husband's office, and a voice filled with matter-of-fact conviction, and evidently conveying some expected message, gave me a weather report for some mysterious places referred to as X and Y. Rather astonished, I jotted down this, to me, quite incomprehensible message. But I noticed from the confused manner of the secretary, who had just come in, that this was something I was not supposed to know anything about! However, she must have told my husband; for, from that day onwards, I frequently took down such reports—sometimes by actual request. It was now presumed, so I thought, that they had acquired an innocent appearance to my mind.

Once or twice a week my husband drove to Augsburg to practise flying. Contrary to the strict regulations of war time a new leather flying suit was acquired, much admired by our little boy and a cause of some astonishment to me! At the same time, in a manner equally contrary to the otherwise strictly observed war regulations, a large brand-new radio apparatus appeared in the work-room of our home in Harlaching and was used behind closed double-doors. It could not have been a case of listening in to foreign stations, because my husband received this news in written form from the official listening-in sources. On one occasion, moved by an understandable womanly curiosity, I looked at the dial to see where it was tuned in and found it was Kalundborg. This was far from supporting my Pétain thesis—but, after all, what was the significance of a reading that might have been accidental ?[10]

Ilse Hess developed her own theory of what was afoot; she believed
her husband was planning a special mission to Pétain in order to achieve
'a lasting peace with France.' She knew of his deep respect for the
Marshal.[11]

Hess was concerned about the radio signals he would need to keep
him on course during his dangerous flight north. Croneiss told her
subsequently what her husband had arranged:

> As my husband had not been able to make use of any official guiding
> signals, he took to using the interval signals from Kalundborg and,
> during the weeks when he made his preparatory flights, he had
> persuaded the head of the Kalundborg station, for some innocent
> reason he supplied, to broadcast a favourite melody at stated
> intervals. The fact that the Kalundborg station was thus drawn into
> the plan gave rise, after 1945, to the presumption that my husband
> had really flown first to Norway and thence under the protection
> of a German bomber squadron to Scotland. In reality he flew quite
> alone, and at that time Croneiss told me again and again what a very
> considerable achievement the purely navigational side of this flight
> must have been.[12]

On the domestic side, Hess revealed that something unusual was
afoot. Ilse Hess continues the story as she experienced it:

> What caused me more surprise than almost anything else during
> those last weeks was the astonishing amount of time—and that in
> the middle of the war—that my husband spent with our son. This
> ran into long hours by the Isar, lengthy visits to the nearby Zoo at
> Hellabrunn and mysterious games behind the closed doors of the
> work-room. All this seemed to me inexplicable in those earnest
> times.

Hess was to make at least three attempts to undertake his mission
to Britain, the first as early as January 1941.[13] According to the evidence
given to James Leasor by the late Karlheinz Pintsch, Hess's adjutant,
who shared with him the secret behind his preparations, the first attempt
in January was abandoned because a fault developed in one of the
ailerons, and the aircraft failed to make sufficient height. A second
attempt, for which the date is not given, failed through bad weather,
and Hess returned to Augsburg. The flight in January took place
shortly after Hess's conversation with Albrecht Haushofer. Pintsch,
together with Hess's detective and chauffeur, accompanied him to

Augsburg, where he was given two sealed letters, one addressed to Hitler and the other to himself; Hess told Pintsch to open his only if he had not returned after four hours. When, four and a quarter hours later, there was no sign of the plane, Pintsch opened the letter and was deeply shocked to read that Hess was flying to Britain for an attempt to bring about peace. Pintsch, wisely or unwisely, broke the news to his companions, and they were discussing this incredible communication when they heard the sound of Hess's plane returning. On landing, Hess ordered them to take him back home, at the same time promising Pintsch some explanation. The moment they were alone, Pintsch gave Hess the unopened letter addressed to Hitler. Hess then explained, quite simply, about Hitler's desire for peace with Britain and the failure of the attempts made through Haushofer to achieve effective contact so that serious proposals could be made. Pintsch began to understand more clearly the reason for the flight, though he failed to see why Hitler could not have been informed of it. Hess went into details—the importance of an ultimate German victory over Russia and the grave risk to Germany were her present war with Britain to escalate into a war with the United States, Britain's powerful ally. Russia would be bound to take advantage of such a situation, and Germany would be crushed from all sides. Hess explained that he was determined to undertake his mission without Hitler's knowledge precisely because of the great risks involved; if he failed, Hitler could disown him without loss of personal prestige; if he succeeded, he might bring about a re-alignment of power which, as he saw it, could save Europe from Communism. Hess concluded that the arrival in Scotland of the Deputy Führer of Germany, a man with a good command of English, would be bound to have a sensational effect, and that the best initial plan would be to use the Duke of Hamilton, the friend of Albrecht Haushofer, as a go-between. The Duke, he imagined, was bound by the nature of his high rank to command the confidence both of the British government and the King, and he could vouch for Hess's identity since he had seen him only five years before. He was determined therefore, to fly direct to the Duke's estate, Dungavel House in Lanark near the west coast of Scotland. Having learned so much, Pintsch was to remain in Hess's confidence until the final flight took place, some four months later.[14]

It has been claimed that Hess, who was interested in astrology, undertook his mission as a result of astrological influences. In *A History of the British Secret Service* (1969), Richard Deacon even goes so far as to suggest that Ian Fleming, the creator of the secret agent Bond, originated a scheme while he was in the Department of Naval Intelligence to lure Hess to Britain by means of a faked horoscope planted on him by an astrologer in Switzerland who was acting as a British agent. This was as firmly as possible denied by Ian Fleming's brother, Peter Fleming, in a letter to *The Times* which appeared on 18 September 1969, and was further discounted by such authorities as Sefton Delmer and Ellic Howe, an historian of astrological beliefs and influence in Europe. Ellic Howe wrote to *The Times*, and his letter, which also appeared on 18 September 1969, explained how the late Ernst Schulte-Strathaus, a member of Hess's staff who knew Hess well and, since he was a student of the occult, discussed astrology with him, had assured Howe before his death that there was no astrological background to the flight. Hess, says Ellic Howe, was more interested in Hitler's horoscope than his own; only Himmler among the Nazi hierarchy took astrology completely seriously; even the story that Hitler deliberately consulted astrologers is a legend. The Nazis, however, like the British, were well aware of the potentialities of astrology as a possible weapon in pyschological warfare, especially in view of the considerable revival of interest in astrology which has taken place in both Britain and Germany during the present century. Except for Himmler, it could be claimed that the régime regarded astrology as a menace, as the celebrated Aktion Hess which took place after the flight was to show. It is true, however, that Albrecht Haushofer was a student of astrology, and took it seriously. Another close friend of Hess who was interested in astrology was Eduard Hofweber, a director of an engineering works in Mannheim. As we shall see, it was the Nazis themselves who decided to make the astrologers appear partly responsible for Hess's 'derangement' when he undertook the flight.

Hess was airborne finally on his mission to Britain at about 5.45 in the afternoon of Saturday 10 May 1941. Ilse Hess, who was not feeling well that day, had not attended the mid-day lunch at which Hess entertained Rosenberg, who left the house early, at one o'clock. Hess had rested briefly, and then taken tea with his wife at 2.30. Ilse Hess herself describes what followed:

He arrived for his tea, having changed his clothes and, much to my surprise, was wearing bluish-grey breeches and high airman's boots, most unusual! Casually he remarked that he had received a call from Berlin in the meantime and would be making a short detour to Augsburg on his way to headquarters. I was even more astonished to see he had on a light blue shirt with a dark blue tie, a colour combination I had so often advocated without the slightest effect! The full significance of this did not dawn until after the flight, when I was being questioned about the clothes my husband was wearing when I last saw him. As I described the breeches, shirt and the rest my questioner gave a sigh of relief, exclaiming, 'Thank God he wore the uniform of an officer of the Luftwaffe. Whatever they may do to him over there, at any rate they cannot shoot him as a spy!' I could say nothing as to his insignia of rank, but later in looking through his papers we found a bill (unfortunately not paid) from a military tailor in Munich, for the uniform of a captain in the Luftwaffe. But the name of the customer (who was at the same time the debtor) had been carefully cut away.

The reader may think that these small events preliminary to a great and tragic venture are of very minor importance, but they demonstrate the minute care which my husband devoted to each stage of preparation and to each thing needed. Such a degree of attention and accuracy demanded an almost superhuman self-discipline.

When I asked him the meaning of the blue shirt, he smiled and gave the charming explanation: 'To give you a pleasant surprise!' What, I wonder, did he *really* think and feel a couple of hours before he took off on his flight to England? We can only conjecture. I can see my husband standing there before me as if it were yesterday. And I remember so clearly how doubtfully I received this surprising piece of matrimonial gallantry. Tea over, he kissed my hand and stood at the door of the nursery, grown suddenly very grave, with the air of one deep in thought and almost hesitating.

'When will you be coming back?'

'I am not quite certain, perhaps to-morrow; but I should certainly be home by Monday evening.'

I did not believe him—and I said so. Writing later from England, he told me that he turned hot and cold by turns when he heard me say:

'What? To-morrow? Or Monday? I cannot believe it. You will not come back as soon as that!'

Very quickly he dashed out to take leave (so he told me in his letter) of his small son, sleeping after his meal; afraid if he stayed longer I would say more or reveal that I *knew more*.[15]

Hess had already summoned Pintsch by telephone early that morning, telling him to be ready for the afternoon drive to Augsburg, and to check the weather reports and bring them with him. The Mercedes arrived, and Hess left his home on the outskirts of Munich for the last time. He sat in the front seat beside the driver, with Pintsch and the detective in the rear. The distance to Augsburg was about forty miles, an hour's drive and, since they were early, Hess ordered the car to be stopped in a woodland outside Munich. He strolled with Pintsch under the trees while they examined the weather report. Then for a moment he walked alone, savouring the countryside he loved. In a few hours, after all, he might be dead. After this they returned to the car and drove to the airfield attached to the Messerschmitt works. This private airfield was very close to Lagerlechfeld, where Hess had landed his fighter plane after his last mission at the close of the first world war. The airfield research manager, Piehl, supervised the removal of the aircraft from his hangar.

There was a black suitcase in the boot of the Mercedes which Hess had brought from Munich. While the aircraft was being prepared for flight, he changed into a Luftwaffe jacket matching the blue trousers he was already wearing; he had brought the jacket in the suitcase. Over the uniform he wore a set of fur-lined flying overalls; these he had to borrow, since someone else seemed to have taken those he normally wore. After this there was nothing left but to shake hands and leave. He climbed into the plane, starting each of the twin engines in turn, warming them for flight. Piehl gave the signal that all was well, and pulled away the chocks. Hess manoeuvred the aircraft onto the runway and opened up the throttles. Within seconds he was airborne.

Pintsch had his own particular schedule. He was to wait at the airport until 10.30 that night, then make his way back to Munich to catch the night train to Berchtesgaden. In his briefcase was the letter for Hitler.

As the hours of waiting went by, Piehl, who naturally knew nothing of Hess's mission, became more and more concerned because a mist was gathering on the airfield, making landing difficult. The ME 110 was still a secret aircraft, and the fact that Hess showed no sign of returning preyed on his mind. Pintsch had great difficulty in preventing him from telephoning Messerschmitt. Shortly after nine, more than three hours after Hess was airborne, Pintsch telephoned an official number at the Air Ministry to ask on a scrambled line for a radio direction signal to be beamed for the Deputy Führer from Augsburg to Dungavel Hill, some thirty kilometres south of Glasgow. He was told there was a major raid over Britain that night—an action neither he nor Hess had known about—and that a beam could only be transmitted up to ten o'clock. Reassuring Piehl as best he could, Pintsch set out for Munich. Instructing the detective and the driver to garage the car after taking him to the station, he also told them to take one of the smaller, less conspicuous cars and go to a friend's house in the village of Gallspach, change into civilian clothes and wait there until news arrived of the outcome of the mission. At the station, he ordered Hess's private railway coach to be hitched to the midnight train which connected to Berchtesgaden. Isolated and apprehensive, he wandered about in the Munich streets before joining the train just before midnight. His part in Hess's mission was still to be accomplished.

The 900-mile solo flight to the west coast of Scotland was to be the proudest technical achievement in Hess's life. It was indeed a remarkable feat of navigation and piloting, and towards the end it became increasingly hazardous. He was to describe the flight, or moments in it, repeatedly in the letters he sent to his wife; the story can be pieced together from these various letters so that we can follow his five-hour ordeal in some detail as he experienced it after he had left the protection of German-occupied territory:

> The North Sea was illuminated by an evening light of unearthly loveliness, such as is found in the far north. It was utterly lonely. But how magnificent! A multitude of small clouds far below me looked like pieces of ice floating on the sea, clear as crystal; the whole scene was tinged with red. Then the sky was swept clean—alas, much too clean! There was not a trace of the 'dense carpet of clouds at about five hundred metres', predicted in the weather report, and where I had thought to take shelter in case of need. For a moment I even thought of turning back. But a night landing with *this* machine, I reflected—that will never do. Even if I saved myself, the Messerschmitt would suffer serious damage, possibly beyond repair. Then indeed, the cat would be out of the bag; nothing could be kept secret. The whole business would be reported in the highest quarters and then all would be over—for ever.
> So I told myself 'Stick it out, no matter what happens!'
> Then I had a stroke of luck. A veil of mist hung over England. Its surface shone so much in the evening light that nothing down there could be seen from above. I took shelter, of course, at once, flying with the throttle full out and coming slap down from a height of two thousand metres towards the coast at a truly terrific speed.

D

The action of that moment saved me then. There was a Spitfire in pursuit which I out-distanced before I was aware of its presence. I could not look behind; I was too enclosed in my cabin and too dazzled by the reflections. Had I not been tempted to dive for cover, but remained in the clear air at the pace I had been going he could easily have shot me down.

As it was, I crossed the East Coast a little below Holy Island at about ten o'clock and after sunset, flying low over a little town whose inhabitants must have been terrified, so low did I roar past, barely higher than the houses, at some 750 km per hour with my two thousand hp engines at full throttle and the exhaust echoing through the sleepy streets. At this level the visibility was surprisingly good. I could see several miles, but must have been invisible to my pursuer. I took good care not to rise too high, but flew on at not more than sixteen feet from the ground—even less at times—skimming over trees, men, beasts and houses; what English airmen call 'hedge-hopping'. It seems to have impressed them a good deal, according to the Duke of Hamilton and judging by the honour done me in a critique in an English flying journal!

I enjoyed every minute of it! At home, this sort of flying was forbidden, although I did occasionally do a bit of it—but not so drastically as on this flight over enemy territory.

'Father' Baur always said that what he really liked was to fly through barn doors, and it was in this spirit I aimed at the Cheviots, now looming out of the misty evening. This was my guiding point, as previously determined, and keeping within a few yards of the ground I literally climbed up the slope. Never before had I ascended a mountain so rapidly. With a slight alteration of course to the right, I slid down on the other side. On I went over level ground, skimming merrily over house tops and trees, and waving greetings to men working in the fields. The variometer told me I was ascending, until suddenly I was over my next point of orientation—a little dam in a narrow range of hills with Broad Dav the highest summit. Here my course bent to the left.

I had no need to bother with a map; all the details of the course, compass points, distances, etc. were already stored in my memory. At about ten-forty pm I found myself over Dungavel, the country seat of the Duke of Hamilton, my quite unconscious future host, or so I hoped. Yet, to avoid all possibility of error, I flew on to the coast, a matter of a few minutes. The smooth sea lay beneath me, as calm as a mirror, lit by the rising moon. Just off the mainland, a towering rock, five hundred metres high, rose out of the water, magnificently illuminated, a pale reddish colour. All looked so peaceful and beautiful. What a contrast to the hazardous and exciting experience then just about to come—immediately before my *first* parachute jump! Never shall I forget this picture.

I flew a few kilometres along the coast until I reached a small place on a spit of land with what might have been a mole, as on my map. Satisfied that I was on the spot, I turned east again and was able to pick out the railway and a small lake which was shown on the map with a road by it and south of the residence at Dungavel. I made a curve, ready to land by parachute after rising to a safe height of some 2,000 metres. Then I switched off the engines, turned the propeller indicator to zero to check rotation regardless of the following wind, so that I could drop without being churned into mincemeat—such a superfluous precaution! For I found out afterwards that it would be easier to squeeze through a solid wall than to press forward against that prodigious air pressure. The first engine did not dream of stopping but, being ignited by the red-hot cylinders, went on spinning and humming merrily and took no notice of the fact that the ignition was off and that its conduct was against the rules!

However, the motor did come to its senses finally, senses which nevertheless soon sealed its fate.

Now I fastened everything up and opened the cabin roof, with the notion of climbing out—not without some scepticism and with much curiosity but all the same in excellent spirits. It was out of the question! The air pressure was something that cannot be imagined, even when the machine was going so slowly; and it pressed me up against the back partition as if I were screwed to it. In spite of all the care I had taken to find out about *everything* from my good friends at Messerschmitts, there was just *one* thing I had overlooked. I had never asked about how to jump; I thought it was too simple.

When I think back to that time, I find it astonishing that I never once thought of using the landing gear to slow down the machine. With no motors running, I had sunk lower and lower. Then I suddenly remembered that Greim had once mentioned that one had to turn the machine over on its back and allow oneself to fall out! I then began to turn the machine over but, although I had done all sorts of acrobatics in the air, this was the one thing

I had never done with this plane. And yet even that was lucky, because I instinctively pulled the joystick as if for a semi-loop instead of setting it for horizontal flight. Coming right over, the centrifugal force held me inside. But, with my head hanging down, had I slid out even a very little, the pressure of air would have broken my neck and spine. But the centrifugal force is immense with such a machine; it made the blood drain from my head and I began to 'see stars'. I was just able to think: 'I am only just above the ground and flying straight down. Soon the crash must come! Is this the end?'

Then everything went black and I passed out. There I sat hurling earthwards, upside down, with no power of control. A desperate, indeed, hopeless situation! The next moment I had recovered consciousness, with full clarity of mind, and found myself staring at the speed guage: the pointer stood at zero. I flung myself away and at the same moment the machine dropped like a stone.

I pulled at the parachute; the strands held me up, and I hovered in the air; an indescribably glorious and victorious experience all things considered. While unconscious, I had done what I *should* have done, had I been conscious. I had brought the plane out of its semi-looping curve to finish almost perpendicular on its tail. The power of the swing spent, the machine stood motionless, immediately before plunging. Momentarily it had thrown me into a position for the blood to flow back into my head.

A second later would have meant death—Kismet!

So there I was, swaying about in the air, the mist barely illuminated by a full moon which sent no more than a thin reddish light through the night. The sudden checking of speed when I reached the ground was sufficient, after my previous experience, to send the blood again from my brain into my legs, so that I stumbled forward and once more all was as black as night; in short, I had my second 'black-out'. This time I recovered consciousness very slowly. Had it happened this way when I was in the machine, it would have proved fatal. Everything around me was swimming; I finally awoke, my expression, I dare say, resembling that of Adam when, having been formed from earth, he saw the world for the first time. For at first I had not the remotest idea of what had happened to me or where I was. Only gradually did it become clear to me that I had reached my goal—or rather a new beginning. Alas, more of a *beginning* than I dreamed.

... When I was flung out of the machine, I was thrown with great force against a part of the tail, which I struck with my right foot just below the ankle, practically the pulse of the foot, so to speak; and the contact with another object so much harder than itself caused such a terrific extravasation of blood that my leg turned black and violet up to beyond the knee ...

I had an additional compass fitted so that, if the two others should differ, the third would indicate which had gone wrong. But they all three gave the same indications with no wavering—including the fourth rather primitive one on my wrist, which was intended to guide me after my jump, when I stepped out of the parachute to make my way to Dungavel. However, in this respect also, things did not go quite according to plan; for in the struggle to get free of my plane—which lasted some time—I landed a couple of hours march from Dungavel.[16]

The single unidentified German plane was spotted by an Observer Corps look-out as it crossed the North-Sea coastline. The report that it was an ME 110 was passed on to duty officers in the RAF plotting room in Inverness, who did not believe what they heard, because no ME 110 could, in their view, have flown so far with any hope of getting back to Germany. As it happened, the arrival of the Messerschmitt was reported to Wing-Commander the Duke of Hamilton at Turnhouse, who sent a flight up to track the aircraft. They returned with the report that it had crashed.[17]

Hess, as we have seen, had landed some distance from his target of Dungavel Hill. As he shook himself free from his parachute, he was nearer Glasgow than Dungavel. Tom Hyslop, a lieutenant in the Renfrewshire Constabulary, was driving along the Eaglesham road around 10.45 that evening in a police car with his daughter, who was serving in the WAAF, when he picked up on his police radio receiver the message: 'A single enemy plane has crossed the Clyde and is flying inland towards Glasgow. It is difficult to identify, but is definitely hostile and may be in difficulties. All police are to watch in case it lands. Message ends.' He stopped the car to listen. For a while there was silence, and then they heard the approaching roar of Hess's Messerschmitt as it passed close overhead, followed by the crash as it landed in a field off the Eaglesham road, about a mile from Hyslop's car.

At the same moment David McLean, head ploughman at Floors Farm, a bachelor living in a whitewashed cottage with his mother and sister, heard the plane immediately overhead—at first with its strange-sounding engines alive and then, suddenly, with its sound succeeded by silence. Pulling the blackout from his window, McLean stared out over the moonlit landscape, and saw the white outline of a descending parachute. He realized it must be a German pilot baling out, so he dressed hurriedly, calling out to the women, who were both in bed, that he was going out after the pilot. He ran from the farmhouse to the fields nearby, and caught up with Hess as he was struggling to free himself from the billowing parachute. As soon as he was clear of it, he tried to stand up, staggering momentarily because of the pain in his ankle.

'Are you German?' McLean called out.

'Yes,' said Hess. 'I am German, I am Hauptmann Alfred Horn. I want to go to Dungavel House. I have an important message for the Duke of Hamilton.'

Hess was determined at this stage not to reveal his identity. He had no idea where he was after his black-out; he certainly did not realize that he had landed almost thirty miles from Dungavel Hill. As he spoke there was a sudden roar in the distance, and a bright sheet of flame ascended from the aircraft, lighting up the surrounding landscape. McLean asked if he was alone, and unarmed. Hess replied that there had been no one with him and that he carried no weapons.

The farm was not far from Eaglesham House, a secret radar centre for the Royal Signals disguised as a searchlight unit. McLean sent another man who had appeared from the farm to get help from Eaglesham House; meanwhile he gathered up the parachute at Hess's request, and helped him to hobble along towards the cottage. Soon he was standing inside the cottage accustoming his eyes to the light as the blackout was adjusted. In front of him stood a little old woman clasping her dressing-gown to her. She was McLean's mother.

'Are you German?' she asked.

Hess clicked his heels and bowed.

'I am German,' he said.

'Ma Gawd,' said Mrs McLean.

They took him into the living-room and sat him in the best chair. To cover their curiosity and confusion, they resorted to the old British custom of making tea. McLean was as much in awe of his feat of capturing a German pilot single-handed as Hess was at the success of his landing. But when Hess asked again to be taken to the Duke of Hamilton, McLean said he must leave all that to the soldiers who would soon be

here. Mrs McLean brought in the tea served in her best china. Meanwhile outside in the darkness, Tom Hyslop and the soldiers from
Eaglesham House had met and were searching in vain in the fields for
the pilot. To break the silence in the cottage, Hess produced a photograph of his three-year-old son for the McLeans to see. He was far more
at ease than they were.

McLean was beginning to measure up his prisoner. He realized the
man was wearing a uniform of exceptional quality, but above all he was
impressed by the fine pair of fur-lined boots. Although Hess persisted
in withholding his identity, McLean sensed this was a man out of the
ordinary. Hess merely admitted to being plain Captain Alfred Horn.

Two Signallers arrived, followed almost immediately by a Special
Constable and a member of the Home Guard. The Special Constable
brandished a first world war revolver, which actually belonged to his
friend in the Home Guard. 'Hands up,' he cried. The Signallers, radar
experts rather than warriors, momentarily obeyed. Hess remained
calmly seated with the beginning of a smile on his face. No one knew
quite what to do, so the round of obvious questions started all over
again—are you alone? are you armed? will your plane explode? and so
forth. Since the Signallers were quite unable to take any unauthorized
person, let alone a German, into Eaglesham House, it was difficult to
decide where Hess should be taken. The local police station was only
another cottage. It was decided finally to drive him to the Home Guard
hut at Busby, two miles or so north, and nearer to Glasgow.

Hyslop arrived at the cottage only after Hess had gone. He was
curious about the crashed plane, which he had found in a field nearby.
The wreckage was still smoking from the fire. He noticed that the
machine-gun barrels were packed with grease, a clear indication that the
aircraft had not been intended for attack.

Hess was driven by his captors in a small, shabby car to Busby, on
the southern outskirts of Glasgow. If anything, in spite of the Special
Constable's bravado, they felt somewhat over-awed and outclassed by
this tall, imperious man with the bushy eyebrows and calmly polite
manner. The Home Guard centre turned out to be a brick-built hall.
Hess's recollections were scarcely complimentary to his captors; he
generalized somewhat widely concerning them when recalling the
incident for his wife some four years later:

A civil official appeared at the head of a troop of soldiers—a man
who had quite evidently, judging by the smell, been celebrating

Saturday with good Scottish spirits, probably having taken an extra shot when he heard that a German parachutist had come down. At any rate he staggered about in a cloud of alcoholic vapour, marching me off and prodding me all the while in the back with a large revolver, his finger never leaving the trigger. As I listened to his incessant belching and stumbling, I felt there must have been the finger of God intervening between his shaking hand and the impending shot. A little later the leader of the military asked me to enter a house, but the alcoholic official protested energetically against this and prevented my entry, poking his revolver, this time, into my stomach. I certainly did not move a muscle at this delightful little game with Fate but urged the two to unite in deciding what to do. Finally we did enter the house, where a really nice little Tommy made all well once more by offering me a bottle of milk which he had no doubt brought for himself. After five hours flying and two 'black-outs', I expect I looked as if I needed it—as indeed I *did*, for on top of the somewhat exciting adventures of the last few hours I now knew that I was under arrest. Little did I know for how long![18]

Hess had decided to adopt a pose of relaxation, and to the astonishment of everyone laid himself flat on the floor in a Yoga-like state of disassociation, his muscles free of all tension. They thought for a moment he had fainted. He came to when Hyslop arrived with some Army and RAF officers, who searched him and gave him his first formal interrogation. Hess stood firmly by the name of Horn. The officers looked in some wonder at the collection of drugs he carried in his pockets, including an elixir from a Tibetan Lamasery for his gallbladder complaint. He also carried vitamins and sedatives.

Hess was next taken by Army truck to Maryhill Barracks, Glasgow, where he was housed in the sick-bay. By now it was Sunday morning and he was beginning to grow impatient of the disregard paid him when he demanded, first of one officer, then another, to be taken to the Duke of Hamilton. This seemed far more important to him than the medical attention needed for his ankle. He was also concerned that he would be recognized before the time came to reveal himself. He was to describe the situation, again very loosely, some four years later:

Some RAF officers arrived during the night to take a look at the phenomenon which had landed in their country—this being part of their 'duty' as they made clear or at least asserted. An army major with them stared at me for a good while and then, speaking in first-rate German, said that I was the image of Rudolf Hess. He had often seen Hess in Munich, he said. I replied very coldly that it was no news to me that I looked like Hess; and in fact it was very painful to me. The major understood perfectly.[19]

Meanwhile, the Duke of Hamilton at Turnhouse was curious why this Captain Horn of the Luftwaffe was pressing so hard to see him personally on a 'special mission'.[20] He arranged to drive over to Maryhill Barracks early on Sunday morning, accompanying the official Interrogating Officer when he went to see Hess at the Barracks. The official report of this meeting made by the Duke follows:

On Sunday 11 May at 10.00 hours I arrived at Maryhill Barracks with the Interrogating Officer, who first examined the effects of the prisoner. These included Leica camera, photographs of himself and small boy and some medicines, also visiting cards of Dr Karl Haushofer and his son, Dr Albrecht Haushofer.

I entered the room of the prisoner accompanied by the Interrogating Officer and the Military Officer on guard.

The prisoner, who I had no recollection of ever having seen before, at once requested that I should speak to him alone. I then asked the other officers to withdraw, which they did.

The German opened by saying that he had seen me in Berlin at the Olympic Games in 1936 and that I had lunched in his house. He said, 'I do not know if you recognize me, but I am Rudolf Hess.' He went on to say that he was on a mission of humanity and that the Führer did not want to defeat England and wished to stop fighting. His friend Albrecht Haushofer had told him that I was an Englishman who, he thought, would understand his (Hess's) point of view. He had consequently tried to arrange a meeting with me in Lisbon (see Haushofer's letter to me dated 23 September 1940). Hess went on to say that he had tried to fly to Dungavel and this was the fourth time he had set out, the first time being in December. On the three previous occasions he had turned back owing to bad weather. He had not attempted to make this journey during the time when Britain was gaining victories in Libya, as he thought his mission then might be interpreted as weakness, but now that Germany had gained successes in North Africa and Greece, he was glad to come.

The fact that Reich Minister Hess had come to this country in person would, he stated, show his sincerity and Germany's will-

ingness for peace. He went on to say that the Führer was convinced
that Germany would win the war, possibly soon but certainly in
one, two or three years. He wanted to stop the unnecessary slaughter
that would otherwise inevitably take place. He asked me if I could
get together leading members of my party to talk over things with a
view to making peace proposals. I replied that there was now only
one party in this country. He then said he could tell me what Hitler's
peace terms would be. First, he would insist on an arrangement
whereby our two countries would never go to war again. I questioned
him as to how that arrangement could be brought about, and he
replied that one of the conditions, of course, is that Britain would
give up her traditional policy of always opposing the strongest
power in Europe. I then told him that if we made peace now,
we would be at war again certainly within two years . . . to which
I replied that if a peace agreement was possible the arrangement
could have been made before the war started, but since, however,
Germany chose war in preference to peace at a time when we were
most anxious to preserve peace, I could put forward no hope of a
peace agreement now.

He requested me to ask the King to give him 'parole', as he had
come unarmed and of his own free will.

He further asked me if I could inform his family that he was
safe by sending a telegram to Rothacker, Hertzog Stra. 17 Zurich,
stating that Alfred Horn was in good health. He also asked that
his identity should not be disclosed to the Press.

Throughout the interview, Hess was able to express himself
fairly clearly, but he did not properly understand what I was saying
and suggested that I should return with an interpreter and have
further conversation with him.

From Press photographs and Albrecht Haushofer's description of
Hess, I believed that this prisoner was indeed Hess himself. Until
this interview I had not the slightest idea that the invitation in
Haushofer's letter to meet him (Haushofer) in Lisbon had any
connection at all with Hess.

The Duke realized that there was little more he could achieve at this
stage with 'Horn', whom he was certain by now was indeed, as he
claimed to be, Hess himself. After he had left him, having promised to
return with an interpreter at some later stage, he advised the officer in
charge of the sick-bay at the Barracks that he had probably got an

important prisoner and that he should be moved from Glasgow and placed under double guard. Hess was accordingly moved to the military hospital in Buchanan Castle, Drymen, some eighteen miles north of Glasgow and near Loch Lomond.

Taking a photograph of Horn for further identification, the Duke drove to Floors Farm, Eaglesham, to examine the crashed Messerschmitt, before going back to Turnhouse, where he immediately requested special leave in order to free himself to make a secret report in person either to a senior official at the Foreign Office or to the Prime Minister himself. With some difficulty, since he could explain nothing over the telephone, he eventually reached the ear of John Colville, the Prime Minister's secretary, and it was agreed he should fly south at once to Northolt in a Hurricane, where a car would meet him during the afternoon.

Pintsch had arrived in Berchtesgaden at seven o'clock that morning. Leaving the sleeping compartment, he telephoned Albert Bormann, the brother of Martin Bormann, and asked for an immediate appointment with the Führer. He met with more or less the same obstruction as the Duke of Hamilton, but at least got transport from the station to the Berghof. He was acutely aware of the difficulties which would face him once Hitler opened the letter explaining that Hess was in Scotland. But his instructions had been to place the letter personally in Hitler's hands. He was scarcely aware of the beauty of the mountain scenery as the car transporting him turned and twisted up the mountain road flanked by Alpine heights and precipices.

Albert Bormann promised on his arrival to work him somehow into Hitler's schedule of meetings.[21] Fortunately, Hitler had an appointment with Dr Fritz Todt, Minister for Armaments, at eleven o'clock, and Pintsch managed to prevail on him to allow him a few minutes of his time. When Hitler came downstairs and greeted him and the Minister, Todt yielded place, and Hitler took Pintsch into his thickly-carpeted study with its vast, sliding windows revealing the panorama of the Alps, and its massive desk beside which stood Hitler's giant globe of the world.

Hitler put on his spectacles and broke the seals on Hess's letter. As he read his face grew stern and grave.

'Where is Hess now?' he asked.

'Yesterday evening, Mein Führer, he flew from Augsburg to Scotland to meet the Duke of Hamilton,' said Pintsch, formally.

'At this particular moment in the war that could be a most hazardous escapade,' said Hitler coldly.

He returned to the letter, reading it through carefully and slowly. Then he summoned an adjutant and sent him to check where Göring and Ribbentrop were. While the adjutant was gone, he read the letter through again. The adjutant returned to report that Göring was in Nuremberg and Ribbentrop in Fuschl. Hitler ordered that they be summoned at once to Berchtesgaden on a matter of the highest urgency. Pintsch stood to attention, waiting the pleasure of the Führer, who disregarded him and, as if alone, began to spell out the letter again, reading it word by word in a whisper. It emphasized the need for an alliance between Germany and England, followed by the pacification of Europe.[22] Hitler's voice dwelt on the last words in the letter: 'And if this project—which I admit may have only a small chance of success— ends in failure and the Fates decide against me, this can have no detrimental results either for you or for Germany: it will always be possible for you to deny all responsibility. *Simply say that I was out of my mind* . . .' Hitler's voice stopped, and he looked out over the mountains. The sun was pouring into the room. Pintsch, his senses alert, standing forgotten behind the Führer, became aware of the scent of flowers in his nostrils. It came from a bowl of blooms on the desk.

At this moment Eva Braun came in. Sensing that there was trouble, she said in a quiet voice that lunch was ready. Hitler merely nodded. Pintsch, still disregarded, joined the silent procession which moved through to the dining-room. Here Todt, Hewel (who was on Ribbentrop's staff), and Karl Bodenschatz, Göring's adjutant, stood waiting. Others present at the lunch were Eva Braun, Ernst Udet, and Martin Bormann. Just before they went in, Bormann had asked Pintsch what was wrong. When Pintsch told him, he had backed away, as if trying to avoid any physical contact with this bearer of ill-news. 'That's nothing to do with me,' he had said. 'Don't involve me.'

After lunch (vegetables and yoghurt for Hitler; soup, meat and fruit for the rest) Hitler drank down his last draught of mineral water, and got up, dismissing the gathering. Then he walked round the table to Pintsch's place. With a nod, he sent Bormann out to fetch in men from his personal guards. Bormann returned with two captains and placed Pintsch under arrest, pending an enquiry into his part in the flight. He was to remain in captivity for three years.

That same Sunday morning a Scottish journalist, Eric Schofield, general manager of the Glasgow *Daily Record*, was walking to Eaglesham with his dog when he noticed an unusual amount of excitement among the people in this normally quiet place. He soon learned the news as Eaglesham knew it—that a German pilot of an exceptional kind, exceptionally dressed and speaking good English, had landed by parachute and had been captured. Schofield also gathered he was asking to see the Duke of Hamilton. Sensing the beginnings, at least, of an unusual story, he telephoned the duty reporter at *The Daily Record* office, Max McAuslane, and told him to send a reporter to conduct interviews and take photographs of the plane. McAuslane, impressed himself by the stranger features of the story, telephoned the editor, Clem Livingstone, who, although he lived thirty-six miles from Glasgow, decided that his place was at his desk. Meanwhile, the chief reporter, John Simpson, had gone out with a photographer to investigate the story on the spot. When he returned with his copy, McAuslane himself took it round to the official Censor at 4.30 in the afternoon. When the Censor banned this seemingly harmless story, McAuslane realized there was even more behind it than he had suspected. But there was no more he could do for the moment.

By this time the Duke of Hamilton had reached Northolt. Here he found an important message waiting for him in a sealed envelope; he was instructed to fly immediately to Kidlington, near Oxford, and close to Ditchley, where the Prime Minister was spending the weekend, though this particular information was not included in the message. Only when he arrived at Ditchley Park, an eighteenth-century mansion owned by Ronald Tree, and used by Churchill as secret headquarters at weekends when the moon was full and the German bombers active, did the Duke learn who had summoned him. The Duke arrived just as Churchill and his advisers were finishing dinner; the Prime Minister received him in the company of Sir Archibald Sinclair, Minister for Air. At first the Prime Minister quite plainly did not believe the story, and insisted on leaving the matter over until he had seen his film of the evening—*The Marx Brothers Go West*. The Duke slept throughout the film, but recovered sufficiently to endure the Prime Minister's subsequent grilling which went on until two in the morning. Hess's identity, if indeed this was Hess, had to be proved to the hilt.

In Berchtesgaden, Hitler held close conference with Göring, Ribbentrop and Keitel as soon as they reached the Berghof during the afternoon. Some of those present, or in the vicinity, have given graphic accounts of the atmosphere as Hitler's attempt to grasp this unexpected event took its toll on his introspective and egocentric nature: Paul Schmidt, Hitler's special interpreter, who was present at the time, says, 'Hitler was as appalled as though a bomb had struck the Berghof.' Jodl, denying that Hitler could have known anything about Hess's intentions, said in the cells at Nuremberg, 'I never in my life saw a man in such a fury as when Hitler heard that Hess had flown to England. He was in such a rage he was fit to burst . . . He was afraid the Italians would think he was negotiating peace behind their backs and leaving them in the lurch, Keitel, too, recalls the tense atmosphere at Berchtesgaden:

> Hitler was walking back and forth with me in his big study, and we talked, and he was touching his forehead and he said, 'Hess must have had a mental derangement . . . I can't recognise Hess. It is a different person.' Hess . . . had a very fine sensibility, I remember in the morning after this news reached us . . . it was delivered only after Hess had arrived in England . . . he ordered all the Gauleiters and Göring to meet for the purpose of communication to them and discussing with them the repercussions of this fact . . .
>
> Naturally, in the beginning, the question was, first, 'We don't even know that he arrived . . . Did he ever get there ? . . . Göring, how is this business ? Can he do it with this type of plane ?' And all these considerations must have been dominant during the first and second day. They rendered the presentation of the matter to the press very difficult.[23]

Albrecht Haushofer was also summoned to the Obersalzberg; he was picked up by the Gestapo and flown to Hitler's residence. On his arrival he was told to dictate to a stenographer any background information he could give about the kind of contacts in Britain Hess might be seeking out. The report survives, twelve pages typed on the special Führermaschine, the typewriter with lettering large enough for Hitler to read without using his spectacles. The report went over the old ground of the attempted contacts through Lisbon, and listed certain eminent men Hess might attempt to see.[24] After completing his task, Albrecht Haushofer was confined for three months' detention, and then released.

Göring, who felt nearest among the Nazi leaders to potential blame for the careless way in which Hess had enjoyed access to a secret aircraft, telephoned Messerschmitt and demanded an interview with him in Munich; Messerschmitt gave his own account of this meeting, which took place the following day, Monday 12 May:

> Göring pointed his baton at me and shouted: 'As far as you are

concerned, I suppose anybody can come and fly off with one of your machines!' I pointed out that Hess was not 'anybody', but was the *Stellvertreter*. 'You should have known that this man was crazy.' I replied drily: 'How could I be expected to suppose that one so high in the hierarchy of the Third Reich could be crazy? If that were the case, Herr Reichsmarschall, you should have procured his resignation!' Göring thereupon roared with laughter and exclaimed: 'Messerschmitt, you are quite incurable! Go back to your factory and get on with your construction. I will help you out of the mess, if the Führer shall seek to make trouble for you.'[25]

What followed was a period of impasse—who was going to be the first to break the news and announce either Hess's departure from Germany or his arrival in England? Each nation waited for the other to make the first move. From Hitler's point of view there was always the possibility that Hess had never managed to reach Britain; even so, his disappearance would at some stage have to be explained. Meanwhile—there was silence.

Even Ilse Hess knew nothing, except that her husband had departed on some unexplained tour of duty and not returned home. Sunday followed Saturday with no news, and so did Monday, 12 May. No one from the Obersalzberg made contact with her or her household.

It was Hitler in the end who decided to make the initial announcement. Ribbentrop, for one, advised this, thinking it would be wiser if Germany's allies heard the news first of all from Germany, and not from Britain. It was worded, not by Goebbels (who, rather significantly took no part at this stage[26]), but by Otto Dietrich, who was, as we have seen, at the Berghof. Hitler ordered Dietrich to prepare a guarded statement for release by Munich radio on Monday evening, the very day on which he finally decided on the much-postponed date for the attack on Russia—22 June 1941. The statement about Hess was put out at 22.00 hours[27] and was repeated in the press the following day, Tuesday 13 May:

It is officially announced by the National Socialist Party that Party Member Rudolf Hess, who, as he was suffering from an illness of some years' standing, had been strictly forbidden to embark on any further flying activity, was able, contrary to this command, again to come into possession of an aeroplane.

On Saturday, 10 May, Rudolf Hess again set out on a flight from Augsburg, from which he has not so far returned.

A letter which he left behind unfortunately shows by its distraction traces of a mental disorder, and it is feared that he was a victim of hallucinations.

The Führer at once ordered the arrest of the adjutants of the Party Member Hess, who alone had any cognizance of these flights, and did not, contrary to the Führer's orders, of which they were fully aware, either prevent or report the flight.

In these circumstances it must be considered that Party Member Hess either jumped out of his aeroplane or had met with an accident.

Hitler approved the introduction of the idea of Hess's insanity—according to Walter Schellenberg of SS Security, as a result of Bormann's advice.[28] But the idea had been planted by Hess himself and was to become the motif of his existence for the next five years.

The floodgates of comment and speculation were immediately opened, and the Prime Minister in Britain was free to issue his own statement at 23.20 hours, as authorized by the Minister of Information:

Rudolf Hess, the Deputy Führer of Germany and Party Leader of the National Socialist Party, has landed in Scotland in the following circumstances.

On the night of Saturday the 10th inst., a Messerschmitt 110 was reported by our patrols to have crossed the coast of Scotland and to be flying in the direction of Glasgow.

Since an ME 110 would not have the fuel to return to Germany this report was at first disbelieved.

However, later on, an ME 110 crashed near Glasgow, with its guns untouched. Shortly afterwards a German officer who had baled out was found with his parachute in the neighbourhood suffering from a broken ankle.

He was taken to hospital in Glasgow where he at first gave his name as Horn, but later on declared that he was Rudolf Hess. He brought with him various photographs of himself at different ages, apparently in order to establish his identity.

These photographs were deemed to be photographs of Hess by several people who knew him personally. Accordingly, an officer of the Foreign Office who was closely acquainted with Hess before the war has been sent up by aeroplane to see him in hospital.

The agencies fed this statement to the press under the inaccurate heading of 'Rudolf Hess in England'. This gave Livingstone his cue at the offices of the Glasgow Record to scoop the world with the story already in his file of Hess in Scotland. His edition went out overnight with the heading 'Rudolf Hess in Glasgow—Official', while all those wanting to use the story had to contact and credit the *Daily Record* office, whose lines were hot until the following midday, Tuesday 13 May.[29]

Meanwhile, the Hess case had been discussed by the British Cabinet at its Monday morning session. As a result Ivone Kirkpatrick, then Controller of European Services at the BBC, was summoned to the Foreign Office and given the substance of the Duke of Hamilton's report. Since Kirkpatrick had served as First Secretary at the British Embassy in Berlin from 1935 to 1938, he agreed that he should be able to recognize Hess and, as he hoped, distinguish between him and any impostor who might have been sent on some special errand from Germany. He then received instructions to fly north that evening with the Duke of Hamilton and identify the prisoner, who was by now in the military hospital at Buchanan Castle. They flew from Hendon in a slow Flamingo aircraft which had to refuel on the journey, and only reached Turnhouse at 21.40 hours. They had had no lunch, let alone dinner, and were settling down to assuage their hunger when the telephone rang and the Foreign Secretary himself, Anthony Eden, demanded that Kirkpatrick proceed without delay by car to Buchanan Castle and identify Hess, since the German radio had just announced that he was missing; he was even told to leave his steak untouched and drive to Buchanan Castle immediately. They did not arrive there until midnight, having lost their way in the darkness.

Italy, Germany's closest ally, received the news of Hess's flight with suspicion. Count Galeazzo Ciano—Mussolini's son-in-law and since 1936 (at the age of only thirty-three) his Minister for Foreign Affairs—directed a well-informed and serpent-like gaze on the European scene. He wrote in his diary for 12 May:

A strange German communiqué announces the death of Hess in a plane accident. I cannot conceal my scepticism about the truth of this version. I even doubt whether he is dead at all. There is something mysterious about it.[30]

Ilse Hess, still without any information about her husband on Monday evening, was feeling better after her indisposition and decided that she would see a film that same night in the room the household used for private projections. Dressed in a housecoat, she went downstairs for the film. At this point, she tells her own story:

What the film was about I cannot remember, for it had barely started when I was called away. At the back of the big room where our audience—our little entourage of adjutants, chauffeurs and servants —was assembled, I saw there was some kind of disturbance and there I found my husband's youngest adjutant in a distraught state standing by the door. Politely but earnestly, he begged me to 'put on my things', meaning slightly more formal clothes—a request which, from the confused and excited manner in which it was made, seemed to me senseless. Then a swift dread crossed my mind and I cried:

'Something has happened to my husband!'

It was some time before I could gather that somebody—not anybody in the room there—had heard over the German radio that 'The former Stellvertreter of the Führer has come down while flying over the North Sea, and is presumed dead.'

I can still remember replying, 'Nonsense!' in an angry tone to the white faced adjutant. Not for one second did I believe anything really tragic had happened. In moments of extreme spiritual tension there comes to us, from regions lying outside the field of reason, a knowledge that will not let us be deceived.

I then did what I had never done before, for with us public affairs and private interests were kept apart. I demanded a call to Obersalzberg 'on State affairs'; and asked for a first priority call.

While waiting for the call, I learned more of the report on the radio which had caused alarm and agitation in every German home. The manner in which this report referred to 'mental aberration', the reference to alleged 'breach of faith' over the pledge not to fly again —these aroused a passionate resentment in me, as may well be imagined. I had fully intended to speak to the Führer and give him a piece of my mind. But I was unable to make that contact, and after much hither and thither I found myself at last speaking to the then Reichsleiter Bormann, who told me he knew absolutely nothing. This turned out to be true, but I did not at the time accept his word. I admit I hardly let him open his mouth, but expressed my indignation with an emphasis and a rhetoric I had never employed before or since in that quarter. Bormann promised to arrange for me to receive an early visit from a Ministry official. Quite exhausted,

if not soothed, I brought my one and only first-priority State phone
call to an end.

I then got through to my husband's brother in Berlin. Alfred
Hess, like myself, did not accept the report of his brother's death;
and this helped—for, in spite of my own confidence, I was not without the need of being comforted. Two close friends came to visit
and offer their help, but they knew no more than I did—only what
they had heard on the radio—and then long after midnight: Dr
H, the promised Ministry official, arrived. My hope that he would
be able to enlighten me was bitterly disappointed. It seemed that at
Obersalzberg they expected *me* to enlighten them. For the first time
I found myself face to face with one of those incredulous persons
who refused to accept my statement that I knew nothing of my
husband's plans. I insisted to the dumbfounded Dr H that all
members of 'the Hess staff' should know their chief well enough to
feel sure that he would never discuss State secrets with his wife. The
term 'State secrets' produced a powerful reaction. Up to this point,
the emissary had been somewhat confused but, if a little pale, had
remained polite and not unfriendly; but now he turned to ice and
informed me that if a single word of what I (supposedly) knew should
leak out, I would be arrested. He then turned on his heel and left the
room.

To-day I cannot recollect all the endless things we discussed,
conjectured, pondered over, or rejected as absurd during that
long night. Three times we listened in to repetitions of the original
announcement—each time slightly altered—yet in the end remaining
much the same. We disbelieved it entirely.[31]

It was after midnight, in the first hour of Tuesday, 13 May, that Ivone
Kirkpatrick and the Duke of Hamilton were led by the Commandant at
Buchanan Castle up a winding stair to what had once been a servant's
bedroom. Kirkpatrick takes up his own version of the story in his
memoirs, *The Inner Circle:*

A door was opened, and there fast asleep on an iron bedstead I saw
Hess. He was dressed in the grey flannel pyjamas issued to soldiers in
hospital and the familiar brown army blanket covered his recumbent
form. Lighting the bare room was a naked bulb with a white enamel
shade. In order to diminish the glare an old newspaper had been
wrapped around the whole contraption.

Accustomed as I was to the pomp and splendour in which the Nazi nabobs lived, I surveyed the scene in silence. Then we woke the prisoner up and after a moment of dazed uncertainty he recognized me and gave me a warm welcome. Two hard wooden chairs were produced for Hamilton and myself and we were left alone with Hess. He asked me to remove the newspaper from the lamp and seizing a large packet of manuscript notes embarked on a long and evidently well-prepared discourse of Germany's grievances against England. He traced the history of Anglo-German relations since the beginning of the century and sought to prove that Germany's legitimate aspirations had always been thwarted by the treacherous brutality of British policy. This oration had not reached its culminating point when the Foreign Secretary telephoned to enquire how I was getting on. I left the room to speak to him and was able to say that I had identified the prisoner as Hess without any doubt whatsoever.

On returning to the bedroom I found Hamilton comatose and Hess itching to get on with his speech. By three am the bundle of notes had almost all been used and he was evidently reaching the end of his peroration. But my patience was exhausted. I cut him short and summarily demanded that he should define the object of his visit. He replied that it was to convince the British Government of the inevitability of a German victory and to bring about a peace by negotiation. He explained that Britain's position was now completely hopeless. We had been expelled from the continent of Europe and could never recover a footing there. We stood alone and our strength must decline, whereas Hitler's would expand with the aid of all Europe's resources including those of Russia. There were therefore two courses open to us. The first would be to continue our ineffective resistance. But in that case, he must warn me, Hitler would be very angry with consequences appalling to our people. Here he drew a vivid picture of Germany's capacity, untrammelled by any warlike operations, to concentrate on an enormous programme of aircraft and submarine construction. The aircraft would be used to encompass the systematic and pitiless destruction of our industries and dwellings. The whole island would be reduced to rubble and millions of our people killed. Meanwhile the submarine fleets would completely blockade the island. The inhabitants who escaped the bombs would perish of starvation.

I asked Hess whether Hitler still intended to invade Britain. He looked rather sheepish and said he really did not know. The Führer, who was a tender-hearted man, might be reluctant to expose his soldiers to the sight of so much suffering. On the whole, he was disposed to think that the most likely plan would be to isolate us, destroy our towns and leave the survivors to starve until the Government sued for peace. Even when we had surrendered it was by no means certain that food would be made available for our famished people. He must beg me not to follow this suicidal course, because there was a way out which promised honour, safety and a glorious future. He could claim to be in the Führer's closest confidence of which I must be aware. He was therefore in a position to speak with complete authority, and could assure me that the Führer, who had always entertained a high regard for Britain and her Empire, would be prepared to conclude a magnanimous peace on the following terms: German hegemony on the continent of Europe and the return of the former German colonies; British hegemony in the overseas Empire which would remain intact and would be guaranteed by Germany. Thus the German Army and the British Fleet would rule the world. This Anglo-German combination would be so strong as to enable us without risk or trouble to see the Americans off; and that would be an advantageous thing for the whole world. There was, however, one condition to this offer. The Führer, understandably enough, would not negotiate a peace with Mr Churchill. He assumed that in view of the generous character of his proposals, having regard to our military position, this would present no difficulty even with Mr Churchill. So now it only remained to open negotiations with myself. At this point he produced a dirty little scrap of paper on which he had written the name and number of a German prisoner of war. He said that he would require this man as secretary and general assistant in the forthcoming negotiations.

Except to correct some of Hess's wilder deviations from the truth I did not interrupt his speech which lasted until nearly four am. By that time the Duke, who had been unable to follow Hess's German language, was nearly asleep and I was very hungry. So we took our leave and went downstairs to eat a dish of scrambled eggs prepared by the night sister. In the middle of this meal a BBC recording van arrived at the castle door and demanded alternatively a recording by Hess or one by myself. It was sad not to be able to reward such enterprise.[32]

After the scrambled eggs, Kirkpatrick and the Duke drove back to Turnhouse, where they arrived only at six o'clock; at eight-thirty he telephoned the Foreign Office to give a brief report of what Hess had said. 'I was told that the Government were embarrassed by the whole affair and did not know exactly how to handle it,' he wrote. He was told to fend off the press with such superficial details as what Hess was wearing or eating; an exaggerated statement appeared in the press later that Hess was breakfasting on chicken and white wine, and this caused a furore. Kirkpatrick later that morning dictated a full report of what Hess had said 'to a charming and competent WAAF stenographer, who was clearly thrilled at joining the small band of people in the secret.' The report was flown to London that afternoon.[33] Kirkpatrick was required to stand by for further instructions about Hess.

Hitler, most anxious to save face, sent Ribbentrop to Italy on Tuesday 13 May to make personal contact with Mussolini and Ciano. Ciano regarded the flight by now as 'a very serious matter: the first real victory for the English.' Ciano's diary is as illuminating as it is characteristic on the subject:

Von Ribbentrop arrives in Rome unexpectedly. He is discouraged and nervous. He wants to confer with the Duce and me for various reasons, but there is only one real reason: he wants to inform us about the Hess affair, which is now in the hands of the press all over the world. The official version is that Hess, sick in body and mind, was a victim of his pacifist hallucinations, and went to England in the hope of facilitating the beginning of peace negotiations. Hence, he is not a traitor; hence, he will not talk; hence, whatever else is said or printed in his name is false. Ribbentrop's conversation is a beautiful feat of patching things up. The Germans want to cover themselves before Hess speaks and reveals things that might make a great impression in Italy. Mussolini comforted von Ribbentrop, but afterwards told me that he considers the Hess affair a tremendous blow to the Nazi regime. He added that he was glad of it because this will have the effect of bringing down German stock, even with the Italians.

Dinner at home with von Ribbentrop and his associates.

The Germans are depressed. Von Ribbentrop repeats his slogans against Great Britain with that monotony that made Göring dub him 'Germany's No. 1 parrot'.

It seems that Bismarck [Prince Otto von Bismarck, Counsellor at the German Embassy in Rome], who hates von Ribbentrop, emphasized every phrase of his Minister with heavy kicks under the table at Anfuso [Ciano's secretary], to whom he finally said: 'He is such an imbecile that he is a freak of nature.'[34]

Mussolini's own original speculations on the flight introduced an entirely new theory, that Hess had been on his way to Ireland in order to start a revolt there. Ribbentrop left the following day, Wednesday, 14 May, for Germany. Mussolini, already disturbed at the way he was being treated by Hitler, took the Hess affair very seriously.

The furore in the press over the chicken and wine which Hess was quite wrongly supposed to be enjoying in Scotland led Churchill to issue instructions to Eden on Tuesday, 13 May about the manner in which Hess was to be treated:

> On the whole it will be more convenient to treat him as a prisoner of war, under the War Office and not the Home Office, but also as one against whom grave political charges may be preferred. This man, like other Nazi leaders, is potentially a war criminal, and he and his confederates may well be declared outlaws at the close of the war. In this case his repentance would stand him in good stead.
>
> In the meanwhile he should be strictly isolated in a convenient house not too far from London, and every endeavour should be made to study his mentality and get anything worth while out of him.
>
> His health and comfort should be assured, food, books, writing materials, and recreation being provided for him. He should not have any contacts with the outer world or visitors except as prescribed by the Foreign Office. Special guardians should be appointed. He should see no newspapers and hear no wireless. He should be treated with dignity, as if he were an important general who had fallen into our hands.[35]

That same Tuesday Professor Karl Haushofer came to see Ilse Hess in a state of distress even deeper than her own. Frau Hess wrote:

> It was incomprehensible to me that my husband's fatherly old friend, Professor Karl Haushofer, when he came to see me on 13 May, should be fully convinced that my husband was dead. He saw further than I did into the real meaning of things, because he had been told by his son, Albrecht, about the preparations for negotiating through Geneva and Madrid. And, since these feelers

were without a doubt extended with the knowledge of Hitler, Haushofer—contrary to my own conviction—persisted in the view, right up to the day of the trials in Nuremberg when his evidence was taken, that Hitler had 'dispatched' my husband, or as he maliciously put it 'sacrificed him'.

The old man was deeply shaken and filled with despair over the death, as he supposed, of his old friend, and after he had gone away I felt that, for the first time since the fateful evening, I was utterly exhausted. It seemed that the whole world, hitherto firmly established, had collapsed about me. The only real thing in this silent phantom-like process of disintegration was my little boy. I took him in my arms and instantly fell into a deep sleep. Perhaps I slept for hours before an excited hubbub and cries of joy ringing through the house awakened me. The second bulletin, telling of my husband's safe landing in Scotland, taken from the English news, had just come through on the Munich radio.

Our spirits soared, at least for a while, to almost excessive heights. The disintegrating world seemed to piece itself together again! Rudolf Hess *alive*—even in a place like Scotland, so improbable to us at this time—was a fact that protected us against all doubts and untruths.

It could not, however, save us from its consequences. The little world that had hitherto belonged to us became a magician's circle enclosing us and preventing our return to the old ties. Adjutants, orderlies, secretaries and chauffeurs, my brother-in-law Alfred Hess, together with Albrecht Haushofer, were all arrested; some of them vanished for years into concentration camps, and were not set free until 1943 and 44. All of us ceased to be members of a group and became objects of arbitrary control. It was indeed a bitter draught we had to swallow day after day, week after week, year after year![36]

Ilse Hess first learned of her husband's safety only on the morning of Wednesday 14 May, when the news was released officially on the German radio. She was not herself arrested, as so many of the members of Hess's staff had been on 11 and 12 May—with the notable exception of Martin Bormann, who was by now far more the trusted member of Hitler's entourage than he was Hess's deputy.[37] By a decree of 29 May 1941, less than three weeks after Hess had left Germany, he was to be invested by Hitler with the powers previously held by the Deputy Führer, but now stripped from him.

At four in the afternoon of 13 May Hitler addressed a conference of Reichsleiters and Gauleiters, whom he had individually summoned to the Obersalzberg by telegram sent the day before. This read:

Most urgent and to be dealt with forthwith . . .

The Führer has just given orders to issue the following official statement: Owing to an illness progressing for some years, Party-comrade Hess had been under strict orders by the Führer to abstain from any flying activity. In contravention of these orders, he has recently managed to secure possession of an aircraft. On Saturday, 10 May, at 18 hours Partycomrade Hess started from Augsburg on a flight from which, so far, he has not returned. A letter he left behind shows traces of mental derangement indicative of Hess having been subject to illusions. The Führer has ordered the immediate arrest of the adjutants of Partycomrade Hess, who, having been aware of the flights as well as of the Führer's orders refrained from stopping or reporting the flights. Under the circumstances the National Socialist movement cannot, unfortunately, rule out the probability that Hess crashed the aircraft or met with some accident. By order of the Führer all Reichs—and Gauleiters are to appear on the Obersalzberg on Tuesday, 13. 5. at 16 hours. As from 12 hours cars are available for them at the Hotel Schottenhamel near the station. Any inquiries are to be directed by telephone to Dr Hansen, Berghof or Partycomrade Friedrich in the Führerbau. The Führer has decided that the functions of the Stellvertreter des Führers and his office are to be continued under the name Partei-Kanzlei.

(Signed) Reichsleiter M. Bormann

Dietrich writes of this conference:

He took occasion to mention that cases of mental illness had already occured in the Hess family. In this connection it is politically significant and a typical example of Hitler's secrecy about his own intentions that he did not so much as hint at the possibility of an imminent clash with Russia. Yet this meeting in the middle of May was the last conference of Party leaders before the beginning of the campaign against Russia.[38]

Hans Frank was also present at this conference; his private opinion was that Hess (whom he had always liked, though despised for what he regarded as his weakness, especially in his handling of Bormann) had undertaken the flight in order to reassert himself with the Führer, since Goebbels and Göring appeared to him far more influential than himself. Frank describes the catastrophic effect of Hess's departure on Hitler. 'When we, all the Gauleiters and Reichsleiters, were received at the Berghof,' he enters in his memoirs, 'Hitler was evidently in torment. I had not seen him for some time, and I was deeply shocked by his utter depression. With a very low voice, and hesitantly, he spoke to us after Bormann had read out the letters left by Hess. Hitler described the flight as utter lunacy, and then inveighed against the astrologers whom Hess had protected. "It is high time to destroy all this nonsense of star-gazing," he said ... Hitler never recovered from the personal injury which Hess's departure meant for him ... From the moment of Hess's flight a kind of iron curtain descended between Hitler and the German people.'[39]

On 14 May, Kersten, who had been attending Hess for his stomach complaints, was questioned concerning Hess. He recorded in his diary the following day:

> Yesterday I was arrested for five hours and was personally inter-rogated by Heydrich. He asked me in the form of a direct question whether I had encouraged Hess in his friendly feelings towards England. I replied that I had not spoken with him on political, only on medical, matters. Heydrich laughed and said: 'I don't believe a word you say, for I know that you are not on our side. But the day is coming when you will tell us the truth for once.'
>
> After an interrogation lasting five hours, Heydrich had to let me go. I've just heard that all doctors who had treated Hess in recent years have been arrested. I also heard from a trustworthy source that during Heydrich's interrogation Himmler rang up and ordered my immediate release. That must be right, for towards the end of it Heydrich was called from the room and I was left alone for ten minutes. Then he said that the Reichs-führer had guaranteed me but that I should hold myself at their disposal.[40]

Taking his cue, most probably, from Hess himself ('simply say that I was out of my mind'), Hitler decided that this would be the simplest line to adopt in order to divest this seeming defection of its worst danger both inside and outside Germany. It is interesting to see how Goebbels, reacting fiercely against what he regarded as Dietrich's gaffe in referring in the first communiqué to Hess's supposed mental disturbance, came round to elaborating this idea himself once he took control of the news.

His immediate reactions are recorded by his aide, Rudolf Semmler, in the diary he kept secretly during the war:

> Everyone is shaken by the Hess affair. Goebbels says it is more serious than the desertion of an Army Corps. Yesterday afternoon the Reich and Gau chiefs were summoned urgently to the Führer at Berchtesgaden. Goebbels talked alone with Hitler. Hitler was in tears and looked ten years older.
>
> Goebbels sharply critized yesterday's communiqué. The sentence about the mental condition of Hess will cause anger among the people. If he was suffering from delusions, how could he remain the Führer's Deputy? This highly unskilful announcement was composed by Dr Dietrich, a member of Hess's staff, with a certain Party official call Bormann. It was amended by Hitler. Goebbels says the Führer is not always a good psychologist, and he is angry that his advice should not be asked in such cases.
>
> Goebbels tells his departmental chiefs: there is no reason to fear that the Hess affair will cause any upheaval in the Party or in the State. For press and radio the following is the directive for the next few days: dramatize the military news, even if it seems unimportant. Divert people's attention as quickly as possible from this unfortunate occurrence. Work up into sensational stories any murders or traffic accidents.[41]

Ivone Kirkpatrick was instructed on Wednesday 14 May to continue discussions with Hess, however unfruitful they might appear—largely, it would seem, because the Government needed time to work out some kind of policy in relation to this unexpected mission. The longer Hess could be kept talking, the longer the publishing of any committed statement could be postponed. Accordingly Kirkpatrick and the Duke returned to Buchanan Castle.[42] Hess was still very friendly but, according to Kirkpatrick, beginning to show signs of depression that, by his fourth day in Britain, there was no indication that the negotiations he had come to conduct were to be started. He felt, too, that he was not being properly housed or treated, having regard to his status in Germany. He even began to show the first signs of the persecution complex which was to develop so strongly while he was in Britain and later, again, in Germany —for example, he said that the sentries outside his door had been issued with specially heavy boots in order that their stamping might annoy him. He did not like the naked light bulb in his room, and he felt the medical attention he was receiving was inadequate. He requested the return of the drugs he had brought with him and which had been confiscated, and he asked for the loan of books, including, strangely, Jerome K. Jerome's *Three Men in a Boat*. He also wanted a fragment of his aeroplane to keep as a souvenir. This prompted Kirkpatrick to ask him to give some account of his flight, which he did. When Kirkpatrick asked him directly whether he had initiated the flight entirely on his own he replied that he had done so; the only person with whom he had discussed it, he said, was Professor Haushofer. He went on to discuss the position of Iraq, as Germany's ally, and the danger that existed for Britain if the war were not brought to an end. After this interview, Kirkpatrick, who had by now become bored by these prolonged one-way conversations, withdrew to Turnhouse, only to be told from London that he must continue with the meetings and even move over to Drymen for the purpose.

The third and last interview took place on Thursday 15 May. According to his memoirs, Kirkpatrick determined on this occasion to draw Hess out concerning Germany's intention regarding Russia. Hess assured him that Hitler had no aggressive intentions whatsoever, and reverted to his complaints about the way he was being treated. In his official reports, however, there is no mention of Russia, only in the first interview, that of 13 May, and no mention at all that Hess began to complain that there was a plot to poison him. He wanted the officer of the guard to taste his food for him.

Meanwhile, orders had been given that an infantry battalion should be stationed in the grounds of the Castle in case Hitler should be planning some spectacular rescue operation by German commandos. On the following day, however, Friday 16 May, further orders came through suddenly that Hess was to be taken south in the greatest secrecy and confined in the Tower of London. At 18.00 hours he was taken by military ambulance and driven to Glasgow, where he travelled by train to London. Hess himself, in letters written many years later to his wife, says that he was 'placed at first in the officers' quarters by the White Tower . . . The little house and also, apparently, a portion of the furniture were seventeenth-century—quite charming . . . Looking out of the window, I could see the English guardsmen doing their daily drill with endless endurance and a precision that would have done credit to Prussians, accompanied by resounding music. I could have managed very well, however, without the bagpipes—and so could many of the English, as they told me!'[43]

Kirkpatrick returned to London the following day, Saturday 17 May; his reports were already in the hands of Sir Alexander Cadogan at the

Foreign Office. On 16 May Churchill ordered a resumé of the interviews to be made so that he could forward a full account of the Hess incident to Roosevelt the following day. Churchill sent this account of the interview to the President on 17 May, and then added for good measure:

> Hess seems in good health and not excited, and no ordinary signs of insanity can be detected. He declares that this escapade is his own idea and that Hitler was unaware of it beforehand. If he is to be believed, he expected to contact members of a 'peace movement' in England, which he would help to oust the present Government. If he is honest and if he is sane this is an encouraging sign of ineptitude of the German Intelligence Service. He will not be ill-treated, but it is desirable that the press should not romanticize him and his adventure. We must not forget that he shares responsibility for all Hitler's crimes and is a potential war criminal whose fate must ultimately depend upon the decision of the Allied Governments.
>
> Mr President, all the above is for your own information. Here we think it best to let the press have a good run for a bit and keep the Germans guessing. The German officer prisoners of war here were greatly perturbed by the news, and I cannot doubt that there will be deep misgivings in the German armed forces about what he may say.[44]

By 15 May Hitler was determined to develop the idea of Hess's alleged insanity in every communiqué issued. He promoted this at a conference of his generals held that day. A series of press statements issued officially on 13 May and on subsequent days, included these sentences:

> Party Member Hess, because of an illness of many years' standing which was becoming worse, and who had been forbidden by the Führer to do any flying, went against this order and obtained an aeroplane on Saturday, 10 May. At 6.00 he left Augsburg in the plane and has not been heard from since. A letter which he left behind shows from its confused writing the unfortunate traces of mental derangement and it is feared that Party Member Hess has sacrificed himself to a fixed idea.
>
> As far as it is possible to tell from papers left behind by Party Member Hess it seemed that he lived in a state of hallucination as a result of which he felt he could bring about an understanding between England and Germany. It is a fact that Hess, according to a report

from London, jumped from his aeroplane near the town to which he was trying to go and was found there injured. The National Socialist Party regrets that this idealist fell as a victim to his hallucinations. This however will have no effect on the continuation of the war which has been forced upon Germany. Dr Karl Haushofer, head of the Geo-political Institute, Willi Messerschmitt, Frau Hess, and others were arrested.[45]

Goebbels had by now recovered and was deeply involved. He was very worried about the propaganda potentialities which the story held for the British, and he was puzzled why they were doing so little with it. He did not appreciate the tactic of virtual silence in the matter which Churchill and his advisers adopted. This gave him no propaganda cues. According to Semmler:

The British seem unaware that Hess is a trump card in their hands. This is Goebbels' view of the affair, which has now been a world sensation for five days. Now it is losing interest. He said that Hitler and himself at first held their breath in dismay at the thought of the gigantic catastrophe which Churchill could have brought about if he had used the Hess story with real propaganda skill. One had only to think of the false statements and views with which Hess could have been made to credit Hitler, statements which might have wrecked our friendship with Italy and Japan without our being able to put up any defence.

Yesterday Hitler wrote Mussolini a very cordial letter of friendship, the gist of which was that the Hess affair would not affect the relations of the Axis.[46]

The campaign against Hess was now fully under way in Germany. By 21 May Goebbels, like the excellent advertising agent he was, appeared fully convinced of the story he was selling; Semmler continues:

It was always the same in our totalitarian state: no sooner has a leading personality fallen from favour than everything derogatory and evil that can be found out against him is assembled with feverish energy and a flood of the meanest criticism pours over his name. Let none believe that the man was a few days before highly respected, honourable and irreproachable. One is suddenly asked to believe that the devil himself has for years been hidden in this person, who has suddenly dared to differ from Hitler.

In Hess's case the game is being played with masterly skill. To-day

Goebbels told us, to our surprise, that he had long thought Hess crazy: to prove it, one only needed to look once into those wild, bushy-browed eyes. At the slightest touch of cold or illness Hess would consult all kinds of quacks and cranks.

Goebbels then described the comedy of Hess and his wife trying for years to produce an heir. No one knew for certain whether the child was really his; it was said that for psychological reasons he had become impotent. Hess was said to have gone with his wife to astrologers, card readers and other purveyors of magic, and to have drunk all kinds of mixtures and potions before they succeeded in having the child.

Frau Goebbels recalls that Frau Hess assured her five or six times over a number of years that she was at last going to have a child generally because some fortune-teller had said that she would. When the child arrived, Hess danced with joy in a way which reminded those who saw him of the birthday rites of South American Indians. All the Gauleiters were ordered to send bags of German soil from each Gau to the Führer's Deputy. This soil was then spread under a specially built cradle so that young Hess could start life symbolically on German soil. Goebbels added that he himself had thought seriously—as Gauleiter of Berlin—whether it would not be better to send a Berlin pavement stone. In the end his gardener brought him a little heap from the manure bed which he then sent off in a sealed official package.

Evening parties at the Hess home had been so boring that most people refused invitations. Generally fruit juice and peppermint tea were offered and the conversation was as thin and dull as the drinks. The host regularly broke up the party at midnight, much to the relief of his guests.

Now the Gauleiters are coming along one by one and complaining of the primitive administrative methods of their former chief. They say it was impossible to work properly with him, because he would often not understand what was put to him and never had the courage to make independent decisions. It is worth noting that three or four weeks ago no Gauleiter would have dared to make such complaints.

In its most extreme form, the story was developed by Walter Schellenberg, Himmler's head of secret intelligence, the SD.

It is astonishing how Hess, with the complete assurance of a

fanatic or madman, believed in old prophecies and visionary revelations. He would recite whole passages out of books of prophecies,
such as Nostradamus and others that I cannot remember, and also
referred to old horoscopes concerning his own fate, as well as that of
his family and of Germany. At times there were signs of uncertainty
which must have represented a change to a depressive state. All this
he expounded time and again in the most elaborate manner to his
wife. She seemed to accept these potions of his and expressed her
agreement with them, but whether this actually represented her
personal beliefs, or whether she did so out of consideration for him,
I cannot say.[47]

This was the campaign which was finally to lead to the wholesale
arrest of astrologers the following month.

The 'nine days' wonder' of Hess's flight drew to a close by the beginning of his second week in Britain. It was evident little was going to
come of it. Kirkpatrick, back in London, was summoned by the Prime
Minister to a 'small meeting' at which Churchill was at first 'in a
distinctly bad temper because he was afraid that the Government might
be thought to be embarking on peace negotiations'. He 'growled' at
Kirkpatrick: 'If Hess had come a year ago and told us what the Germans
would do to us, we should have been very frightened, and rightly. So
why should we be frightened now?' Kirkpatrick, while claiming that
Hess in the end appeared to be representing no one but himself, thought
that he should be interviewed by someone of Cabinet status, since it was
unlikely he would part with any further information to anyone more
junior. It was agreed finally that Lord Simon, the Home Secretary,
should see him, along with Kirkpatrick. This did not happen, however,
until 10 June, almost three weeks after Hess's removal on 21 May to
Mytchett Place, a Victorian mansion near Farnborough, which was to
be his place of confinement for the next thirteen months. Two detach-
ments, one of the Coldstream Guards and one of the Scots Guards,
were detailed to watch over him, under the command of Lieutenant-
Colonel A. Malcolm Scott. The house was hastily fortified in three days
against any possible German commando attack, and concealed micro-
phones were installed to monitor anything Hess might say either awake
or in his sleep.

For Kirkpatrick, the interviews with Hess were largely to be associated
with frustration. To achieve his first interview he had had to sacrifice a
much-needed steak; for the second, he lost a pleasant opportunity to

1 *Left*. Schoolboy at Godesberg

2 *Above*. Hitler's Secretary, 1924

3 *Below*. At the wedding of Bormann and Gerda Buch, 2 September 1929

4 & 5 At Hitler's
chalet,
Obersalzberg

6 *Right*. With Professor Haushofer

7 *Below*. March 1933: Hitler marches to the Reichstag to take his seat as Chancellor. Second from left is Roehm, with Gregor Strasser and Hess on the right of Hitler

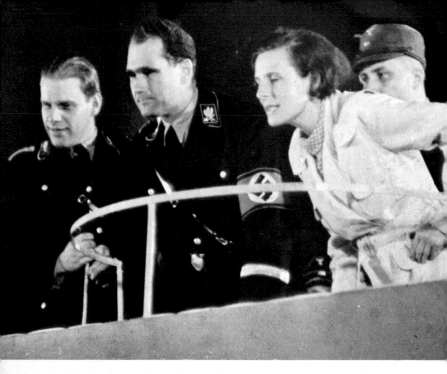

8 With producer Leni Riefenstahl rehearsing the Nuremberg Party Rally, 1934 (see page 60). Behind Leni Riefenstahl is Bormann

9 Hitler Youth Rally, Nuremberg, 12 September 1938. Baldur von Schirach and Hess stand behind Hitler

10 Propaganda portrait of Hess addressing Hitler Youth on the Führer's birthday, 20 April 1940

11 *Right*. With Wolf Rüdiger a few days before the flight to Scotland

12 *Below*. Wreckage of the Messerschmitt 110 after the flight

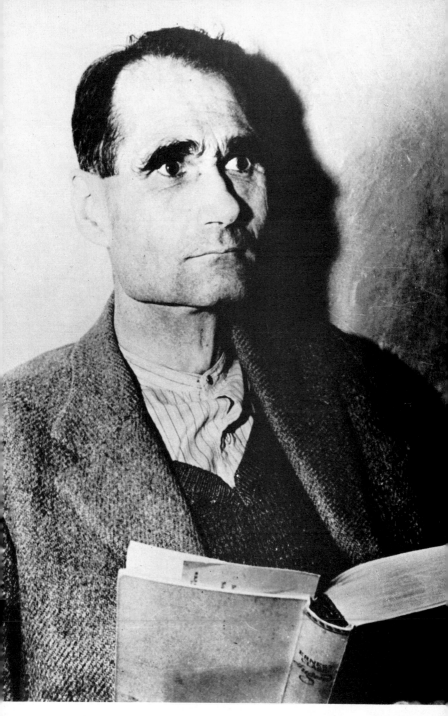

13 In captivity, 1945

14 Nuremberg—from left to right: Goering, Hess, Ribbentrop and Keitel

15 Letter written by Hess from the Allied Prison at Spandau, dated 17 May 1970

accompany the Duke of Hamilton on a visit to the newly commissioned carrier, *Victorious*; on 16 May he was about to play a round of golf with the Commandant at Buchanan Castle when the message came that Hess was to be moved south at once, and the game had had to be abandoned. He had just reached Ireland to conduct some urgent private business when he was summoned back to accompany Lord Simon[48] on his visit to Hess, which had to be incognito since the Government did not want it known that a member of the Cabinet was involved in an interview with the prisoner. Accordingly, Simon became 'Dr Guthrie' and Kirkpatrick, 'Dr MacKenzie' for the purpose of the visit, and the only people at Mytchett who knew the truth were two specially detached German-speaking officers. Hess, of course, knew the rank of the man he was to face, and had decided he should wear his smart Luftwaffe uniform for the purpose. When Simon and Kirkpatrick arrived, however, Hess appeared to have developed a certain unaccountable shyness at meeting a Cabinet Minister. According to Kirkpatrick, when they arrived Hess was still in bed, claiming he was not well enough to meet them. To pass the time while Hess made up his mind, the distinguished visitors were given lunch.

Hess decided to get up and put on his uniform. The visitors went upstairs to a room which had been prepared for the conference where they found Hess waiting for them. Hess seemed 'strangely pleased', says Kirkpatrick, to see him again, and he was formally introduced to Simon.

No real sense came out of this meeting, in spite of the presence of an interpreter. Simon's subsequent official account of what Hess said was made public in April 1946 at the Nuremberg Trial:

> My coming to England in this way is, as I realize, so unusual that nobody will easily understand it. I first thought of this plan in France in June last year. I admit that, when I saw the Führer at that time, I was convinced, as we all were, that sooner or later we should be victorious over England. In discussing the position with the Führer, I expressed the view that we should as a matter of course demand from England the return of what was taken from us by the Versailles treaty (such as the value of our trading fleet). He believed that the war could give rise to an opportunity to come, at last, to a real under-standing with England, such as he himself desired ever since he began his political career. I can bear witness to the fact that ever since I knew Hitler (from 1921 onwards) he had always spoken of the

necessity of coming to an understanding with England, and said that as soon as he came into power he would aim at doing this. He told me then, in France, that in his opinion no hard conditions should be imposed in case of victory over a land with which an understanding was desired. I thought that if this were only realized in England it might be possible that a desire for understanding would develop in England also. After the end of the war in France, Hitler made an offer to reach an understanding with England; but this was turned down. This served to make me more sure than ever that my plan must be put into practice.

Then there were acts of war between England and Germany, in the course of which the former suffered more damage than did Germany; so that I felt England could not give way without suffering a severe loss of prestige. I then said to myself: 'This is the moment when your plan must really be carried out, for if you are over in England this might prove an occasion for England to enter into discussions, without loss of prestige.' It was my opinion that, apart from the conditions necessary for an understanding, there was a certain general mistrust to be overcome. I was confronted by a very hard decision. I do not think I could have arrived at my final choice unless I had continually kept before my eyes the vision of an endless line of children's coffins with weeping mothers behind them, both English and German; and another line of coffins of mothers with mourning children.[49]

Kirkpatrick, who had heard much of this before and was no doubt jaundiced at having to return from Ireland to hear the same routine statements all over again, referred to the meeting as a 'Mad-Hatter's Tea Party', an 'unequal struggle' in spite of Simon's attempts to 'lift the conversation on to a reasonable plane'. According to Churchill, Hess also spoke of the hopelessness of Britain's position once Hitler decided to launch an all-out attack upon her. To this, Simon replied (says Churchill): 'I do not think that that particular argument will be very good for the British Cabinet, because, you know, there is a good deal of courage in this country, and we are not very fond of threats!'

With this interview, Hess's quixotic mission finally collapsed, and he himself gradually succumbed to despair. Churchill, obviously, retained a lingering regard for Hess; his motives, he writes, were naive, but 'certainly neither wicked nor squalid'. His mission he describes as a 'devoted and frantic deed of lunatic benevolence'. Hess was henceforth to drop out of the history of the struggle with Nazism, and to suffer acutely from the impotence of his position, creating a new drama within his mind.

A book has been published recently which claims,[50] without actually putting forward any documentary evidence, that Hitler knew of the mission all the while, and much has been made of Hess's references, in conversation with his wife, to the conditions attaching to the award of the Bavarian Max Josef Order and the Austrian Maria Theresa Order. These he described to her as follows:

> Both these decorations are given only for acts of bravery carried out on personal initiative. In the case of the Maria Theresa Order something further is required: if one acts independently on one's own responsibility in a manner directly *contrary* to what has been clearly commanded by one's superiors, and the action is successful *then* one gets the Order—but if one is so unlucky as to fail, then one gets shot.[51]

In the hands of the British he did not get shot, as he would very possibly have been had his mission taken him to the East. Stalin was to regard the presence of Hess alive in Britain as a lasting grievance, a grievance which is not forgotten to this day. For Hitler, the evidence is entirely that the flight came to him as the profoundest shock. He accounted Hess among the most loyal of his supporters. There is also sufficient evidence, however, to show that he never regarded Hess privately as a traitor, only as a deeply misguided man. Certain of Hess's immediate associates were called upon to suffer so that the régime might save its face; Pintsch, for example, who had real knowledge of the exploit, was detained for three years, only to be released to serve on the Eastern front, where he was taken prisoner by the Russians. Albrecht Haushofer, as we have seen, was confined for only three months, and then released unconditionally. Karl Haushofer, Willi Messerschmitt, even Frau Ilse Hess were never arrested at all, in spite of public statements to the contrary. Only one strange aspect of this strange affair remained to be enacted—Hitler's purge of the astrologers, the so-called Aktion Hess. This represents the final face-saving act on behalf of the Party and the régime. The astrologers became, like the Jews, the scapegoats. They were represented as driving Hess out of his mind.

Most of the Aktion Hess arrests took place on 9 June 1941. On 6–7 June Bormann had issued a decree to Gauleiters aimed not only against astrologers but faith-healers, fortune-tellers, clairvoyants, graphologists, and even Christian Scientists and Rudolf Steiner's Anthroposophists— in fact, all practitioners in the medical or psychological sphere who might be described as unqualified practitioners, whether working professionally for money or as amateurs without gain. All these people were held to be actual or potential enemies of the Reich. Schulte-Strathaus had already been arrested on 12 May along with other members of Hess's staff, and was kept in prison until 1 March 1943, but on 9 June F. G. Goerner of Mannheim, one of Germany's leading professional occultists, and also a trained engineer and friend of Hofweber, the astrologist who was one of Hess's associates, was taken by the Gestapo. Goerner had had an extensive number of Jewish clients before the war, and the Gestapo had been aware of him for a considerable time. Goerner was grilled by the Gestapo in Mannheim about Hess's flight, about which he knew nothing, and he was put under arrest. This case was typical of the hundreds of arrests which took place at this time and which represented a purge of practitioners of the occult following Hess's flight. At the same time, their libraries were confiscated, and the circulation of occult literature was forbidden.

Only once during the weeks following Hess's departure does the record show that Hitler revealed any trace of feeling for the loss of the friend who had for twenty years been so close to him. In the spring of 1942, about a year after the flight, Ilse Hess visited Frau Elsa Bruckmann, widow of the publisher Hugo Bruckmann of Munich, who had died shortly before. The Bruckmanns had been close friends and supporters of Hitler in the early days, and he had called on her to express his condolences on the death of her husband. He found her designing a headstone for Hugo Bruckmann's grave, and Elsa Bruckmann told Frau Hess what Hitler had said. 'We all have our graves and grow more and more lonely,' he had declared, 'but we have to overcome this, and go on living, dear gracious lady. I have been deprived of the only two human beings among all those around me to whom I have been truly and inwardly attached: Dr Todt is dead and Hess has flown away from me.'[52] When Elsa Bruckmann had dared to rebuke him for the repeated press reports alleging Hess's insanity, Hitler had shown no resentment. He had merely said, 'Is it not enough, what I have just said to you, and to you only, about my real feelings. Is this not enough?'

4

'DAGGER OF THE MIND'

WHETHER or not any commando attempts to rescue or establish contact with Hess were ever planned, anticipating Otto Skorzeny's brilliant rescue of Mussolini in 1943, none actually took place.[1] Nevertheless, the British Government had to assume such an attempt might at any time be made, especially during the initial period of Hess's detention. Mytchett Place was therefore put under special guard; the garden was equipped for defence, and was used as a training-ground for troops brought in from outside. The interior was wired up like a cage, and Hess, known as 'Jonathan' or 'J', was never left unattended, his principal companions being three officers from Army Intelligence. Mytchett Place looked, and was, a strong-point.

Hess had nothing left to do but to pass the time, to read, to write and to think. The curious circumstances of the flight, the strange array of medicaments which he carried,[2] and the one-track mentality which he increasingly displayed when interviewed, led to constant queries whether he was altogether sane—especially in view of the sensational statements about him which the Nazis themselves published.

Although deeply dissatisfied with the failure of his mission, Hess was relatively content with his new environment. In a letter written some seven years later to his wife, he describes Mytchett Place and its officers very favourably:

> I was surrounded by large sweet-smelling glycineas, while magnificent rhododendrons of all colours flowered in the garden. Had it not been a prison with plenty of barbed wire and sentries to protect me from the hostile public, I could very well have been satisfied. The dining-room and the music-room, as at home at Harlaching, were on the ground floor and opened into the Park. The Commandant, a professional artist in peacetime and a true artist by nature, played Mozart with the most beautiful delicacy. Outside were warm summer nights, while my heart was filled with pain, although I could

133

not guess how long all would last and what lay in front of me.[3]

Hess first came under medical observation at Drymen; his first doctor was Lieutenant-Colonel Gibson Graham, who was responsible for his care up to the time he travelled south with him and eventually confided him to the care of an Army psychiatrist, Major Dicks, on 19 June. Later, at Mytchett, he came under the care of Captain Johnston, and for the whole of the period he was in the care of the British, and later of the Americans at Nuremberg, he was under constant psychiatric observation. In fact, since 1941 he has become, very probably, the most closely observed psychiatric 'patient' of modern times. Expert after expert from several nations has interrogated and observed him, and he no less than they developed an intense interest in 'the case of Rudolf Hess'. In fact, he determined to create his own symptoms of mental disturbance in order to trick them, though his own innate peculiarities of mind formed a ready base upon which to build the more artificial and sensational aspects of his 'case'. When, after the war, his consent had to be obtained to publish a book under the editorship of Dr J. R. Rees about the long series of medical and psychological reports of which he was the subject, he readily consented. He wrote:

> Dr Gilbert brought to my notice your wish for a confirmation from me that I should consider it favourably if the physicians who had me under their care in England and later in Nuremberg published their reports and case histories concerning myself for scientific purposes.
>
> I am therefore informing you that I should welcome such a publication very much. This is not because I perhaps hold the belief that the public would thereby be informed more correctly than hitherto, as Dr Gilbert thought. But I would welcome it because one day it will be regarded as supplementary proof of the fact that in some hitherto unknown manner people can be put into a condition which resembles that which can be attained through a hypnosis leaving its after-effects ['post-hypnotic suggestion']—a condition in which the persons concerned do everything that has been suggested to them, under the elimination of their own will, presumably without their being conscious of it.
>
> For the present case proof would be supplied that even honourable men, physicians and experts, partly of high repute, through the compulsion exercised on their minds, were brought to commit the gravest crimes and at the same time to deliver judgments which contradict the truth, in order that the crimes should be hushed up.

The only condition for giving my consent to the intended publication is that this letter is published with it, and that fully and literally.[4]

This letter provides a possible clue to the strangely dual conditions of mind to which Hess gradually succumbed during his period of confinement in Britain. He had arrived hoping to bring off a great *coup* in the political field for which all Europe, if not the whole world, would honour him. Instead, he was faced with utter rejection—by Hitler and by Churchill alike. He was left, as he saw it, to rot under the care of men whom he increasingly came to distrust, and whom he genuinely believed to be not only determined to persecute him, but if possible assassinate him by poisoning his food over a period of time. Parallel with this, he determined, like Hamlet, to assume an 'antic disposition', to feign madness—partly because it might lead to his speedier repatriation under some form of exchange of sick prisoners-of-war, and partly because it enabled him to wash his hands of any further responsibility for the war. He wanted to 'drop out' of any further involvement in the whole business. Thus his feigned madness can be said in some measure to be the product of his own psychological peculiarities, and to give some measure of support to those psychiatrists who believed him to be genuinely disturbed, though not in any technical sense 'insane'. The case developed into a more or less successful campaign conducted by Hess against the array of alien psychiatrists he believed to be pitted against him, while at the same time, like Hamlet, he became more and more involved in other, perhaps lesser forms of disturbance which were undoubtedly genuine. He suffered acutely, for example, from what has been called 'prison psychosis', and the delusions of persecution which go with it. Though his successive attacks of amnesia were feigned, his delusions of persecutions and his melancholia were not. Also, he was to make two attempts at suicide while he was in Britain.

His delusions of persecution had already begun to manifest themselves during his interviews with Ivone Kirkpatrick, and he proved difficult to handle during the train journey by sleeping-car to London, objecting at one stage violently (according to Dr Graham's report) to having an officer guard in his compartment and a light kept on all night. At the Tower itself, he behaved rationally and reasonably, except that on 19 May he addressed a letter to Germany in which, says Dr Rees, 'he toyed with the idea that his death was being encompassed'.

At Mytchett, according to Dr Graham, 'he was extremely agitated . . .

and told me he was convinced he was surrounded by Secret Service agents who would accomplish his death either by driving him to commit suicide, committing a murder staged to look like suicide, or by administering poison in his food.' In conversation, he reiterated a great deal of the Nazi mythology—he 'never tired of talking of his Führer, whom he regarded as a God'—and his desire to fulfil his 'mission'. He became depressed, and Dr Graham on 23 May put in a request for the services of a psychiatrist. On 28 May, when told of the sinking of the *Bismarck* he complained of pain in the back and took to his bed. His mood was now up and down, assertive at one moment, depressed at the next, overeating while at the same time concerned that the food he consumed in such quantity might be poisoned. He complained that the noise in the garden and in the corridors was deliberately enhanced to prevent him from sleeping. On 31 May the case was finally handed over to Major Henry V. Dicks, a German-speaking psychiatrist of the RAMC on the recommendation of Brigadier Rees, the consulting psychiatrist who had visited Hess at Mytchett on 30 May and to whom he had complained of depression and insomnia, and expressed his resentment at the locks, bars and wiring by which he felt hemmed in. Mychett Place was, indeed, a forbidding looking place. Among Dr Graham's final observations on Hess before he returned to Drymen are the following:

1 Although no evidence of mental instability was noted at the beginning of my care of Rudolf Hess, as time went on his behaviour and reactions led me to form the opinion that one dealt with a psychopathic personality.
2 He showed marked hypochondriacal, paranoid tendencies, apprehension and delusions of persecution. Simple incidents were misinterpreted and given a sinister meaning.
3 From such knowledge as I possessed of his flight to this country, his mission was the outcome of his mentally disordered state. The short account of his life he gave me suggested, even as a young man, an abnormal mentality. He showed a lack of sane grasp of affairs, and his motives were vague and incoherent.[5]

Dr Rees, following his visit on 30 May, agreed. In his initial report he wrote:

While this man is certainly not to-day insane in the sense that would make one consider certification, he is mentally sick. He is anxious and tense; he is of a somewhat paranoid type, i.e., he has suspicions for which there is no sufficient indication in his situation and which persist despite very full explanations. He has an abnormal lack of insight or self-criticism. He is also of an introspective and somewhat hypochondriacal type. He is obviously an intelligent man, and the consequent impression is of a somewhat confused condition in which there are both hysterical and paranoid tendencies. Whilst his judgment on ordinary matters of fact might be sound, his appreciation of more intangible problems would be unsound because of the intrusion of his own personal emotional difficulties. This man gives me the impression of being lacking in balance, a psychopathic personality, to use a technical word, and also of being someone who, because of the added depression due to his circumstances, might take impulsive action such as an attempt at suicide despite his alleged promise to the Führer not to take his life. . . .

His moodiness and his tendency to slip easily into hysterical symptoms, as after the *Bismarck* news, and his tendence to posturing, are worthy of note. I was told that while the troops were parading in the garden he was on the terrace and that he gave the most curious display by doing what was practically a goose step down the path in front of them as though to demonstrate his own military status and technique. . .

In my opinion Hess is a man of unstable mentality and has almost certainly been like that since adolescence. In technical language I should, on my present acquaintanceship, diagnose him as a psychopathic personality of the schizophrenic type, i.e., a tendency to a splitting of his personality. He is, as many of these people are, suggestible and liable to hysterical symptom formation. Because of his constitutional make-up and the kind of life he has led of recent years, he is at present in some danger of a more marked depressive reaction now that he feels frustrated.

The exact legal position of Hess as a prisoner was still undefined. It was uncertain whether he was a prisoner of war or a prisoner of State. It was important not to let him feel he was being treated as a mental patient. The Army Political Intelligence officers in charge of him were present to obtain what information he might have to offer about Germany's war plans, and the Army psychiatrist placed in charge of the 'case' which Hess gradually came to represent was not there ostensibly to effect a 'cure', but rather to assist the Intelligence officers in obtaining information.

Dr Rees gives a description of Hess's appearance when he first saw him at Mytchett Place:

It is fair to say that the first glimpse of Hess produced an immediate reaction—'typical schizophrenic'. He was found sitting behind a table littered with papers, his skull-like face wearing a profoundly unhappy, grim expression, with his eyes staring into infinity. The contrast between photographs previously seen in the illustrated papers and the man as he now appeared was prodigious. He was gaunt, hollow-cheeked, pale and lined; whereas the full face produced an impression of baleful strength, the profile disclosed a receding forehead, exaggerated supra-orbital ridges covered with thick bushy eyebrows, deeply sunken eyes, irregular teeth which tended to be permanently bared over the lower lip in the manner of 'buck' teeth, a very weak chin and receding lower jaw. The ears were misshapen and placed too low in relation to the height of the eyes. In parenthesis it should be added that a subsequent examination showed the palate to be narrow and arched. The whole man produced the impression of a caged great ape, and 'oozed' hostility and suspicion. . . .

With the establishment of rapport, even during this first interview, the private personality of Hess left one with the impression of pathos rather than hostility. He began complaining that he had come here with the best of intentions and had received scurvy and unchivalrous treatment by the nation it was his intention to save from certain destruction. He revealed a split between his 'official' attitude as an important representative of the strongest power of Europe and his private simplicity. His personal equipment was of the simplest; his watch was of steel, his linen and other personal accoutrements simple and modest. He produced pictures of his wife and little son and described his interests as those of a mountaineer who had no greater wish than to return to a little chalet where he could devote himself to the education of his child and to countrified pursuits. His interests had been in philosophy and matters of health and welfare. He took a special interest in a rehabilitation centre for disabled industrial workers which he said was his own creation. There was a schoolboy-like pride in his attitude when he related details of his flight, which he said was made secretly without the Führer's knowledge.[6]

In view of Hess's interest in the countryside, the psychiatrist was surprised to find, when they walked round the garden, that Hess did not appear to know the names of the commonest flowers. He shared no knowledge whatsoever of British life or society, and seemed convinced that his present treatment was due entirely to Churchill, who was deliberately preventing him reaching (through the Duke of Hamilton) the friendly Court circles which, he believed, would be only too ready to receive peaceful overtures from Germany. In the mess, his fear of poisoning became evident; he would insist on changing his plate, for instance, with that of another officer; he would preserve pieces of bread and cheese and take them up to his room for analysis in the future. He was never served anything other than normal army rations, though the press enjoyed making occasional references to the luxurious living in which it was supposed he was indulged. But it was true that he frequently ate ravenously what was provided for him. He always refused the wine with which officers in the Brigade of Guards were still regaled. He was especially careful over drinks, and in any case rejected alcohol. In his attitude he was alternately haughty and simple, irritating and pathetic, resentful and then responsive and grateful, especially for the medical care taken of him.

By the time he had reached Mytchett, the slight injuries to his ankle and back caused by his leap from the aircraft were virtually cured. It was his stomach pains and other internal and psychological symptoms which disturbed him continually at this stage, and the highly intelligent officers in charge of him found him a very dull companion. He was kept supplied with drugs, and everything was done (for example, in the serving of food) to lessen his suspicion of the supposed evil intentions of his guards. He was given sedatives and sleeping-tablets to overcome his insistence that the noisiness of his environment was a deliberate part of the treatment which he was now beginning to believe was a Jewish conspiracy against him, the same influences which, he now felt, were contaminating his food so that he should endure intense discomfort after meals.

He took to composing lengthy documents, written in indelible pencil (with carbon copies) and addressed to the British government and to the Swiss Minister in Britain, as chief representative of the Protecting Power.[7] He also began to plan the elaborate mountain residence he hoped to establish in Germany after the war. However, when he learned that, on 10 June, a British Minister was at last coming to meet him, he showed, as we have seen, what almost amounted to fear that he could not face so demanding an occasion. The Intelligence officers had the impression that Hess suffered from some kind of inferiority complex when it finally came to measuring up to reality. He insisted that the Intelligence officers (whom he appeared to trust far more than the psychiatrist, since they were, he considered, the King's representatives) should have the specimens of food he collected analysed. Eventually, however, when the Lord Chancellor, Lord Simon, arrived, he pulled himself together and drank a great deal of milk before the interview. Afterwards, he was found in a state of collapse in his sitting-room. He was persuaded by the psychiatrist to drink glucose and eat cake, but only after the psychiatrist had himself tasted both. Then Hess ate the cake ravenously. Later, he started on the composition of a series of valedictory letters addressed to his relatives, and even to Hitler himself, expressing complete unquestioning loyalty to him. He was preparing for death, he alleged, and he ended his letter to the Führer: 'I die in the conviction that my last mission, even if it ends in death, will somehow bear fruit. Perhaps my flight will bring, despite my death or indeed partly because of my death, peace and reconciliation with England.'[8]

From this letter it is uncertain whether he expected to be poisoned, and so die a martyr's death, or whether he anticipated death through suicide. His delusion of poisoning increased to the extent that he promised Dr Dicks great rewards in money after the German victory, if he would frustrate the plots of the poisoners. On 15 June he reached some state of crisis, shouting at the psychiatrist, 'I am being undone, and you know it!' He was trembling as he paced about the room.

During the early hours of 16 June, Dr Dicks was wakened and summoned to Hess's bedroom since he could not sleep. The bedroom, sitting-room and bathroom allocated to Hess were on the first floor, reached by an oaken staircase constructed round a square open space. A wire grille had been erected caging in the upper landing on Hess's side of the staircase-well, and a locked gate in the grille gave access to the stairs. An armed sergeant of Military Police guarded this gate in the grille, which was exactly opposite to Hess's bedroom door, while the officer on guard during the night spent his time in Hess's sitting-room, punctuating his period of duty by occasional visits to the bedroom. Dr Dick's bedroom was on the other side of the landing, which was not wired in. As Dr Dicks moved across the landing to the door of the cage, the sergeant opened it to admit him, while the officer in charge stood to one side. Suddenly Hess emerged in full Luftwaffe uniform and rushed through the open gate of the grille—his face was distorted with distress, his eyes staring and his hair dishevelled. Dicks thought for the moment Hess was about to attack him; but Hess swerved round, and leapt over the banisters, falling down the well of the staircase to the stone floor below. A second guard who was climbing up the stairs carrying a cup of tea for his colleague, dropped the cup with a crash, and drew his revolver. Dicks, gathering his wits, cried out, 'Don't shoot!'

The whole building sprang to life as every available guard rushed to the spot where Hess lay, writhing and groaning. Hess was very little injured, his fall being to some extent broken because his body struck the handrail of the staircase as he fell, fracturing the bone of his left thigh. He was fully conscious, and annoyed at the failure of his clumsy attempt to take his life;[9] but he was rational and business-like in trying to organize his treatment. He was in great pain, but he could not be given morphia until, an hour and a half later, the army surgeon arrived to diagnose his injury. In spite of this, he became almost hilarious. He was mortified, however, when the surgeon cut open his Luftwaffe breeches with scissors. The guards carried him to his bedroom to await the arrival of mobile X-ray equipment.

Hess's recovery from his injury followed normal lines. When his recuperation, both physical and mental, was assured, it was decided that he should have some access to the news, and he was allowed to read *The Times*. He was now far more rational, and agreed that his previous fears of poisoning, and so forth, were probably subjective. However, by 19 June his delusion of persecution began to return. On 22 June he received the news of the German invasion of the Soviet Union with a wry smile and the remark, 'So they have started after all.' He remained wholly confident of a German victory. He made further written depositions about his care addressed to both the King and to Parliament. He alleged that a number of the officers surrounding him were being hypnotised and used by an evil power to bring about his destruction; they were, he claimed, insane.

On 17 July Major Dicks gave place to another psychiatrist, Captain Johnston, since Hess's English was regarded as sufficiently good not to require any longer the services of a German-speaking psychiatrist. Johnston, on their first meeting, found Hess, who was still confined to his bed, 'gaunt, hollow-eyed and anxious.' He claimed to Johnston that he had attempted suicide because he felt he was going mad. He was still writing lengthy addresses, declaring those around him to be hypnotised, still planning his future houses—one to be built in Scotland, one in Sussex, and one in Germany—still rousing curiosity by his odd behaviour—such as lying on his back with his fingers in his ears while he was thinking, or so he claimed. Then, on 6 September, he was further disturbed when he learned that a second member of the Cabinet was to visit him. He said he was too ill, but nevertheless he met Lord Beaverbrook for an hour on 9 September.

Lord Beaverbrook, a close friend of Churchill, had been sent to see Hess in order to give the Prime Minister a commonsense (as distinct from technically psychological) answer to the question whether Hess was sane or insane. Beaverbrook came back with the answer that he was undoubtedly sane—he just held certain peculiar views in such matters as Hitler and health. Otherwise, Hess advanced the usual arguments and Beaverbrook the usual counter-arguments. 'A victory for England,' said Hess to Beaverbrook, 'will be a victory for the Bolsheviks.' If Russia were not broken by the combined forces of Britain and Germany she would come to dominate Europe, and then the world. Later that month, Beaverbrook met Stalin in Moscow as head of a delegation from Britain to discuss arms supplies to the Soviet Union. Stalin, deeply suspicious of the Deputy Führer's continued presence in Britain, raised the question of Hess, as Beaverbrook has recorded:

> In Moscow, Stalin said to me: 'Britain means to make peace with Germany, leaving Russia to fight alone.'
> I asked him: 'What makes you think that?'
> 'Hess is your line of communication with Hitler,' he said.
> 'Oh, no,' I said.
> 'Why then do you not shoot him?'
> 'He must be tried,' I answered.
> 'Why did he come to Britain?'
> That was the question I was waiting for. I produced the transcript of my conversation with Hess, and also a memo he sent me in his own hand, proposing that Britain should make peace with Germany on our terms providing we would join a German-British attack on Russia. I told him that Churchill had rejected the plan with contempt.[10]

By November Hess was permitted to move into his sitting-room; now that his fractured thigh-bone was almost healed, the fear that he might attempt suicide again was revived, and his bedroom was equipped with various precautions against further attempts. Meanwhile, he went on writing—producing on 21 November a whole packet of documents wrapped in tissue-paper and sealed in an envelope with tallow from a candle. About this time, too, he began to complain of loss of memory. Eventually, on 4 December he claimed his memory had completely disappeared, and that this amnesia had been deliberately induced by his enemies. On 12 January 1942 he spent three and a half hours with Dr Hans Fröhlicher, Head of the Swiss Diplomatic Mission in Berlin, to whom he gave samples of food and drink for analysis. He also asked to have his faeces and urine analysed independently. Fröhlicher saw him again for a lengthy interview in April.[11]

During the ensuing months he used to complain of abdominal cramps and headaches. He refused to receive Red Cross parcels from Switzerland on the grounds that they, too, might be poisoned by his 'many enemies in Switzerland'. By June it had been decided he should be transferred to a quieter, more remote area for the duration of the war, and on 25 June 1942 he was escorted to Maindiff Court Hospital at Abergavenny in South Wales. The journey there by car delighted him. He was to remain here until his transfer to Nuremburg after the war in the autumn of 1945.

Maindiff Court Hospital, near Abergavenny, had been prior to the war the admission centre for the county mental hospital; during the war it became an independent institution for service patients. No mental patients as such were housed there. Hess was to live here, solitary but in comfort, for the next three years.

When he arrived and was put in the care of Major Ellis Jones of the RAMC, he was considered to be in a good physical condition except for being rather pale and thin following his long period of confinement and refusal, after recovering from his suicide attempt, to take outdoor exercise. During the summer he behaved quite normally, ridding himself for a while of the delusions that he was being poisoned, and was even allowed brief excursions by car into the surrounding countryside, where he was permitted now and then to walk. In his letters to his wife which look back on his confinement in England, he gives some descriptions of these excursions, which obviously meant a great deal to him:

> I wrote to you once from there describing the peculiar beauty of the district, especially the astounding play of colour on the hills and mountains and the ever-changing effects of light . . .
>
> With Abergavenny as a base, I took short and long walks and occasionally motor trips further afield. Not very far away is the White Castle, a well-preserved large castle, with five immense round towers in the surrounding wall. It dates from the eleventh or twelfth century, and looks exactly what I thought a medieval castle should

be, when I was a boy! In the courtyard of the castle, a most carefully tended lawn, and around it, between the wall and the moat, ancient trees and a multitude of flowering shrubs, such as lilac and elder. Several times I paid a visit to Llanthony Abbey, a Gothic church now in ruins, save for the aisle which is intact in parts. The church was probably sacrificed to the destructive fury of Cromwell. I can well understand that English people do not like to be reminded of their 'Ironsides', their feelings in this respect are very mixed. Thus—as I soon became aware—it was not tactful to draw parallels between Cromwell and a certain other person.

This district is, like nearly the whole of England, a huge park; although here in Wales this impression is somewhat diminished by the grim-looking hills, usually bare of trees and often covered with crumbling stones. How often I yearned for great stretches of real forest, as we have them in Germany. I felt rather like a man who is fed all the time on super-refined foods and longs for good solid country food—such as pork and dumplings—or one who would prefer honest black bread to a diet of cakes and biscuits.

In the areas that are ploughed up for crops, hedges surround the fields and border the roads. This is a real land of hedges, such as might have been planned and planted by *Zeitalter des Lebendigen*. The hedges consist of blackberry bushes and small hazelnut trees, together with a good deal of white and red hawthorn, and wild roses mixed with all sorts of bushes not known to me. I gathered large quantities of blackberries for weeks during the summer; I might be said to have made a 'blackberry cure'. Nobody in the district bothers to pick them, for they have enormous masses of such things. Nor did I neglect the hazelnuts, which were also ignored and left to anyone who cared to take them.

A thing that pleased me very much was the widespread love of great old trees, which were often preserved, even when no more than hollow stumps. They told me about a small farmer who sold his farm at a low price on condition that an old tree that stood there should never be cut down.

The behaviour of the people I met on my walks was, with very few exceptions, beyond reproach. In the villages and small towns through which I had occasion to pass, the inhabitants would run to their doors to gaze at the German who had come down to them from the sky; but they were often quite friendly, and one of the officers who had been assigned to me informed me that large numbers of the population had hoped that my mission would be successful and the war brought to an end—that would have been splendid!¹²

Only when Brigadier Rees decided to visit him on 25 September, did Hess suddenly relapse into the psychotic condition already familiar at Mytchett Place. Every symptom recurred—the stomach cramps associated with the delusions of poisoning, the persecution by noise (in this case, the local trains), the intense sense of fatigue. These symptoms prevailed to greater or lesser degree until October 1943; during that month his amnesia returned and remained with him until 4 February 1945, when he reported to Major Ellis Jones that his memory had returned, and then proceeded to claim that everyone from the King of Italy to Winston Churchill, Anthony Eden, Brigadier Rees and even he himself were subject to hypnosis by Jewish conspirators. During the afternoon he made a second attempt at suicide, stabbing himself in the left lower chest with a bread-knife after having changed into his Air Force uniform. The wound, in fact, proved slight; two stitches were sufficient to close it. The doctor's report then adds: 'In an agitated state he maintained that his amnesia had been simulated.' The following day he gave the reason for this second attempt as realization that 'it was all over for Germany', that Europe and Britain would be over-run by the Russians, and that he himself would never be allowed to leave the country. The Jews, he claimed later, had put the bread knife in his way so that he would stab himself.

Between 4 and 12 February he took no food, and drank only water. He was determined, he said, to starve himself to death. When threatened with forcible feeding, however he finally gave way and took food. He was never now left alone, and he occupied himself with reading. He claimed that his amnesia was returning, but nevertheless he retained a ready enough memory for trifles, and he always showed interest in the many photographs of his family and the portrait of Hitler he kept on the wall of his room.

On 15 February, eleven days after the second suicide attempt, Lieutenant-Colonel Dicks revisited Hess, and in the course of his report wrote of him:

I find the patient at much the same level of mental and physical health as when I left him three and a half years ago, i.e., intellectually vigorous and alert; somewhat grandiose and overbearing when acting 'officially', simple and rational, indeed sociable in private; rather egocentric, fussy and suspicious. His suspicions follow lines which can almost be called a stereotyped formula in his normal milieu and the patient retains some critical insight into them, as before.[13]

Contact between Hess and his family by letter began only in January 1942. The delays in getting the letters through to their recipients in Germany often lasted months, and Ilse Hess did not receive the first letter from her husband until some six months after his flight. The letters were sent through Switzerland (as the Protecting Power), but frequently suffered prolonged delay because of censorship and other restrictions, not only in Germany and Britain, but in Switzerland itself.[14]

Most of the letters which have been published are addressed to his wife. It must be remembered that Hess has always had to write since 1941 with censorship in mind. It is also true that some of the letters of a later date written after he had been returned to Germany, reveal more about his reaction to confinement in Britain than those written while he was there. Many of these refer repeatedly to his flight—a feat of which he was always to remain proud. They have already been quoted. Many of them are about his son, Wolf Rüdiger, whom he calls by the pet name of Buz:

> Oh! how I rejoiced to know that the little chap still remembers his Dad; that he still knew where all the splendid toys were put away— the puffing trains, wheels rattling on the rails, with which we secretly amused ourselves in my study during those days before I left. I often think of the things I intended to tell him and show him, following up the bent of the 'technical, geographical and scientific' Buz.

And again:

> According to all that I have heard about the tendencies and occupations of the little fellow, I feel that his gifts lie in the direction of technical science. Unchecked by paternal authority, he will now be able to develop this talent, an opportunity denied to me, apart from little flights over the sea—〰〰〰.[15]

His letters are full of a slightly self-conscious humour; he and his wife had the habit of indicating laughter or jokes in their letters by using a wavy line 〰〰〰—what they called their laughter-line.

In one letter, written from Abergavenny, he was able to give his wife a clue to his whereabouts. He wrote on 16 July 1943:

I have broken off my habit of resting after the chief meal. Sometimes I have the opportunity of taking a walk in the neighbourhood, which is beautiful. When the weather is good I enjoy little rests on the way, selecting spots where there is as enjoyable a view as possible. The colours of this landscape are unusual and attractive. An essential part is the red earth, lying between meadows and fields of green turning to yellowish tinges when ripe, and matching the autumn trees. Every cloud-shadow at once changes the effect of the colours and with it the whole impression. It can happen that a distant mountain, dominating the background, changes within a few minutes, under the influence of the light, from darkest violet through dark blue to olive and emerald green, with reddish brown and yellow turning to bluish grey. Further, I found that the colours are more beautiful in autumn and winter than in other seasons. On the one hand, this had something to do with the softer light and, on the other, with the ploughed up fields which look even redder against the green of those left unploughed in the winter. I am quite ready to believe, as I am told, that artists are especially attracted to this district.[16]

His devotion to Hitler remained undisturbed by his own fate and his open rejection in Germany: On 4 September 1943 he wrote to Ilse:

It makes me very happy to see, again and again, from your letters that nothing has changed in your *inward relationship* to the man with whose destiny we have been so closely linked in joy and in suffering, for more than twenty years. You have changed no more than I myself have changed. One must never forget that these times have placed him under a nervous strain, hard to imagine—a strain responsible for states of excitement, in which decisions have been made which would not have been made in more normal times. Writing thus, I am not thinking of myself—not in the least—but of my lads. As regards myself, I was prepared for anything.[17]

After the war is over, he writes again on 18 June 1945:

Very few people have been privileged, as we were, to participate, from the very beginning, in the growth of a unique personality through joy and sorrow, hope and trouble, love and hate and all the manifestations of greatness—and, further, in all the little indications of human weakness, without which a man is not truly worthy of love.[18]

The simulated amnesia presented a certain embarrassment to Hess. If he had lost his memory, how could he write to a wife the recollection of whom was presumably lost to him? He managed, however, to produce at least one very rational letter which set out to explain what was happening; he writes on 15 January 1944:

> I have been sitting here for, literally, several hours wondering what I can write to you about. But I get no further; and that I regret is for a very special reason. Since, sooner or later, you will notice it or find out about it, I may as well tell you: I have completely lost my memory. The whole of the past swims in front of my mind enveloped in a grey mist. I cannot recollect even the most ordinary things. The reason for it I do not know. The doctor gave me a lengthy explanation, but I have already forgotten what it was. He assured me, however, that all would be well again. I trust he is right.
>
> Moreover, that is the reason why I can't actually write a sensible letter; for *that*, memory is needed—more than one might think. It is different though, if one has a letter in front of one to answer, providing subject matter and stimulus. Your last letter reached me on 13 September of last year![19]

He reiterates, in a letter of 26 February, the need for some stimuli to his memory from home to which he can respond. In this way he managed to some extent to circumvent the 'amnesia' without revealing his deception to the psychiatrist. According to Dr Rees, most of the letters of March 1945 refer to the recovery of his memory.[20]

Only after the trial at Nuremberg was over did he feel free to comment on his subterfuge to his wife:

> Since, for the greater part of my stay in England, I was 'suffering from loss of memory', my laziness in letter-writing is at last explained and can be excused.
>
> Towards the end this farce went so far that I allowed myself to be given injections against loss of memory. At first I made some resistance, but I saw there was nothing else for it if I did not want to strengthen the suspicion they had that at the very least I exaggerated my trouble. Luckily, it was admitted beforehand that it was not certain the treatment would recall lost ideas. The worst of it was that as part of the treatment I was given a narcotic, and under its influence had to answer questions supposed to 're-unite the conscious and subconscious'. So I was faced with a double danger: I might reveal

things that, as a German, I should hold secret (very likely the intention of the instigator of the injections!); or I might let the cat out of the bag concerning my loss of memory!

In the long run, as I have said, I had to give way. But, by calling up every scrap of will-power, I managed not to lose consciousness whilst pretending to be unconscious—and they gave me more than the normal dose. To every question I simply said: 'I do not know', with a pause between each word, speaking softly in a flat, absent-minded voice〰〰〰. After a long time, I was able to recall my own name, which I breathed in the same flat manner. Finally, I thought it time to return to consciousness and woke up, eyes full of astonishment, to return slowly to life. It was a real drama. Add: a *complete* success! They were now utterly convinced that my memory was quite gone . . .

How completely the experiment with the narcotic convinced my doctors that my loss of memory was genuine is shown by the fact that when at a later date, for special reasons of my own, I thought it best to reveal my trickery, the medical gentlemen at first refused to believe that they had been taken in. Only when I repeated to them all the questions that had been put to me when I was 'unconscious' and when I played over again the comedy of 'awakening', using the same mode of speech and flat voice, were they forced to admit that I had brought off a terrific 'leg-pull'〰〰〰〰.[21]

It can be assumed that a considerable measure of the symptoms Hess developed at Mytchett Place and at Maindiff Court were, when not actually feigned, exaggerations of real disorders of mind and body on which he played for the purpose he had in mind—one of which undoubtedly was the possibility of being sent home in an exchange of prisoners of war. He refers to this in one of his letters written after the trial, and referring back to this period of confinement in England: 'I now began to hope that I would at last be exchanged and sent home; but it came to nothing.' However, it must also be assumed that a certain measure of the symptoms were genuine—the nervous pains, the depressions, the insomnia, probably to some extent the delusion of persecution. Although his confinement was never less than comfortable, to be suddenly and permanently deprived of the outdoor activities—the mountaineering, the walks, the sport and flying to which he had been used all his life—was more than merely irksome to him. Also, he was a family man, and missed his wife and child acutely. But above all, the failure of his great mission preyed on his mind and on his pride. He gives the clue himself to his state of mind in a letter to his wife which looks back over the span of a decade to this period in Britain. Writing as late as 1950, he says:

> In view of the nine months of being perpetually on the alert, of repeated false starts, involving wrenching myself away from my family and then having to come back and repeat the mental torture— in view of all this, it is possible that I had become really not quite normal![22]

5

NUREMBERG

HESS was escorted to Nuremberg by air on 10 October 1945, by Dr Ellis Jones, accompanied by an army officer, a sergeant and a British official. It was a rough passage and Hess was among those who were airsick. The Commandant of the prison at Nuremberg, Colonel Burton C. Andrus, was in charge of the security of all the high-ranking Nazi prisoners, who were confined there both before and during the trial which was to last so much longer than anyone at the start foresaw. Hess in fact remained in Nuremberg jail from 10 October 1945 until his final removal to Spandau on 18 July 1947, along with the rest who had received sentences other than the death penalty. His fellow defendants at the future trial had arrived during September. Speer, in fact, has recorded that he saw Hess led in after his arrival. 'He appeared in a grey-blue tweed coat and was handcuffed to two American soldiers. He seemed absent-minded as well as truculent. For years I had been used to seeing all these prisoners in pompous uniforms, and either aloof in manner or spilling joviality. The scene now seemed to me absolutely unreal; at times I thought I was dreaming.'[1]

An American psychologist, Dr Douglas M. Kelley, whose duty it was to keep the prisoners under constant observation, has described Hess's reaction after Andrus had explained to him the details of the prison regulations. Hess had objected violently to the regulations requiring him to surrender all his personal possessions:

Hess finally agreed to relinquish everything except a number of small parcels. He insisted that these contained material for his defence, including drugs and food which he had brought from England for chemical analysis by an impartial chemist. He offered to permit a guard to remain in his cell twenty-four hours a day, provided these items could be left with him.

In the end Colonel Andrus impressed on him that his rights and privileges were no different from those of any other German prisoner

151

and that his precious parcels would be sealed and locked up in the presence of witnesses. Hess accepted this ultimatum and was escorted to the cell which was to be his home for more than a year.

On arrival at the jail, Hess was, physically, in good shape, but thin. He was dressed in his Luftwaffe uniform, though without insignia. However, his heel-clicking stiffness and somewhat incongruous flying boots—high and black, thickly lined, and made of soft leather with two zippers on each—lent him a military bearing that no array of insignia could have given.

Psychiatrically, he was alert and responsive. His approach was reserved and his general attitude formal, but he gave the impression of making a real attempt at co-operation. His stream of thought was curtailed as a result of his amnesia, the majority of his responses being, 'I do not know,' or 'I cannot remember.' He claimed to be unable to remember his birth-date, birth-place, date of leaving Germany, or any fact or detail whatsoever of his early life.[2]

Hess was determined to maintain his amnesia as a principal line of defence against the death sentence he was sure was coming to him at the trial. Apart from the amnesia, he behaved normally and achieved an IQ of 115/120 in the various tests given him. On 16 October, Kelley asked Mr Justice Jackson, the principal American prosecutor, for permission to try to break Hess's amnesia, which he was convinced was partly malingering, by the use of drugs inducing a hypnoidal state. Not only did Hess himself refuse to be hypnotised, but Jackson refused to grant permission for this to be done, on the grounds that any danger whatsoever which might be involved was not advisable in the case of a prisoner of Hess's prominence. Eventually three Russian, one French, three British and three American psychiatrists all agreed with Kelley that 'Hess's basic personality pattern was hysterical and paranoid.' They also agreed that if Hess maintained his amnesia it would be a hindrance to his defence.

Nuremberg jail was a three-storey block with cat-walks serving the opposite lines of cells on the second and third storeys, which were reached by circular stairways at each end of the block. The major Nazi prisoners, however, were kept on the ground floor. The cells were nine by thirteen feet, reached through a door in which an observation inlet some fifteen inches square gave the guards a permanent view of the prisoner except when he was seated on the toilet. After the suicide of Robert Ley on 25 October 1945, a guard was put on duty at each cell door twenty-four hours a day. During the night the cell light was dimmed, but never extinguished. Not less than once a week, prisoners were ordered to strip and stand in a corner of the cell while it was thoroughly searched. Prisoners were exercised separately in the prison yard, and kept incommunicado except for the barest instructions from the wardens; they were permitted a shave once a week, and were shaved by a German barber; their food was served in mess tins. Hess was exercised, and walked to and from the interrogation room handcuffed to a guard. This was because of his history of attempted suicide. Along with most of the other prisoners, he was glad of the constant opportunity to talk which the interviews with the psychologists involved.

The trial itself, the International Military Tribunal, began on 20 November 1945, and lasted 217 days. Its constitution was determined at a conference of the prosecutors appointed by the principal Allies, Britain, the United States, France and the USSR. Sir David Maxwell Fyfe, Attorney-General of the United Kingdom, presided, and on 8 August 1945 the trial was proclaimed by general agreement and a Charter was drawn up establishing the Tribunal and determining its procedure, based broadly on an amalgamation of British and American practice in courts of law. The trial, the first of its kind in the history of law, was presided over by Lord Justice Lawrence of Great Britain. For its organisation it was entirely dependent on a complex system of multi-lingual translation through headphones, and it was recorded for world audiences on film and by radio. No trial before or since has been attended by so much publicity, and mass coverage by the press, radio and news-reels. The Nuremberg Palace of Justice was even to have a novelty shop selling souvenirs of the trial.

The United States bore the heavy costs of the Tribunal, and was responsible for its administration, including the guarding of the prisoners by picked men of the American First Division. The vast mass of captured official documents of the Third Reich was largely in American hands, and these were examined against time, selected and translated into English, French and Russian, and then reproduced for circulation to the prosecution teams and the defence counsel. This documentation formed the raw material on which the trial was based, supported now and again by film records. At its maximum, the American prosecution staff reached as many as 600, while behind the British prosecution team was a staff of some 160.

Major Airey Neave, later to become a London barrister, and a protagonist for the release of Hess from Spandau, was responsible, thirty days before the trial began, for serving the defendants with the 24,000 word document, translated into German, which formed the indictment. It had been prepared in October in Berlin by the Chief Prosecutors as the official indictment by eighteen countries which by then adhered to the Charter setting up the Tribunal. The defendants were to be charged under four main headings—The Common Plan or Conspiracy, Crimes against Peace, War Crimes, and Crimes against Humanity. Not only were the defendants to be accused as individuals, but also as key members of one or more of the indicted Nazi organizations through which the régime had functioned—the Reich Cabinet, the Leadership Corps of the Nazi Party, the SS and the SD, the Gestapo, the SA, and the General Staff and High Command of the German Armed Forces. All of these establishments were to be put on trial as criminal groups. The charge of Common Plan or Conspiracy included the breaking of treaties, the planning and waging of wars of aggression, the ill-treatment of civilian populations, racial persecution, the theft or destruction of property, and such counts as did not necessarily come under the other prime headings. Major Neave served this document on Hess, as he did on the other prisoners, and arranged for the selection of their defence counsel from the list of German barristers eligible. Hess's defence counsel initially was Dr Günther von Rohrscheidt of Berlin.

On 30 October, Hess's numerous sealed packages brought from England were opened in his presence. They were made up mostly of scraps of food which he had alleged caused his mental collapse, weakening of the heart, constipation, and the like. Other packages contained documents he had written.

Various attempts were made to revive his memory. On 8 November he was shown some news-reels involving himself. On 16 November he was confronted by his two secretaries, Hildegard Fath and Ingeborg Sperr.[3] Hildegard Fath, who knew Hess and his family far better than Ingeborg Sperr, seemed to excite a little recognition in him, but he soon covered this up. An eye-witness report of this meeting emphasizes the curious situation these confrontations created:

> Hess was seated with his back to the door and Fräulein Hildegard Fath was brought in. Hess appeared to recognize her, but demonstrated little emotion and later denied ever knowing her. She expressed considerable emotional response and discussed his family, showing him several pictures of his son. He apparently was little interested and he told her that he had lost his memory. The second

secretary was next brought in and Hess evidenced even less reaction on seeing her. At one time, however, during the interview an incident of significance occurred which was noticed by Colonel Schroeder and myself. Hess was asked about a matter to which he replied: 'I do not remember.' Whereupon, his secretary took up one of the pictures and said: 'Here, maybe this will help you to remember.' Hess immediately waved his left hand at her hurriedly and said in a very low voice: 'I do not want any help.' He later denied this, but it was obvious to all present that he did not want to run any risk of giving himself away.[4]

Hess was also confronted by his former colleagues, Göring, Haushofer and Bohle. He was able to show no sign of recognition.

Meanwhile, the medical and psychological experts reported on Hess; their examination was initiated by a request from his counsel for a ruling with regard to his competence to stand trial. A multinational panel of eminent medical men interviewed Hess on 14 November, and subsequently submitted their individual reports as national groups between 17 and 19 November. These were collectively submitted to the court on 24 November by which time it was already in session. The specialists agreed collectively that Hess was 'not insane in the strict sense of the word', that his amnesia did not prevent him from understanding what was going on around him, and that it might well disappear with changing circumstances. Certain of the individual reports went so far as to suggest the amnesia was self-induced, either hysterically or as a subconscious or conscious inclination towards self-defence. The British spoke of the 'conscious exaggeration of his loss of memory', the Russians of his 'deliberate and conscious tendency toward it'.

The courtroom of the Palace of Justice had been carefully prepared for the staging of this epic drama, mostly with the labour of SS prisoners of war. The windows were heavily curtained, the seating for the prisoners had been built on a rostrum, the blazing lights beamed to give the maximum illumination for the benefit of the news-reels cameramen and the press photographers. The eyes of the world were focused on this confined hall in Nuremberg when proceedings opened on 20 November 1945. Space was provided for 250 journalists, and 150 spectators. But no one anticipated the inordinate length to which the trial would stretch. The case for the prosecution lasted the whole winter, from November until March 1946, corresponding (one might claim) to the range and magnitude of the crimes the régime had committed; the responses from the defence counsel lasted until July, and these were followed by the hearing of the cases against the indicted organisations. Each defendant was permitted a final statement on 31 August. Judgement was pronounced a month later, beginning on 30 September, and the sentences were read on 1 October 1946. The record of the trial runs to some six million words, and the index alone occupies some 1,400 columns; it was taken down by a team of stenographers, mostly women; every word of each simultaneous translation was also recorded. The translators sat behind little glass panels. The reading of the indictment occupied the first day, and the statement of individual responsibility levelled by the Prosecutor against Hess was set out as follows:

> The defendant Hess between 1921 and 1941 was: a member of the Nazi Party, Deputy to the Führer, Reich Minister without Portfolio, member of the Reichstag, member of the Council of Ministers for the Defence of the Reich, member of the Secret Cabinet Council, Successor Designate to the Führer after the defendant Göring, a General in the SS and a General in the SA. The defendant Hess used the foregoing positions, his personal influence and his intimate connection with the Führer in such a manner that: he promoted the accession to power of the Nazi conspirators and the consolidation of their control over Germany set forth in Count One of the Indictment; he promoted the military, economic and psychological preparations for war set forth in Count One of the Indictment; he participated in the political planning and preparation for Wars of Aggression and Wars in Violation of International Treaties, Agreements and Assurances set forth in Counts One and Two of the Indictment; he participated in the preparation and planning of foreign policy plans of the Nazi conspirators set forth in Count One of the Indictment; he authorized, directed and participated in the War Crimes set forth in Count Three of the Indictment and the Crimes against Humanity set forth in Count Four of the Indictment, including a wide variety of crimes against persons and property.[5]

On the second day of the trial each defendant was called upon to state whether he was guilty or not guilty, proceeding in turn to the microphone in the dock. Hess was the next to be called after Göring. He got up and uttered the word 'Nein'; this, declared the President of the Court, amid some laughter from the press, would be recorded as a plea of 'Not guilty.'

Hess adopted the pose throughout the trial of paying little or no attention to the proceedings; he appeared to be sleeping most of this first day in court, but later on he was usually reading books. He is described by a journalist, R. W. Cooper, who reported the trial:

> Everything about him was vaguely 'queer'—the dark cragginess of the man; his rabbity grin; an air whether real or simulated of taking not the remotest interest in what was going on around him as, disdaining the use of earphones, he sat between Göring and Ribbentrop usually buried in a Bavarian novel. Sometimes his burning eyes would rove round the court and glancing up to the visitors' gallery he would smile sardonically.[6]

On 29 November, a lengthy film assembling the atrocity sequences shot in the concentration camps by American Army cameramen was shown. The reactions of most of the defendants were very marked, some like Fritzsche, Funk and Frank being reduced to tears. Hess merely looked bewildered, and after the film was finished he was heard by the psychiatrist, Dr Gilbert, to remark to Göring that he did not believe it. In his cell afterwards, Hess merely kept repeating, 'I don't understand.'

On 30 November in the late afternoon Dr Günther von Rohrscheidt's submission that Hess was unfit to plead was heard in the courtroom, which was cleared for the purpose. He asked for the proceedings to be temporarily suspended so far as Hess was concerned. He had to admit, however, that 'Hess himself thinks he is fit to plead, and would like to tell the Court so himself.' Rohrscheidt said, 'I believe that the defendant is quite incapable of making himself understood in the manner that is to be expected from a mentally normal person.' He referred to Hess's refusal to undergo narcotic analysis, declaring that 'he disapproves of such violent methods' and that he regarded himself as already fit to plead. He also felt it would be against the spirit of the Charter establishing the Court to try him *in absentia*, since the charges against him were so grave; in any case, Hess had told him that he wanted to be present. Rohrscheidt concluded by saying that if the Tribunal did consider Hess fit to plead, they should first of all permit him to be placed in hospital for a more thorough and prolonged examination than had been possible on 14 November.

A lengthy discussion of the various medical reports followed.[7] Each prosecutor summed up his position:

General Rudenko (for the Soviet Union):

I consider that the findings of the experts are quite sufficient to declare Hess sane and able to stand his trial.

Sir David Maxwell Fyfe (for Great Britain):

It is part of his defence, and it may well be 'I don't remember anything about that at all.' And he could actually add to that: 'From my general behaviour or from other acts which I undoubtedly have done, it is extremely unlikely that I should do it.' That is the defence that is left to him. And he must take that defence, and that is my submission.

The Tribunal (Mr Biddle): So even if we assume for the purpose of argument that his amnesia is complete, and that he remembers nothing that occurred before the indictment, though now understanding the proceedings, you think he should be tried?

Sir David Maxwell Fyfe: I submit he should be tried. That is my submission as to the legal position.

Mr Justice Jackson (for the United States):

I respectfully suggest that a man cannot stand at the bar of the Court and assert that his amnesia is a defence to his being tried, and at the same time refuse the simple medical expedients which all agree might be useful.

He is in the volunteer class with his amnesia. When he was in England he is reported to have made the statement that his earlier amnesia was simulated. He came out of this state during a period in England, and went back into it. It is now highly selective. That is to say, you cannot be sure what Hess will remember and what he will not remember. His amnesia is not of the type which is a complete blotting out of the personality, of the type that would be fatal to his defence.

So we feel that so long as Hess refused the ordinary, simple expedients, even if his amnesia is genuine, he is not in a position to continue to assert that he must not be brought to trial. We think he should be tried, not in absentia, but that this trial should proceed.

But Rohrscheidt, doing his best for this most difficult of 'clients', stuck to his case:

The defendant Hess is suffering from amnesia, which, as all medical experts admit, exists. They all agree, however, that this amnesia is caused by a pathological condition of his mind. The result is that the defendant is not insane, but has a mental defect In a legal sense, I think, from this it can be deduced that the defendant cannot disdain responsibility for his actions, because at the time when the acts he is charged with were committed, he was certainly not mentally insane, consequently he can be held responsible. But there is a difference, according to German law at any rate, when the question is whether the defendant is at the moment in a position to follow the trial, that is, whether he is capable of participating in the proceedings. This question should, in my opinion, as I have already said, on the basis of the medical reports, be answered in the negative. He is not capable of pleading his case.

In the midst of all this argument, Hess himself asked to be allowed to make his statement. The few words he spoke were among the most sensational of the trial:

In order to forestall the possibility of my being pronounced incapable of pleading in spite of my willingness to take part in further proceedings, and in order to receive sentence alongside my comrades, I would like to make the following declaration before the Tribunal, although, originally, I intended to make this declaration during a later part of the proceedings:

Henceforth my memory will again respond to the outside world. The reasons why I simulated loss of memory were tactical. The fact is that it is only my ability to concentrate that is somewhat reduced. However, my capacity to follow the trial, to defend myself, to put questions to witnesses or even to answer questions, is not being affected thereby.

I emphasize that I bear the full responsibility for everything that I have done or signed as signatory or co-signatory. My attitude, in principle, that the Tribunal is not competent, is not affected by the statement I have just made. So far in conversations with my official defence counsel I have also simulated loss of memory. He has, therefore, represented me in good faith.[8]

The hearing was immediately adjourned. The following day, the President announced that in view of what Hess had said the Tribunal was of the opinion that he was capable of standing trial, and that no further medical examination would be necessary. The trial proceeded, and Hess returned to his book-reading. Off stage, however, he appeared unusually pleased by the sensation he had caused, and the vast 'press' which he received.

Dr Gilbert found Rohrscheidt completely nonplussed; he did not know where he was with Hess. Göring at first thought it all very funny, a joke at the expense of the psychiatrists and the Court itself. Von Schirach was amazed; Ribbentrop bewildered. In court, Göring soon resented Hess becoming the centre of attention; in the moments of conversation now available to the defendants during the recesses and other intervals, Hess enjoyed giving Göring details of his flight. In his cell, Dr Gilbert reports that he was very cheerful. He told Gilbert that he had decided to make his statement in case he was not going to figure any longer in the trial. To Kelley, visiting him in his cell after his revelation, he appeared like an actor who had just left the stage following a particularly fine performance.

'How did I do? Good, wasn't I?' is what Kelley reports him as saying. 'I really surprised everybody, don't you think?' But both Gilbert and Kelley considered that his recovery was, in a sense, a delusion, and that his mental condition was still unsound and his memory uncertain. As psychiatrists they were not prepared to lose him so easily. Kelley also claimed that Hess admitted he was nervous during the film shown him before the trial because Kelley had persisted in watching his hands. 'It made me nervous to know you had learned my secret,' he said. When shown old scenes, Kelley had noticed, his hands had tended to tighten. Later, according to Kelley, he made a further statement that much of his amnesia had indeed been real, after all. He admitted his brain tired easily. Kelley persisted that Hess was a case of what he called a 'self-perpetuated hysteric'. He was to resort to his amnesia pose at intervals throughout the rest of the trial. Once, early in January 1946, he said to Gilbert: 'The first period of memory loss was really genuine . . . But the second period I exaggerated somewhat. It wasn't entirely loss of memory.'[9]

As the great weight of evidence against the régime was accumulated in the Court by the Prosecution, the prisoners, able to mix now more freely and talk among themselves as well as to the psychiatrist Dr Gilbert (Dr Kelley having retired after the first month of the trial), let their thoughts drop in conversation both in and out of their cells. Hess was content, for example, to let Gilbert think what he liked about the simulation or otherwise of his amnesia. He appeared, however, disturbed by what had happened during the régime, especially after he had left the country.

'It is just incomprehensible how all those things came about,' he said to Dr Gilbert. When the psychiatrist asked him, 'What do you think of Hitler now?' he is reported to have replied, 'I don't know—I suppose every genius has a demon in him. You can't blame him—it is just in him.' He continued to reflect on the idea, says Dr Gilbert, but was apparently unwilling to say more, except, 'It is all very tragic—but at least I have the satisfaction of knowing that I tried to do something to end the war.' Later, on the 27 December, according to Dr Gilbert, 'he admitted he was disillusioned about a lot of things that have come to light in the trial, which he did not know about during his imprisonment in England. I suggested that he must have been greatly disturbed by the turn of the war after America came in. "Yes, that was quite a shock. When I flew to England I really was sure we would win," Hess reflected, without any show of emotion.'[10]

Later in January 1946 he refused any longer to accept Dr von Rohrscheidt as his advocate. He sent the following letter of explanation to the Court, dated 30 January:

> In the *New York Herald Tribune* [European Edition] date 27 January, 1946, there is a report of an interview given by my former defending counsel, Rechtsanwalt Dr von Rohrscheidt. This contains a passage in which strictly confidential instructions given by me to Dr von Rohrscheidt in respect of my defence are given publicity, while at the same time it is emphasized that these were my instructions.
>
> This constitutes a breach of confidence and an offence against the secrecy to which an advocate is pledged; it is a grave professional offence which, in normal times, would lead to a denunciation before the governing chamber of lawyers.
>
> I therefore hereby place on record that I no longer have any confidence whatever in my former advocate.
>
> At the same time I draw the attention of the Court to the fact that I have now been a whole week without a defending counsel, while I have not been permitted to take advantage of the right to which the Statute entitles me of pleading my own case. In consequence of this state of things, I was prevented from questioning even a single witness of all those who came forward during this period—although, again, I was entitled by the Statute to do this.[11]

Rohrscheidt had in fact been the victim of an accident, and on 23 January Hess, speaking through Dr Horn, counsel for Ribbentrop, had requested the Court's leave to defend himself. The President had said the matter would be considered, and on 30 January, at the beginning of

F

the afternoon session, he declared that, having been so far represented by counsel, it was in Hess's interest to continue to be so. Accordingly, they appointed Dr Stahmer to represent him. He was replaced, however, by Dr Alfred Seidl, Frank's defence counsel, on 5 February. Dr Seidl was a most able young lawyer, still under thirty.

Hess, in a statement of 5 February in fact designed for his wife, but composed in the third person and written in a form resembling a memorandum for Seidl himself, explained his desire to defend himself, but ended in expressing his confidence in Seidl. Hess wrote of himself:

> He would prefer, as always to defend himself. He is, moreover, convinced—and is glad that this view is shared by others—that he is the best advocate for his cause. His mastery of all the material is superior to that of anyone else and he has in his possession all that is necessary as occasion arises, whereas an advocate would have to consult him continually. As, according to the statutory regulations, a defendant may have several defenders he would, in any case, wish to have a jurist as second counsel for the defence. After his claim to defend himself had been turned down, at first Göring's defending counsel was assigned to him; but he was already overburdened, so Dr Alfred Seidl, who was acting already for Frank, took on the task. Dr Seidl is the keenest and most aggressive of all the defending counsels; and is moreover an old ski-runner who had been up the Kreuzeck with Herr Hess. Finally, he speaks pure Munich dialect. The two last points are not essential conditions for a good advocate but they help to create a good personal relationship which is, in its turn, an essential factor in creating a firm basis of confidence. Herr Hess is extremely glad to have the services of Dr Seidl in his defence.[12]

Seidl had little time to prepare the defence, since the Prosecution's case against Hess opened on 7 February, the counsel being the British barrister, Lieutenant-Colonel J. M. G. Griffith-Jones. He began by outlining Hess's career and the positions he had occupied in the Party and in the government of the Third Reich as Minister without Portfolio and Deputy to the Führer. He emphasized Hess's close alignment with Hitler, especially in his advisory supervision of the laws and decrees which followed Hitler's seizure of dictatorial power after the passing of the Enabling Act of March 1933. He quoted from Hess's speeches to show his support for this method of government, and then referred case by case to many of the more significant decrees Hess had signed which gave him arbitrary control, for example, over official appointments in the Civil Service, control in education, control over the administration of the Adolf Hitler Fund for German Industry. He made it clear that Hess shared in the responsibility for the persecution of the Jews by signing the Law for the Protection of Blood and Honour, the Nuremberg racial decree of September 1935, and decrees depriving the Jews of their civil rights. He showed how Hess had participated in Hitler's plans for war, signing the decree for compulsory military service of March 1935, and how he had both supported and publicly advocated rearmament. He had also been responsible for the development of the Party's various organizations for Germans living or travelling abroad and, extending into Nazi activity outside Germany, Colonel Griffith-Jones showed Hess's involvement in the Austrian Anschluss, his fermentation of pro-Nazi feeling among the Sudeten-Germans, and his part in the pressure put upon Poland and Danzig before Hitler's invasion of these territories. Finally, he was to be responsible for assisting in the formulation of certain of the decrees which led to the persecution of the Polish people, both Jewish and otherwise.

Colonel Griffith-Jones then described Hess's mission to Britain, and his attempt to split the Allies in order to further Germany's forthcoming attack on the Soviet Union:

> Presumably when he came over he was not attempting to be funny. One can only conclude from these reports that at that time the people in Germany, and the German Government, really had no kind of idea of what the conditions in England were like at all. Throughout it appears that this man thought England was ruled by Churchill and a small war-mongering gang. It only needed him to come over and make a peace proposal for Churchill to be turned out in the course of two or three days.[13]

He quoted from the official reports of the interviews with the Duke of Hamilton and with Ivone Kirkpatrick, and then he added:

> His humanitarian reasons for coming, which sounded so well on the 10 or between the 10 and 15 May, took on quite a different light, when barely a little more than a month later Germany attacked the Soviet Union. One cannot help remembering an exact parallel between this business and that which took place before Germany attacked Poland, when every effort was made to keep England out of the war and so let her fight her battle on one front only. Here the

same thing appears to be happening, and what is more, we have it from Hess himself, in the course of those interviews, that at that time Germany had no intention at all of attacking Russia immediately. But that must be untrue, because it will be remembered, and the evidence is set out in the trial brief, that as far back as November, 1940, plans were being made, initial plans, for the invasion of Russia.

Hess, Colonel Griffith-Jones concluded, could scarcely be unaware of Hitler's plans, since he was, after all, the Führer's Deputy.

Hess did not take the stand, nor did Seidl intervene other than on one purely formal point. The case was allowed to stand by the defence until their own intervention some six weeks later.

In a letter to his wife dated 25 January, Hess had said, 'The trial is in part horrible and in part monotonous, but every now and then it can be interesting.' Ten days earlier, on 15 January, he had told her, 'I am still exactly the same man, inwardly and outwardly, as my comrades have recognized with joy.'

On 19 February the Russians, whom Göring continued openly to scorn both in the Court and outside it, showed their Nazi atrocity film. Göring, copying Hess, refused to look at the screen and pretended to read a book, yawning now and then, or making a sarcastic remark to Hess, who sat beside him throughout the trial. Göring had been trying since the beginning of the trial to dominate the rest of the defendants, with whom he had been free to talk during the meal intervals in the prison, though on 18 February a new, official order for sitting at meals had been adopted, Göring being forced to eat alone, while Hess was segregated with Raeder, Streicher and Ribbentrop, the group of defendants most on the defensive and least likely to talk other than in very neutral terms. By the weekend of 23–24 February Hess was allowing his memory to lapse to some degree in order, no doubt, to circumvent Gilbert's continued questioning. He revived his complaints of stomach-cramps, and disturbances at night. He could not concentrate, he said, and claimed he could not remember the duration of the trial, witnesses who had appeared, and so forth. 'Do you remember your flight to England and all the circumstances surrounding it?' persisted Gilbert. 'I remember *why* I went, but not the details,' replied Hess. 'Did I ever remember them before?' Later he wrote down some details of the flight, but he represented his memory as extremely vague on all points when Gilbert questioned him in his cell during the weekend of 9–10

March. He liked to lie in his bed day-dreaming. He played the same game with the other defendants, so as to avoid being called as a witness. On the other hand, he said to Gilbert when told that the former Field-Marshal von Blomberg had died, 'I hope none of my witnesses leaves me in the lurch by preferring death.' He claimed not to remember the name of Haushofer. When one of the other defendants told him he had *got* to remember, he merely sighed and said, 'I wish I knew how.' On 24 March he decided not to take the stand on the advice, apparently, not only of his counsel, but of Göring as well.

The case for the defence—put by Dr Seidl, who was to prove the most formidable and effective of the defence counsel—opened in the late afternoon of 22 March and continued on 25 and 26 March.[14] He opened with a statement, which the President rejected, that Hess 'contests the jurisdiction of the Tribunal in so far as other than war crimes proper are the subject of the trial. However,' he went on, 'he specifically assumes full responsibility for all laws or decrees he has signed.' Hess, therefore, did not propose to defend himself against any of the charges which referred, as Seidl put it, 'to the internal affairs of Germany as a sovereign State.' He was only concerned that his counsel should clarify certain points relating to activities of the foreign organizations of the Party, and define as he wanted it defined, the purpose of his flight to Britain.

Later Seidl read extensively from the record of Simon's interview with Hess in England, and then attempted to introduce, without prior warning, the terms of the secret codicil to the non-aggression pact between Germany and the Soviet Union signed in August 1939, in which the delimitation of the mutual sphere of interest in Eastern Europe recognized by Germany and the Soviet Union was determined, more especially the division of Poland after its invasion by Hitler. From Seidl's point of view, the document was dynamite, since it would show, if admitted into Court, that the Soviet Union, as an adjudicating nation, had been guilty of the very crime with which the defendants were being charged.[15] The interchange which followed was a dramatic one, in which finally General Rudenko, the Soviet prosecutor, intervened:

Dr Seidl: On 23 August, at Moscow, a non-aggression pact was concluded between Germany and the Soviet Union, which has already been submitted by the prosecution as Exhibit GB 145. On the same day, that is to say one week before the outbreak of the war and three days before the planned attack on Poland, these two nations also made a secret agreement. This secret agreement essentially contained the definition of the spheres of interest of both nations within the European territory lying between Germany and the Soviet Union.

The President: Dr Seidl, you are not forgetting, are you, the Tribunal's ruling that this is not the opportunity for making a speech, but simply the occasion for introducing documents and calling witnesses. You will have the opportunity of making your speech at a later stage.

Dr Seidl: Yes, indeed. I do not intend to make a speech, but I intend to say a few introductory words on a document which I shall submit to the Tribunal.

Germany, in the secret documents, declared herself disinterested in Lithuania, Latvia, Estonia, and Finland.

The President: Dr Seidl, we have not yet seen the document. If you are going to put in the document, put in the document.

Dr Seidl: Yes, indeed. I can submit the document at once. It is an affidavit of the former ambassador Dr Friedrich Gauss. In the year 1939 he was the Chief of the Legal Department of the Foreign Office. He was present at the negotiations as the escort of the then German plenipotentiary in Moscow, and it was he who drafted the non-aggression pact which has already been submitted as an exhibit, as well as the secret agreement, the contents of which I want to submit now to the Tribunal as facts which are important as evidence.

The President: Well, will you hand in the document?

Dr Seidl: Certainly. However, I intend to read parts of this document later.

The President: Dr Seidl, the Tribunal does not quite understand what this document is, because it is not included in your document book, and it does not appear that you made any application for it or made any reference to it, and it is in German; it is not translated.

Dr Seidl: Mr President, when I prepared the document book for the defendant Hess, I did not then have this affidavit in my possession. It dates from 15 March, 1946. At that time, when the relevancy of the applications for defendant Hess were discussed, I had then no definite knowledge of the context which would have enabled me to make a proper application. The excerpts which I intend to read from this document are short, and it will be possible for them to be translated immediately by the interpreters present here in the courtroom.

The President: Have you a copy for the prosecution?

Dr Seidl: Certainly, a German copy.

The President: I am afraid that would not be of any use to me. I do not know whether it is to all the members of the Prosecution. Have the Prosecution counsel any objection to passages being read from this document?

General Rudenko: Mr President, I did not know about the existence of this document and therefore strenuously object to having it read into the record. I would wish that the procedure established by the Tribunal be observed by the Defence. The Prosecution, in the past, when presenting its evidence invariably presented copies of these documents to the Defence counsel. Counsel for Hess is now presenting a completely unknown document, and the Prosecution—with every reason—would like to familiarize itself with this document beforehand. I do not know what secrets or what secret agreements counsel for the Defence is talking about, and on what facts he is basing his statements. I would therefore, to say the least, define them as unfounded. I request that the document should not be read into the record.

Dr Seidl: The prosecutor of the Soviet Union states that he has no knowledge of the existence of this secret document, which shall be established by this affidavit. Under these circumstances I am compelled to move that Foreign Commissar Molotov of the Soviet Union be called as a witness, so that it can be established firstly, whether this agreement was actually concluded, secondly, what the contents of this agreement are, and thirdly . . .

The President: Dr Seidl, the first thing for you to do is to have a translation of this document made, and until you have a translation of this document made the Tribunal is not prepared to hear you upon it. We do not know what the document contains.

Dr Seidl: As to what the document contains, I already wanted to explain that before. In the document there is . . .

The President: No, the Tribunal is not prepared to hear from you what the document contains. We want to see the document itself and see it in English and also in Russian.

For the moment, therefore Seidl was prevented from introducing his 'bombshell', though he was to do so later, on 1 April, when questioning Ribbentrop in the witness-stand, in spite of Rudenko's attempt to have the matter set aside as irrelevant. He returned to the matter also on 21 May.[16] He next called Bohle as a witness for the defence. The work of the Ausland Organisation was described in some detail with a view to showing that it was quite innocent of fermenting war or acting as a 'fifth column' in foreign countries. Colonel Griffith-Jones put some damaging questions in cross-examining Bohle about the spying in Holland and Norway conducted by representatives of the Ausland Organisation, as well as assistance given by them to German troops after the invasion of, for example, Greece. Bohle could only explain that any activity of this kind was conducted without his knowledge, and certainly without direct instructions from him. The questioning was widened to deal with Hess's activities in relation to the whole problem of 'Germanism abroad'. Colonel Amen for the United States asked questions about the activities of the Bund. Pressed on to whether he had a transmitter at his headquarters in Germany to issue secret instructions or to monitor reports from abroad, Bohle denied that anything of the sort had existed.

Seidl then called to the witness-stand Karl Stroelin, former Lord Mayor of Stuttgart, whose affidavit was read concerning the Auslands-Institut in that city. Stroelin was at pains when cross-examined to state that his Institut did not come under Hess's jurisdiction, though it was concerned with Germans living in foreign countries. Griffith-Jones tried to link the Institut with Hess, with whom it was reported to have co-operated closely. Colonel Amen questioned him about his personal activities in New York City in 1936, when he had addressed a rally of Germans in Madison Square Gardens. Colonel Amen also tried to get Stroelin to admit that members of the Institut, linked with the Bund, acted as spies in the United States. He finally drew from Stroelin a confession that there was a time eventually 'when one was no longer proud of Germany'.

The third and last witness called for the defence was Alfred Hess, who gave further evidence on the Ausland Organisation, affirming that it did not receive orders from Hess to act as a 'fifth column' abroad. The case concluded with a lengthy debate concerning the relevance or not of discussion of the terms of the Versailles Treaty, which was finally ruled inadmissible. Dr Seidl was particularly hostile to the Treaty. His later attempt to introduce the subject on 5 July was just as firmly rejected by the Tribunal.

From the end of March until the end of July, Hess in effect drops from the record. Gilbert has virtually nothing to say of him, and it is evident that he mentally absented himself as far as ever possible from everything which was going on.[17] He even refused to read the news-papers which the prisoners were allowed. He also refused to receive his wife and son in prison, saying it was beneath his dignity, and because he feared that the sight of them would break down his stoicism. But he wrote on 8 May:

> From the room on the second storey where we take our meals during the mid-day interval in the theatrical performance, I enjoy an extensive, beautiful view towards the north-east, as far as the distant heights. My soul reaches out in this direction—not only over this visible landscape, but also towards other blue mountains, not visible at this distance to the physical eye, which mean home and love . . . I never give my autograph to anyone, although I am asked for it several times a day. And no doubt the ensuing high market-value of my writing ∿∿∿ must have the effect of increasing the competition to get hold of specimens ∿∿∿.[18]

He wrote affectionately to his son on 27 July:

> My dear Buz,
>   I thank you for your letter in which you let me know that you have given up the idea of driving the locomotive pulling the tipping-trucks in the Munich rubble-clearing work, in favour of becoming a driver of a real railway train. I give you my full permission straight away! I understand only too well that you want to race along at high speeds. Of course, you could go even faster as the pilot in an aircraft.

The concluding speech was given by Dr Seidl on 25 July, beginning with an historical survey of the period and then proceeding as far as he could to draw the teeth of the prosecution's case against Hess as an instigator of crimes against peace by virtue of the decrees he had signed. He claimed the Prosecution had failed to show that the organizations abroad had received direct instructions from Hess to act as fifth colum-nists or spies. He defended him, too, against the charge of active con-spiracy against Austria and Czechoslovakia; he held neither of these annexations to be illegal. He outlined the problem of Poland in 1939 as it had been seen by the Germans, and what he held to be the very reasonable solution proposed before the war, as a result of which the Poles mobilized. His historical outline, naturally, included reference to the German-Soviet peace-pact, and its sinister 'secret supplementory protocol'. It was a brilliant, if highly tendentious historical survey from the right-wing German, rather than an ostensibly Nazi point of view.

Dr Seidl then defended Hess, taking in order the separate counts under which he had been charged. He based his main plea on the fact that Hitler alone was responsible for all the key decisions which were taken. Hess, he claimed, was a cipher when it came to taking any ultimate decisions; there was, therefore, no 'common plan' as suggested in the first charge. He said:

> The defendant Rudolf Hess, though the Führer's Deputy and the highest political leader for Party matters, did not contribute to or take part in any of the conferences, or any important political or military decisions characterized by the prosecution as being essential to prove the existence of a common plan.[19]

Point by point he cleared Hess of any executive implication in the key decisions taken by Hitler which were recorded in the documents forming the basis for this charge. Often he was not even present when Hitler took these decisions, in spite of his high position in the Party and the State.

The demands for 'Lebensraum' for the Germans and the return of the former German colonies which Hess had made in public speeches Seidl maintained did not constitute a 'common plan of conspiracy'; these, he asserted, were demands couched in 'legitimate' terms, at least by European as distinct from Anglo-American law, as he put it. This he argued at some length.

He further defended Hess against the charge of crimes against humanity, diminishing as far as possible his direct intervention in the laws affecting the Jews and, from 1939, the Poles. He represented that the furthest Hess had gone in the latter case was advocating corporal punishment. He also mentioned (a point which had not been raised by the prosecution) Hess's order to civilians of 13 March 1940 concerning the treatment of parachutists landing from enemy aircraft; he had ordered that they should either be arrested or rendered harmless (that is, he said, 'subdued'). Seidl did not consider such orders violated normal practice.

The defence then turned to Hess's position as a leader in the various political groups indicted as criminal. Seidl said:

> Although the defendant Hess was the highest political leader, and although no action is charged against him which constitutes a crime according to any penal law, he is to be convicted as a member of the allegedly criminal organization of which he was the leader; it

cannot be denied that this is a legal situation which does not happen every day.[20]

To punish Hess on this count, claimed Seidl, was tantamount to accepting 'criminal responsibility without guilt', a factor which 'has hitherto only existed among primitive peoples'. These groups (such as the Reich Cabinet, the Secret Reich Council) existed not as executive bodies capable of collective action, but solely by virtue of Hitler's will, which they existed to fulfil.

Seidl then outlined the purpose behind Hess's flight to Britain, emphasizing this as a 'mission of humanity'. The flight to England alone, said Seidl, proved that Hess was no war conspirator. He said:

> This sacrifice was all the greater as Hess was one of the very few whose relation to Hitler was based on intimate personal confidence. If the defendant decided to stake his position in the Party, and everything that meant a personal bond with Hitler, for the re-establishment of peace, then this must lead to the conclusion that the defendant Hess likewise saw in war the ghastly scourge of mankind and that it must appear quite improbable for this reason alone that it was his intention to prepare the German people for war . . . In undertaking his flight to England, which was linked with his plans for the restoration of peace, the defendant Hess committed his entire person in an attempt which sprang from the desire to avoid further bloodshed at all costs.[21]

After his flight in May 1941, Hess could no longer be considered implicated in events in Germany. He even went so far as to claim that Hess had no advance knowledge of the impending invasion of the Soviet Union.

Mr Justice Jackson then began, on 26 July, the summing-up for the American prosecution. This took the form of a panorama of Nazi crime—'No half-century,' said Jackson, 'ever witnessed slaughter on such a scale, such cruelties and inhumanities, such wholesale deportations of peoples into slavery, such annihilation of minorities.' In his speech he said, 'the zealot Hess, before succumbing to wanderlust, was the engineer tending the Party machinery, passing orders and propaganda down to the Leadership Corps, supervising every aspect of Party activities, and maintaining the organisation as a loyal and ready instrument of power.' Sir Hartley Shawcross followed for the British—he was particularly concerned with Nazi concentration camps and genocide, referring to Hess as one of the instruments of the Nuremberg Laws, a point re-emphasized by M. Dubost, the chief prosecutor for the French. General Rudenko referred to Hess at length, considering him guilty on every count, with the added culpability that he had attempted to avoid his trial and punishment by trying 'to declare himself insane'. The speeches for the prosecution finished on 30 July. The cases against the indicted organizations followed, carrying the trial on to the end of August.

On 31 August came the final statement by the defendants. Their speeches were supposed to be short. Hess, who asked if he might remain seated because of his state of health, spoke second, following Göring. He made a long, rambling speech which the President only interrupted after Hess had been speaking for twenty minutes. With an obvious reference to trials in the Soviet Union during the 1930s, he referred indirectly to witnesses who were, in effect, brainwashed into giving untrue evidence. He proceeded to claim that those in charge of the genocide camps had been hypnotised into carrying out their tasks, like those who had guarded him in England, and that those men had 'strange eyes . . . glassy and like eyes in a dream.' He referred to the Boers done to death by the British in their concentration camps in South Africa half a century ago. He then set about swearing a mighty oath to speak the truth. When told he must conclude his statement by the President, he said:

> I was permitted to work for many years of my life under the greatest son whom my country has brought forth in its thousand-year history. Even if I could, I would not want to erase this period of time from my existence. I am happy to know that I have done my duty to my people, my duty as a German, as a National Socialist, as a loyal follower of my Führer. I do not regret anything.
>
> If I were to begin all over again, I would act just as I have acted, even if I knew that in the end I would meet a fiery death at the stake. No matter what human beings may do, I shall some day stand before the judgment seat of the Eternal. I shall answer to Him, and I know He will judge me innocent.[22]

After the session, Hess retreated, according to Gilbert, into 'an embarrassed silence in his cell'. On the day he made this wholly irrational speech, Hess wrote very rationally to his wife:

> From your 'Lachlinie' 〰〰〰 I realized that you had taken humorously Dr Seidl's communication to the effect that I had

again lost my memory completely. Meanwhile, you will certainly
have heard through the radio that there has been another 'miracle',
and that I have completely recovered it 〜〜〜〜. Or they may very
well tell you that I have lost my reason; or at least suffer from fixed
ideas. I hope you will see the humorous side of this also. Karli
once said that for the sake of a great cause one must be able to suffer
the pain of seeming to one's people, for a time, to be a traitor. To
this I would add: or seeming to be crazy. After all that I have
experienced and suffered in the last five and a half years, the latest
trick played upon me by the strange fate which guides me cannot
disturb me at all; on the contrary I face it with a quiet and balanced
mind and a smile, with the same imperturbability with which I
shall receive the verdict.[23]

Two days later, on 2 September, he wrote:

It has now been decided that the prisoners here should be graciously
permitted to receive ONE visit from their relations, that is to say they
may be seen and heard through a closely-knit iron wire net. I have
firmly refused to meet either you or anyone else under these conditions, which I maintain to be beneath our dignity. Between ourselves we should have to admit that 'at Landsberg we met under
conditions that were not very pleasant', but there is a vast difference
between sitting side-by-side in the same room for half an hour or an
hour, with no hindrance save the presence in a corner of a good
German soldier of the guard who slept part of the time—or very
kindly pretended to do so—and seeing each other through a wire
net, with guards on both sides who will certainly *not* sleep and,
above all, are not decent German fellows like our own guards.

I agreed at the time, finally, that I would not resist your desire to
attempt to obtain a permit to see me: but I gave way on this point
because I knew definitely that your request would not be granted.
Now the position is rather different and one day you will agree with
me, even if to-day you wish to carry out your plan.[24]

Then, in case no report was allowed to reach the German people
of what he had said in court, he gave his wife the gist of the final statement he had made about Hitler, and about having no regrets for what he
had done.

Judgment was given on 30 September, and the statements concerning
the individual defendants and their sentences came on 1 October.

The judgment on Hess began with the now familiar outline of his offices of Party and State and the various principal decrees which he had signed. The judgment then went on:

> It is true that between 1933 and 1937 Hess made speeches in which he expressed a desire for peace, and advocated international economic co-operation. But nothing which they contained can alter the fact that of all the defendants none knew better than Hess how determined Hitler was to realize his ambitions, how fanatical and violent a man he was, and how little likely he was to refrain from resort to force, if this was the only way in which he could achieve his aims.[25]

It then dealt in some detail with Hess's involvement in Austria, Czechoslovakia and Poland, and finally his flight to England, after which, it was maintained, he showed no remorse for Germany's acts of aggression, and blamed England and France for the war. The judgment concluded:

> There is evidence showing that the Party Chancellery, under Hess, participated in the distribution of orders connected with the commission of War Crimes; that Hess may have had knowledge of, even if he did not participate in, the crimes that were being committed in the East; that he proposed laws discriminating against Jews and Poles; and that he signed decrees forcing certain groups of Poles to accept German citizenship. The Tribunal, however, does not find that the evidence sufficiently connects Hess with these crimes to sustain a finding of guilt.
>
> As previously indicated, the Tribunal found, after a full medical examination of and reports on the condition of this defendant, that he should be tried, without any postponement of his case. Since that time, further motions have been made that he should again be examined. These the Tribunal denied, after having had a report from the prison psychologist. That Hess acts in an abnormal manner, suffers from loss of memory, and has mentally deteriorated during this trial, may be true. But there is nothing to show that he does not realize the nature of the charges against him, or is incapable of defending himself. He was ably represented at the trial by counsel appointed for that purpose by the Tribunal. There is no suggestion that Hess was not completely sane when the acts charged against him were committed.

The Tribunal finds the defendant Hess guilty on Counts One and Two [the Common Plan or Conspiracy; Crimes against Peace]; and not guilty on Counts Three and Four [War Crimes; Crimes against Humanity].

In the afternoon the sentences were proclaimed individually, each prisoner mounting in turn to the courtroom to learn his fate, and then returning to his cell. While Göring was near to emotional breakdown at his death sentence, and asked to be left alone in his cell, Hess, according to Gilbert, 'strutted in, laughing nervously, and said that he had not even been listening, so he did not know what the sentence was—and what was more, he didn't care. As the guard unlocked his handcuffs, he asked why he had been handcuffed and Göring had not. I said that it was probably an oversight with the first prisoner. Hess laughed again and said mysteriously that he knew why.' In court he had not even put on his ear-phones. An appeal against his sentence of life imprisonment based on Hess's alleged insanity was entered by Dr Seidl, but rejected as were all pleas for clemency on behalf of the defendants. The day of execution was fixed for 16 October, while the day before, 15 October, it was announced that those serving sentences in detention would be removed eventually to Spandau prison in Berlin.[26]

After the sentences had been passed, the President announced that the Soviet member of the International Military Tribunal, Major-General I. T. Nikitchenko, wanted to record his dissent from the decisions which had been taken. It was his view, for example, that Schacht, Papen, and Fritzsche, who had all been acquitted, should have been convicted. For many reasons, which he outlined in a document which the President announced would be annexed to the Judgment and published, the Soviet member thought Hess should have been condemned to death. Hess may not have committed personally the crimes against humanity with which he was charged, but he was responsible for the preparations which led to them; in particular he was party to the setting-up of SS formations in the occupied territories. His statement ended: 'Taking into consideration that among political leaders of Hitlerite Germany Hess was third in significance and played a decisive role in the crimes of the Nazi régime, I consider the only justified sentence in his case can be death.'

This pronouncement was to have serious consequences for Hess in the future, and accounts, in part at least, for Soviet intransigence when, years later, appeals for his release from Spandau were to be put forward.

On 2 October, the day after sentence had been passed, Hess wrote to his wife:

> I am greatly surprised, for I had reckoned with the death sentence. If I attached any importance at all to the judgment of the court, I might feel satisfied so far. As it is, however, there is no question of being or not being satisfied. I find myself in a state of most perfect calm, disturbed only by the thought that I cannot convey my own state to comrades who cannot feel in the same way about the matter. In accordance with my refusal, on principle, to recognize the court, I paid no attention—ostentatiously—when the judgment in my case was announced: I did not put on the earphones through which the translation was given, and I did not listen to what the President said in English.
>
> As a matter of fact it was quite a long time before I discovered, accidentally, what the sentence had been.[27]

And again on 5 October:

> I am the essence of peace and quiet; but I am pained by the thought of the spiritual suffering of comrades who will suffer the death penalty, and more especially of their families.

With many of his former colleagues now dead, Hess was left with nothing to hope for but confinement for the rest of his life, his occupation the few menial tasks allotted to him, and otherwise reading what books he could get and writing whatever he cared to write. He resented not having been allowed to complete the reading of his lengthy, prepared statement in the court. During October he borrowed a typewriter from the American Army authorities and carefully typed out what he had wanted to say. It came to forty-nine pages. Then at the top he typed in both English and German: 'To be transmitted in the most secret way to Sir Oswald Mosley in London. A *very* high gratification will be granted later on. (Signed) Rudolf Hess.' He felt that Mosley would be the only person he could trust to publish it.

The statement was handed over, but never delivered. The American Deputy Commandant at the prison took it back with him to the United States. The document was eventually to be acquired by *The Sunday Times*, and Professor H. R. Trevor-Roper was to give some account of it in that newspaper on 24 May 1970, almost a quarter of a century after it was written.[28]

The argument is that already partially developed at Nuremberg, but here carried to its logical, but wholly irrational conclusion, namely that the Jews had managed, for their own nefarious purpose of dominating the world, to bewitch everyone—not only those who defeated Germany, but even the Nazis themselves.

In Hess's opinion the horrors of the concentration camps could only have been perpetrated by people acting under hypnosis. The hypnosis, spreading like a vast, mysterious network enclosing an ever-increasing section of humanity, finally reached Hitler himself, leading him to develop the gas-chambers for the Jews' own destruction. It was indeed a powerful, as well as a self-consuming magic.

To what extent did Hess, whose letters to his wife and others remained so rational, really believe this fantasy? Was it—in the form, first, of his statement in court and, later, in this further elaboration of his arguments—a part of his campaign to obtain release from prison on the compassionate grounds that his mind was disturbed? Throughout the whole of Hess's strange story lies the dilemma of knowing where his own peculiarities and obsessions end and his assumed disturbances begin. But in the letters, both published and unpublished (in so far as we have seen the latter), none of these fantasies ever appears. It could well be that they were Hess's secret weapon, a part of his fight for liberation. If, however, the document reflects his actual beliefs, then the repeated statements of the psychiatrists about Hess's mental condition would appear to be correct, and the document represents a strange flight into fantasy resulting from some form of prison psychosis. The eminent psychiatrist Professor Bürger-Prinz, who has made a special study of Hess's case, accepted our suggestion that the document was Hess's means of coming to terms with the shock from the revelations about the concentration camps produced at the trial. He terms this a case of 'hysterical escape mechanism'.[29]

6

SPANDAU

AFTER the death of those who had had to face execution,[1] the defendants who had received various terms of imprisonment were confined at Nuremberg jail until July 1947, when Spandau prison in Berlin was ready under four-power agreement to receive them. The men who remained in confinement along with Hess were Walter Funk, Karl Dönitz, Erich Raeder, Baldur von Schirach, Constantin von Neurath, and Albert Speer.

Hess, as we have seen, refused to let his wife and child visit him in jail. This was not because he lacked affection for them, but rather for a variety of reasons which led him to feel that neither they nor he could gain from any personal contact made under prison conditions. Apart from the wounding of their pride, it might lead to emotional difficulties he did not want to face. He preferred to keep their relationship alive through sending and receiving letters. He wrote to both of them.

Ilse Hess had a very difficult time. She moved in 1945 to a small villa in Hindelang in the Bavarian Alps, the Allgäu, where the French authorities found her and put her under arrest in May 1945. Her son, who was now eight years old, was cared for by her mother. No charge was preferred against her; it seemed sufficient that she was Rudolf Hess's wife. She endured a brief confinement in a French military camp on the shores of Lake Constance—a fourteen day period she describes much later in a letter to her husband written in May 1947; here she acted as a go-between for the German lady whose villa was requisitioned for the use of a number of French officers and their wives. She kept herself busy with domestic work, and impressed the French guards, who had not thought an ex-Minister's wife would be prepared to work in this way without being driven to it.

Later, re-arrested in June 1947 and confined by the Americans in the Labour and Internment Camp at Göggingen, near Augsberg, she came, she says, to understand why Hess refused to receive family visits so long as he was imprisoned. She wrote him on 7 June 1947 from the camp: 'I must admit that now I begin to understand why you always rejected the idea of a visit from us. It is, basically, nothing but a devilish form of torture.'

Hess's letters of advice to her during this period of imprisonment, when her case was handled by Dr Seidl, are interesting for the light they throw on his conception of behaviour while both in prison and on trial; on 4 June 1947, writing from Nuremberg, he said:

> Your arrest is only what I have long expected; and I was fully prepared for it. In fact I am prepared for anything and nothing can surprise me. Nevertheless my feelings when I heard of this were such that I need not and indeed *will* not put them down in writing. But I should like to tell you about my conception of personal honour, as held for many years: the honour of an individual cannot be injured, or even touched, by any acts of expression on the part of another. He who attempts this does an injury to his own honour. Honour can suffer solely as a result of dishonourable conduct on the part of the individual himself. Accordingly, many things that might well get on the nerves of others pass me by.
>
> Since you now find yourself in a situation in which your own acts and all attempts to steer your own course must be confined within very narrow limits, I will again remind you of an idea of which I have often spoken: there are events which take their course upon a level where we cannot exert any influence, or at times when we must be left out because, not being able to anticipate them, we are always too late . . .[2]

And again on 26 June:

> About the conduct of your case: It does not matter in the least by whom you are represented or if anyone represents you, whether you are taken to see Seidl or decide not to see him. Nor will it make any difference what you say or how you say it, whether you fly into a temper, turn sullen, or maintain a silence like that of an Egyptian tomb before it has been opened to enjoy the benefits of our civilization. All the various modes and types of defence matter only so far as the *outside* public is concerned, if they are not too drastically 'cut' in the press, or distorted, like my own final words were before the court, which made me smile when I saw them in print.
>
> Nor will it make the slightest difference if witnesses appear on your behalf and speak with the tongues reputed to be proper to angels. You must remain equally indifferent if witnesses are called

against you to swear to evidence that is pure fiction, as happened in many cases (that can be proved) in the great trial itself. False evidence moreover counts for nothing; it can do no more than impart a more or less decorous appearance to a *show* of justification for the sentence. Even if no false evidence were given, the result would be exactly the same. I tell you all this so that you may be prepared and, when the time comes, be able to take it all with the same sense of humour you showed about the statement by the prosecution. It is your *inward* attitude that will count.

Above all, never forget that I wrote to you about personal honour. You must attain to the point when you can take everything that comes with an inward smile—and then shake it off you with the feeling 'That's that!' The decent people in the outer world (and who else matters?) do not, in spite of all, believe in this nonsense. The others need not bother us; for them a bit more falsification or a little less, and what is the difference? Nothing can stop the victory of truth when the time is ripe.

Concerning the judgment to be expected, for once I do not stand alone. Dr Seidl takes precisely the same view; that you are my wife, that you were one of the earliest Party members, that you held the Golden Badge of Honour, not as an ornament but because you had been a member from the beginning—all that will be quite enough to get you a term in prison no matter how the trial will go, and quite apart from anything to do with your attitude or any statements by the defence. Seidl and myself differ on one point only: he thinks it possible that the sentence may be considered served whilst awaiting trial. However, we shall see what we shall see!

Meanwhile, we may have to go through some more difficult times; but that, too, is part of what fate has in store for us. If in consequence the boy is separated from your influence for a few months, this must not be taken too tragically. He has such good stuff in him that this experience will not decisively influence his future. The grave troubles that have fallen to his lot, also, in his early years, will counteract other influences and tend to the good. This or that tendency which may not be quite what we would like will be ironed out as he grows older. I think I remember writing to you from England about a family I knew who, on principle, left their children to themselves, influencing them as little as possible—even taking little notice of real naughtiness—and the experiment turned out extraordinarily well.

After all, you have laid a sound foundation: seven years, not reckoning the earliest, with *such* a mother. That will yield lasting results—believe me! 〰〰〰.

To sum up: the defence is a matter of indifference. All sorts of incomprehensible charges will be trumped up, and very possibly equally incomprehensible statements will be made by witnesses. The verdict will be detention of some kind. That is not important. The main thing is that you should be prepared from the very beginning to look upon the whole affair as a theatrical performance. Theatre, theatre, nothing but theatre! But *not* with a tragic end.

Their constant concern was for the effect of all this on Buz, though they were satisfied he was taking things well and was being well looked after by the family. Three days before his final transfer to Spandau, Hess wrote to Ilse:

I wish you would contemplate this transfer with a smile, as I do, whenever it may actually take place. I must admit, however, that this is very difficult for you, since your belief in the inevitability of fate is not so absolute and unshakable as mine, and thus your attitude towards the question of my removal must be fundamentally different. But, believe me, neither ministers with special powers, arbitrary judges, nor Allied courts of Russian commissars can make our fate. That belongs solely to ourselves—to accept it for what it is, and through acceptance to shape it.[3]

Spandau prison was only agreed between the Allied Powers as the place of confinement for the seven Nazi leaders after a period of debate. The Americans would have preferred to keep the prisoners in Nuremberg. The British were prepared to have them, if necessary, in their zone. The Russians wanted to confine them in the Ploetzensee prison in Berlin, where many of the officers involved in the attempt on Hitler's life in July 1944 had been cruelly hanged from meat-hooks amid blinding lights with the film-cameras turning. In the end Spandau prison on the Wilhelmstrasse in the British sector of Berlin was chosen. It was designed to hold some 600 prisoners; now it was to be reserved for the seven.

They were removed from Nuremberg shortly after being wakened at 04.00 hours on 18 July 1947. Their few belongings were soon packed in kit-bags. Then, each of them handcuffed to an American military policeman, they were driven in two ambulances under heavy guard to the local airfield, where they were flown to Gatow Airport in the British sector of Berlin. From here they were taken in blacked-out cars to Spandau, where they were received at 11.00 hours.

Spandau is divided into two security sectors, an outer and an inner prison. The outer walls, fifteen feet high, were covered with high-voltage electric wiring which could bring death at a touch. Machine-gun posts disposed around the walls pointed downwards into the courtyard which had access to the inner prison complex with its own security walls. After passing through the administrative area of this inner complex one reaches the inner core of the prison, which includes the Prison Director's office, the Allied conference room and the visitor's room. Steel security doors lead finally to the cell block, with the prison chapel. On the further side of this inner prison complex lies the prison garden, bounded by its own inner walls together with the main outer wall of the prison, with three of the machine-gun posts looking down on the prisoners when they were working in the garden.

On 18 July, the newly arrived prisoners were led through the succession of gates, doors, courtyards and corridors. They were told to strip, and were medically examined by doctors representing each of the four occupying powers. Their persons were also thoroughly searched in case they were concealing any phials of poison. The special wardens, representing in nationality all the four Powers, faced their prisoners for the first time, and the comparatively easy-going life in the American-controlled prison at Nuremberg was replaced by the far stricter regimen of inter-Allied control designed to satisfy the differing conceptions of strictness of the American, British, French and Soviet Prison Directors. They were given their prison numbers—Hess was number seven, the number of his cell.

The regulations were strict. They rose at 06.00 hours, washing (without speaking) two at a time; they breakfasted at 06.45; they cleaned their cells and made their beds at 07.00 hours; at 08.00 they worked on other jobs which were assigned to them, such as general prison cleaning and tending the kitchen garden. At midday they ate again. In the afternoon, after a brief rest, they worked until 16.45 hours. They had their supper at 17.00 hours, and the lights in their cells were extinguished at 22.00 hours. There was a routine security search of each cell twice daily. The prisoners were shaved three times a week, and they bathed initially only once a week.

The cells, newly painted and clean, were only 2·5 by 1·5 metres in size, and contained a simple bed (with bed linen), a small table, a shelf and a wash-basin.[4] The cells were lofty, with an inaccessible barred window high in the outer wall and a light covered by a metal grille in the ceiling. Here they were isolated for more than twelve of the twenty-four hours. They had to maintain a monastic silence, and were only permitted to speak to one or other of the chief warders. The prison warders were international and were not changed, but the guards themselves were changed monthly, each of the four nations in turn taking over control of the prison. Hess wrote his first letter to his wife from Spandau on 3 August 1947:

We are not allowed to send a letter, such as I now send, more than once in twenty-eight days. I realized in Nuremberg that I would not be allowed to go on writing so frequently and looked upon the fact that I was able to do so as signifying some change before long. In this same twenty-eight days we may receive not more than *one* letter, but at present there is no limit as to length. Conditions: it must be written clearly in Latin characters . . . My number is now the lucky seven.

There is a positive side, however: the 'rooms' are newly painted and fresher and cleaner. And just imagine, I have a pillow, one with a pillow-case, and a mattress covered with white linen—the first seen since I left England! Again, I possess a chair and need no longer pretend that the edge of the bed is a sofa. A drawback is that the white linen covering of the mattress means more trouble washing—and we have to do that ourselves. ～～～～.

Yesterday for the first time I was in the line-up for washing, with Doenitz. I imagined myself as Gudrun by the shores of the North Sea, but she, I am sure, breathed an air with more ozone in it. How we scrubbed, soaped, rinsed and wrung out! We did our level best. But I fear that a good housewife would have cast despairing and pitying glances to heaven, to see our methods.

In fact our present profession carries with it all sorts of activities! Our education as market gardeners makes rapid progress. It is voluntary, but we all take part. True, this progress is very irregular because there are so many gaps in our knowledge. With some guidance from the French guard—who presumably retired as a *rentier* at the age of around forty and now potters about in his little plot for the benefit of Madame's kitchen—I am already quite an expert in tomato-growing.[5]

Ilse's reply from her prison camp shows something of the family sense of humour, serious but genuine:

Not only have I got your first letter from Spandau, but also an extremely 'witty' reporter has already written something about your arrival there, saying (which soothed me a good deal) that you were the most cheerful inmate of the new abode besides being the one who wrote 'tender' letters to his wife—adding that you made use of little wavy lines 〜〜〜 to indicate a pause for laughter! 〜〜〜 〜〜〜 〜〜〜. You see this makes me laugh like anything, by post. Who would have thought that the good old Hess 'laughter-line' would attain to fame in the newspapers? Not even in the long years when you were in England, when it proved the cause of two important visits paid to me . . . they felt sure I must be 'up to something 〜〜〜 that I was attempting, impudently, to communicate with you by some secret code or other!

Soon Hess's letters were full of accounts of his gardening activities, growing tomatoes and other vegetables and even tobacco plants, and gathering walnuts in October. The rest of his spare time he spent reading, and his letters contain many points of interest arising from his somewhat heavy reading of such authors as Ranke, Seidel, Kolbenheyer and Goethe. His principle interest appears to have been history, but the prison authorities carefully excluded anything relating to German nationalism or contemporary German history. In November he was delighted to receive from England a consignment of books he had gradually, with the help of the Swiss representative, assembled as his library. About 120 books arrived, and formed the nucleus of the prison library. Gardening, reading, and letters, limited at this stage to one a week, were his only pleasure, now and in the future as far as he could foresee it. Daily newspapers were provided, but Hess at first showed no interest in them, since he held them to be propaganda.

That Christmas Buz was allowed to stay with his mother in her prison camp; Hess wrote to Buz at Christmas:

I am very pleased, Buz, my lad, that you are learning to make all sorts of lovely things with your hands, such as metal-work. Mind you learn all that you possibly can! If you learn as a kind of play, as now with your mother in the camp, so much the better . . . And chess—you want to learn that too! Splendid. But don't forget that you need a bit of brains to do that. I learned when I was twelve, with your Uncle Alfred, then a year younger than you are now . . .

Last night I thought of you a lot, with your picture in front of me; very large and real. And, in my mind, I saw side-by-side with it, amongst other things, your mother's head, her hair light and fair like your own. A few days ago was the twentieth anniversary of our formal engagement—how time slips past![6]

The limitation on letter-writing imposed no strain on Hess; indeed, he had written earlier in the year:

No one understands better than I do that, even were it possible, you would not write every day! Not only would I be unable to do the same, but also I should not feel it really right. Like other things, letters are subject to the law of diminishing value when in large supply. They tend to become mere matter-of-course, no longer anything special, and their contents too largely composed of petty daily affairs.

In January 1948 Ilse Hess writes to say how she had had to steel herself to part with Buz after his long visit to her; she felt life in a women's prison camp was not good for him, young though he was. Everyone spoiled him. In February Hess writes about the newly fallen snow in the garden:

How delighted I always was by newly fallen snow! But to-day? It leaves me indifferent: ground, bushes, branches, trees, walls— all are bedecked with white, but I hardly notice them! Perhaps I do not *want* to see them, because I no longer desire to see beauty and allow my spirit to be moved by it. The protective skin round about my soul grows thicker; it begins to develop the rings of years. *Only those who have lost freedom know what freedom means.*

Then in March Ilse Hess writes to say how she suddenly found herself free after her case was heard on 23 March:

I had no idea that my release would come with lightning speed after this date. It had been the general experience that after the hearing of a case, weeks or even months would pass before release. I never thought that I had been taken into custody as a 'security measure' pending investigation and was not included amongst those classed as AA [automatically arrested]. Through the court of justice in the camp it was possible for my case to be settled quickly once the German officials in control there were in possession of the relevant documents. They were then able to set me free—*without* consulting the Americans. And this they did!

All this happened in exactly twenty-four hours, so that it is only *now* that I am gradually realizing the situation—as you may well imagine . . .

Yes, this phase of my life is over. Don't laugh, but I have a yearning for the camp and my companions there and have to get accustomed to life without that comradeship—in spite of Buz. Naturally, to have him again is so lovely that no words can express what I feel . . .

When in the summer she proposed to visit Hess in prison, he still forbade it:

Before I forget! Let me answer the query about the suggested visit, at once: it is meant, I know, very kindly, but I do not wish to have any visits—whether unimportant or otherwise. I cannot give you all my reasons for this decision, and some of them have already been given . . .

Schirach has told us he tried to persuade Hess to break this rule, and Hess indeed much later showed some signs of doing so, at the time his son was taking his final examinations in engineering. Speer, on the other hand, gave as his opinion that Hess, though appearing stubborn, was possibly right.[7] He had found the officially permitted monthly visits a terrible emotional strain. The only visitor Hess received before 1969 was his lawyer, Dr Seidl. Even then, if their business only occupied part of the allotted time (half an hour), he would dismiss him rather than talk for the sake of doing so.

The information given us by Speer and Schirach revealed that the conditions were, initially at least, very severe, more especially during the month the Russians took over guard duty.[8] The interpretation of the rules gradually slackened, in the case of the Russians to a minor extent after the death of Stalin in 1953. In the early days, if they undertook any kind of handywork it was destroyed at the end of the day in their presence. Some of them made paper-bags during working hours, and even these were formally destroyed. Schirach enjoyed producing floral designs, and these had to be burnt. The only creative work permitted was gardening, and this (rather than more prison cleaning) soon became the prisoners' principal daytime activity when the weather allowed it. Each had their individually allocated space; Speer's garden was, he says, about one-hundred metres by fifty. He would spend five hours a day on this allotment. According to Hess, the soil was poor, like sand.

The food, says Speer, was reasonable, changing somewhat with the nation in charge. The British might give them kippers for breakfast, the Russians *Kvas*. As time went on, relations with the guards eased, and communication between the prisoners themselves increased. They first began to break regulations by talking during washing and bathing periods. Later they were able to talk in the garden. But relations between them always remained distant, and they would address each other by their former titles. Speer himself took to writing, and his memoirs were largely written in prison.[9] The periods devoted to reading increased, and Raeder during his confinement in Spandau acted as librarian, issuing the books with all the exactitude of a clerk in a public library.

In their account of Hess himself, both Schirach and Speer affirm that he continued to be a troublesome prisoner. He would cry out in the night for the warders to fetch the doctor on account of his stomach pains, waking the others with his shouting and cries of pain. Schirach felt some of this, at least, was assumed for the purpose of giving his captors trouble. But some of it, also, was without doubt genuine, as perhaps were his continued suspicions that the food was poisoned. Hess appeared very conscious of his senior 'position' among the prisoners, rather like Göring during the Trial at Nuremberg. Schirach's word for Hess's attitude in the prison was 'oysterization'. If he were asked questions he did not want to answer, he would absent himself and retire into his shell. When the later trials began in Germany at the turn of the 1950s and 1960s, while the others would discuss the 'revelations' which the evidence reported at length in the press uncovered, Hess would refuse to read it. 'I don't want to hear anything about it. I can't talk about that,' he would say. At Christmas they were permitted to eat together; once, however, Schirach remembers Hess rising brusquely in the middle of the meal and taking his plate with its portion of turkey away to his cell. As he wrote to his mother, 'I learned to ponder over problems more than I had ever done before, and a great peace filled my heart. Now I am able to understand men who feel impelled to withdraw into complete loneliness, to become hermits.'

Hess was practising being a stoic. 'I am a stoic in the first place,' he wrote in November 1947 to Ilse. Two months later he calls himself an 'intelligent pessimist', who 'in the really big things' is also a ' "crazy" unshakable optimist'. Later in 1948 he discovered Sir Thomas More, whom he regarded as 'a truly outstanding spirit, far ahead of his times'. It is strange that, what with reading and gardening, the years of confinement did not lag for him. 'Time flies so quickly,' he wrote to his mother.

The prisoners were allowed to keep family photographs in their cells. Hess wrote to his wife on 8 May 1949 about Buz:

> Of the photos, I like best the one in which Buz looks keenly into the distance, presumably watching the ski-ing. Yet I don't know *what* he really looks like: less so, the more pictures I see of him. He looks different in each, according to the light, his mood and which way he's looking. Probably he has a very changeable appearance and this is not only due to the photos; his age—entering upon the teens —is one of change. His spelling, however, never changes; it is always perfectly frightful.[10]

What Hess appears to have feared most now was emotion, and a hint of this is given in a later part of this same letter:

> At this very moment I hear Funk—that unique East Prussian character—playing variations on *Alle Tage ist kein Sonntag* on the chapel harmonium . . . Oh! how well I can sympathize with you, when you feel the tears welling up in the presence of absolute beauty, whether you wish it or not, and when even silly little scraps of popular melodies, or perhaps a flower may give rise to the same astonishing reaction. If I could have my wish, the harmonium would be used for firewood, and the sweet smelling lilac bushes, now in full flower, would be cut to the ground!

Earlier, during the spring, he had written to her:

> I detest lilac and all lovely things, as long as I find myself closed in by walls and bars. How strange a thing is freedom. Never again will I shut a bird up in a cage. And now I understand so well why the Chinese and Japanese, when they wish to show gratitude for good fortune, go to the market, buy cage-birds and let them loose. I will do this, too, one day . . .

Ilse Hess was having her difficulties. On her release, her resources were very meagre, and she had to earn what money she could. Eventually, in 1900, she was offered the chance to become the proprietor of a guest-house, Die Bergherberge, in the Hindelang Mountains of Bavaria. A room here with the mountain view he used to love waits for her husband, if and when he is ever released.

During the 1950s certain of the prisoners in Spandau were released;

some, indeed, had their sentences remitted. Neurath was the first to go in 1954; his health was poor, and after serving seven of his fifteen years' sentence he was allowed to leave. Raeder was even more fortunate. He was released in 1955; he was seventy-nine and his health, too, was bad; his sentence of life imprisonment was therefore remitted. Doenitz was only due to serve a ten-year sentence, and he was released in 1956. The following year Funk was freed, his life sentence remitted after he had been at Spandau for eleven years. Speer and Schirach (both due for release in 1966) remained to keep Hess company, but they could look forward to their future freedom while still young enough to enjoy it. Only Hess was left with no hope whatever of the remission of his sentence. In all the cases, except that of Hess, there was general agreement among the four occupying Powers.

Hess, indeed, was to suffer primarily for the high position he had held in the Third Reich. Largely because of this he was regarded by the Russians as deserving the death penalty. The fact that he had received only life imprisonment meant that the Soviet authorities refused to remit his sentence.

The first appeal to the Allied Control Commission was made by Dr Seidl in 1947.[11] The appeal was lodged broadly on the grounds of his poor health, and for humanitarian reasons. The Soviet authorities were mainly responsible for vetoing this early appeal, although Hess had already been in one form of captivity or another for six years. A second appeal addressed to UNO in 1956 met with no success, after Hess had been in confinement for fifteen years. A third appeal in 1957, addressed this time to the European Commission for Human Rights in Strasbourg, was equally unsuccessful, although by then Raeder and Funk, both of whom had been sentenced to life imprisonment, had been released with the consent of the Russians.

The climax of this series of appeals came in 1966, the year of the release of both Speer and Schirach. Once they had gone, Spandau was being maintained as a massive gaol solely to house one solitary man over seventy years of age. The basic annual costs are estimated at 800,000 West German marks (paid by the city of Berlin and the Federal Government), let alone the costs in wasted manpower to the four occupying powers in the provision of prison staff and a unit of guards.[12]

It had been apparent, however, for long enough that Spandau and its prisoners had a symbolic, political significance. It is situated in the western sector of the city, and it gives the Russians from the eastern sector a rightful foothold in the west of which they take sole charge for one month three times a year. Spandau enjoys a status which is almost the equivalent of diplomatic territory, and meetings concerning the conduct of the prison form a useful point of regular contact. The Allies of a quarter of a century ago, after all, have never yet signed their collective peace-treaty with Germany. Secondly, Hess is the last prisoner to be held captive jointly by the Allies who fought the war against Hitler side by side; he is therefore the last prisoner left to represent their joint defeat of Nazism. As Hitler's Deputy he symbolizes the final shadow of the régime on a level far above any of the other former prisoners now released from Spandau. His mission to Britain, which can be given a favourable slant by those who wish to do so, can scarcely appear in the same light to Soviet officials, since Hess was seeking to break up the Allied partnership and bring Britain into the war on the German side against the Soviet Union. They insist Hitler's Deputy must have known about the imminent attack his Führer was to make upon their country. So Hess remained confined still in 1971, at the age of 77, not so much for being a war criminal, but because he is a political figure, and a confirmed anti-Communist. Men who have committed far worse crimes against humanity than he was ever party to have been set free long ago by the individual Allied authorities, as well as by the Russians and by the Germans themselves. But they were men without the special status which belongs to Hitler's Deputy.

On 18 May 1966, Dr Seidl delivered a fourth petition for Hess's release, and addressed it this time jointly to HM Queen Elizabeth of England, the Presidents of the United States and France, and the Chairman of the Soviet Government. It is a document of some 6,000 words. In a preamble, Dr Seidl pointed out in Hess's favour that he was found guilty only under Counts One and Two (preparing a war of aggression) and cleared on Counts Three and Four (war crimes and crimes against humanity). He then went on to claim that the judgment pronounced on Hess was contrary to the principles of Human Rights and Fundamental Freedoms agreed and signed in 1950 at the Convention of the Council of Europe, as well as the principles in the Universal Declaration of Human Rights proclaimed earlier by the United Nations in 1948; more especially the judgment violated the principle of Nulla Poena Sine Lege, that is, the principle that no one should be punished for an alleged offence which at the time it was committed did not constitute a criminal offence under national or international law. He quoted at length Dr Jahrreis's attack on the validity of the trial in this respect, which he had put forward in his speech before the Tribunal on

4 July 1946.[13] In other words, the principal crime for which Hess was judged guilty was the one which the Tribunal had least legal precedent for asserting to be a crime at all—'Sentences against individuals for breach of the peace between states would be something completely new under the aspect of law' (Dr Jahrreis). 'In the unanimous opinion of all distinguished scholars of international law, there did not exist at the time war broke out any principle of general international law under which ministers, commanders-in-chief of armed forces or industrialists could be tried or punished in person under penal law for their participation in the preparations for a war of aggression or for a war in violation of international treaties' (Dr Seidl). A further point in law was that the judges were appointed to the Tribunal only by states which belonged to one of the two sides in the dispute behind the second world war; thus those who created the Charter of the trial, who appointed the prosecutors and also the judges themselves, belonged to the single, victorious side in the war. Dr Seidl then returned to the point of attack which he had tried so hard to establish at the trial, namely the secret terms of the non-aggression pact between Germany and the Soviet Union which, he maintained, made the latter equally guilty with Germany of aggression against Poland—so that the Russian judge was in Dr Seidl's view sitting in judgment on his own nation's case. He then quoted at length from an article in the London *Economist* supporting the view that 'the Nuremberg Trial is only within certain limits an independent judiciary.' Coming to more recent history, Dr Seidl declared that Britain and France at the time of Suez and the United States later in Vietnam were themselves participants in what were technically wars of aggression. Hess, therefore, is being unjustly detained not only in law, but because the nations who set themselves up in judgment upon him and are still his jailers have themselves committed the very crime for which they keep him imprisoned. Finally, he put up the plea of Hess's mental condition, claiming that he was unfit to be detained—'There can be no doubt that Rudolf Hess is suffering from mental illness, namely latent schizophrenia.' He cites a report of Professor Maurice N. Walsh who examined Hess at Spandau in 1948. In conclusion, he adds: 'As the Allied Control Council for Germany and the Allied Kommandatura, Berlin, have been dissolved, and as twenty-one years have passed since the end of the second world war, the victorious powers can, as it is, no longer justify, even on political grounds, continuing the joint administration of a prison at Spandau, Berlin, in the heart of Germany.'

This elaborately argued appeal met with no response whatsoever.

By now, however, it was realized that, left to themselves, the American, British and French governments would have collectively ordered the release of Hess and the abandonment of Spandau some years before. It had always been the Soviet government which had used its right of veto in the matter.

In November 1966, Dr Seidl tried to get certain of the conditions of Hess's imprisonment improved. On 3 November he wrote asking that censorship of the books Hess was allowed to read should cease, that he should be permitted to have a watch (none of the prisoners had ever been allowed to possess one), that he should be allowed to spend longer in the garden than the regulation half hour for exercise and read or write there, that he might be able to see his lawyer once every three months without special permission, that he be permitted an electric bell in his cell, so that he could summon a guard in the case of sudden illness, and given the facilities to make a cup of tea or coffee for himself, that (as a non-smoker) he could have some confectionery to eat, and some latitude in reading-times at night (since he had to give up his spectacles at 22.00 hours when the lights were due to go out, whether he wanted to go on reading or not). He also wanted the right to a daily, not a weekly bath. The last request was granted, but no other changes were made by the authorities to ease the regulations.

Following the failure of these official approaches, a lobby dedicated to campaign for Hess's release was formed both inside and outside Germany. In 1967 an organization known as 'Freedom for Rudolf Hess' was founded in Germany, and collected some 800 signatures from notable people supporting their campaign. In June of the same year, Hess's son, Wolf Rüdiger Hess, then aged twenty-nine and a civil engineer, came to Britain to start campaigning for his father's release. He visited the area in Scotland where his father had landed in 1941.[14] On 30 September 1968 he held a press conference in Berlin at which the French writer, Michel Vercel, reported that he had seen the statutes of the Spandau prison administration, and that, according to these, any one of the four powers had the right to withdraw from the four-power administration of the prison. In his opinion, if one of the powers retracted, Hess would have to be returned to the state which originally placed him under arrest. Since this would be Britain, he could then be released.

In the United States during 1968 a significant exchange of letters took place between Julius Epstein, a research associate at the Hoover Institution at Stanford University, California, and an official Russian spokesman.[15] Dr Epstein's original letter, dated 29 October 1968, was addressed to Chairman Alexei Kosygin:

Dear Mr Kosygin:

I am writing to you in behalf of Rudolf Hess, the last and only prisoner in Spandau.

The Governments of the United States, Great Britain and France have repeatedly demanded his release. The Government of the Soviet Union is the only obstacle to this humanitarian act. Why? The Soviet Government has never publicly stated its reasons for insisting that Rudolf Hess should die in Spandau.

As you know the International Military Tribunal at Nuremberg had acquitted Rudolf Hess of war crimes and crimes against humanity. He was sentenced to a life term of imprisonment for the preparation and carrying out of 'aggressive war'.

Rudolf Hess is seventy-four years old. He has been a prisoner for twenty-eight years!

Innumerable people have publicly declared that Rudolf Hess should no longer be kept in prison. This opinion is in accordance with 'socialist' as well as 'non-socialist' humanitarianism.

Among those advocating his release were Sir Winston Churchill and Hess's prosecutor at Nuremberg, Sir Hartley Shawcross.

To mention just a few of the illustrious people who want Hess released, I mention the following: Professor Hahn, Professor Hensenberg, Martin Niemoeller, André François-Poncet, Sefton Delmer, Jean Anouilh, Bishop Lilje, Ernst Juenger, Francis Noel Baker, Lord Robertson of Oakridge (House of Lords, England), Lord Russell of Liverpool (House of Lords, England), Bishop of Woolwich, England, Archduke Otto von Hapsburg.

These are just a few of the 800 people of all creeds and political standing who have signed a public appeal for the release of Rudolf Hess.

1968 has been declared by the United Nations as 'Human Rights Year!'

May I respectfully suggest, Sir, that you reconsider the Soviet Government's point of view in the light of true humanism?

The reply to this letter finally came from the Russian Embassy in Washington on 17 February 1969. It read:

In connection with your letter of October 29, 1968 in which you

G

raised the question of the prosecution of nazi war criminals I was asked to inform you of the Soviet position on the inapplicability of the term of prescription to nazi criminals.

Our position is determined by the standards of international law as they were stated in the Charter of the International Military Tribunals and in the process of the Nuremberg Trial and were approved by the UN General Assembly resolutions of February 13 and December 11, 1946.

In its statement of December 24, 1964 the Soviet Government pointed out that the FRG being one of the successors of the former Hitler Reich, is legally responsible to punish every war criminal. And nobody can free the FRG from this responsibility. The nazi criminals who plunged mankind into the catastrophe of World War II and spilled a sea of man's blood must not be given a chance to evade justice.

On November 26, 1968 the UN General Assembly approved the text of the Convention regarding the inapplicability of the term of prescription to war crimes and crimes against mankind. This decision has a great preventive meaning and it was fully supported by the Soviet Government.

Yours sincerely,

Alexander Evstafiev,
Press Counselor

In a number of articles,[16] Dr Epstein has alleged that Dr Rees was asked to falsify his official report on Hess by British Prime Minister Winston Churchill; he was in fact certain at the time that Hess was a schizophrenic and insane. Dr Epstein also claims that the American psychiatrist Dr Maurice Walsh in 1948 was ordered to falsify his report to the Berlin Four-Power Commission by the surgeon of the American garrison in Berlin, Colonel Chamberlain. Dr Epstein continues in one of his articles:

> The reason behind Churchill's order to suppress the medical report was that he did not want to repatriate Hess to Nazi Germany. He wanted to keep him in England, so he could be tried after the war as a war criminal.
>
> American Colonel Chamberlain did not want to contradict or embarrass the Soviets who insisted that Hess was sane and should serve his whole lifetime sentence in Spandau.

Assuming these diagnoses are correct, the incarceration of Hess is a violation of Western law and civilized tradition. It is also a violation of Soviet law.

Even if Hess should be sane as most people believe, especially on the basis of his published letters to his wife, he should now be released.

In another article, Dr Epstein adds a further and more humane reason for Churchill's suppression of the medical report. This was that if Hess had been repatriated on the grounds of his mental condition, Hitler might have executed him.

In Britain there have been many supporters for the release of Hess,[17] including Sir Hartley Shawcross (now Lord Shawcross) the Chief British Prosecutor at Nuremberg, and, even more significantly, Lord Justice Lawrence (later Lord Trevethin and Oaksey), President of the International Military Tribunal. Lord Oaksey wrote to Hess's son, Wolf Rüdiger Hess, on 8 January 1968:

'I have on several occasions expressed my opinion that Rudolf Hess has suffered enough and should now be released. I will once more express these feelings to the appropriate authorities and hope very much that it may be of some avail.'

The climax of the campaign in Britain, however, was to come at the close of 1969. On 24 November Hess's condition worsened, and he was removed from Spandau to the British Military Hospital in West Berlin, where he was guarded by four warders (Russian, American, British, French) and a British Army guard of six men. He was now seventy-five years old. Herr Willy Brandt, the West German Chancellor, promised to intercede with the Russians so that Hess might be permanently released from Spandau. At the same time, Hess, now he was out of prison, at last agreed just before Christmas to see his family.

Wolf Rüdiger Hess, then aged thirty-two, and his mother, aged sixty-nine, visited on Christmas Eve the man neither had seen since 1941. The visit was limited to half an hour, in spite of Herr Hess's request that it be increased to an hour. He and his mother were also required to sign a declaration, which Herr Hess regarded as 'nearly unacceptable', forbidding them to comment on Hess's health, or give any account of what transpired during the visit. Other restrictions included any attempt even to shake him by the hand. Both were deeply upset, especially as the meeting had to take place in the presence of the directors belonging to all four nations controlling the prison. Afterwards, Wolf Rüdiger Hess said, 'The reunion was unnerving. For me it was practically becoming acquainted with my father. My mother was also shocked.' Frau Hess is reported as saying, 'I think perhaps after all my husband was right. It might have been better not to have gone to see him.'[18] Their request that Hess's stomach ulcers be examined by a distinguished German specialist, Professor Rudolf Zenker, was again rejected.

The tragic sarabande of protocol meant that no one of the Four-Power officials dared to act without the consent of the others, with the Russians calling the tune. In the United States, three eminent American criminal lawyers issued a statement that the continuation of Hess's imprisonment beyond twenty years contradicted western jurisprudence and the principles of human rights. In Britain, the floodgates of comment opened up after Christmas 1969 when the news of the conditions in which the family reunion took place were reported in the press. Feature articles and editorials began to appear in such newspapers as *The Daily Telegraph*, *The Daily Express*, and *The Times*. Letters of protest appeared in *The Times*, and on 31 December, Mr Airey Neave, now a Conservative Member of Parliament, headed a campaign once again to free Hess from Spandau. Mr Neave, of course, had first met Hess when he had served the indictment upon him in advance of the Nuremberg Trial, and had acted as his adviser whilst he was preparing himself to face it.[19]

At Spandau, the Russian governor insisted that the monthly changing of the guard should continue in Hess's absence, and that even the watch-towers of the empty prison be manned. The Americans moved out at the end of December, relieved by a British officer and twenty-four men of the Royal Regiment of Fusiliers, who, protocol demanded, should continue to examine the empty cells and empty corridors as if there were prisoners present. Mr Neave called this, 'the great Spandau madness'.

On 2 January a further letter by Lord Shawcross was published in *The Times*. It read:

> I have, on other occasions, given my personal opinion (for as Chief Prosecutor for the United Kingdom at the Nuremberg Trial of the major war criminals, I have long since been functus officio) that the continued imprisonment of Rudolf Hess serves no useful purpose whatever.
>
> His life sentence by the International Military Tribunal at Nuremberg was, in comparison with others, by no means a lenient

one. I suspect that all of us on the Western side took it for granted that it would be subject to the sort of commutation recognized in civilized systems of criminal justice and would not literally be for life.

That he should continue to be imprisoned now seems to me to be an affront to all notions of justice and (if this indeed be the fact) that the British authorities in whose hospital Hess now is should accept a Soviet veto on operative procedures which the medical specialists of the United States, France and Britain consider to be necessary in order to safeguard his health is an instance of pusillanimity of a degree to which I had hoped the United Kingdom had not yet fallen in international affairs. I shall say nothing of humanity. Although I still believe that the merciful are blessed.

On 4 January 1970, the diplomatic correspondent of *The Sunday Times*, Nicholas Carroll, commented on the situation in an article headed 'Blockade Fear Keeps Hess in Jail'. He wrote:

It is assumed by the Western Powers that Russia's instant response to a breach of the Four-Power agreements over Spandau affecting Hess would be their withdrawal from the air safety centre . . . Soviet motives in keeping Hess shut up alone in the huge 600-cell Spandau prison are essentially political . . . But Russia is determined to maintain her presence in West Berlin by prolonging the four-party status of Spandau to its full limit. This, in crude terms, could mean Hess's death.

An article by Ian Pocock appeared in the London *Evening Standard* the following day emphasizing the same points in greater technical detail. Since the Russians left the Allied Control Council in 1948, the only two official points of contact left between them and the Western Powers in Berlin concerned Spandau and the vital Air Safety Corridor in which all four nations collaborate in air traffic control over the Berlin area. The changing of the guard at Spandau gives a regular opportunity for informal meals and talks together. *The Daily Express*, in particular, took up the case for Hess's release in editorials on both 4 and 8 January.

Wolf Rüdiger Hess came to Britain again and met Mr Airey Neave on 4 January. They discussed not only the best way to achieve Hess's release but, more immediately, to ease the regulations which restricted his meetings with his family now he was, temporarily at least, away from Spandau. January was the month the British were in charge at Spandau, and because of this Herr Hess felt action could best be taken immediately. Mr Neave agreed to try to press the British Government to take unilateral action and release Hess now he was in their hands and out of prison.

It soon became plain, however, that Britain was not prepared to release Hess without Russian consent for fear it might upset the delicate 'balance of power' in Berlin. The price would be too great for too many people. Herr Hess and Mr Neave spent an hour at the Foreign Office discussing the matter with Mr George Thomson, Chancellor of the Duchy of Lancaster. All that could be promised was that the British, along with the Americans and the French, would continue to press Russia to consent to Hess's release. The last formal request had been made in May 1969. Herr Hess did not even know whether his father was aware of the efforts being made on his behalf—all references to his case in the press are blacked out by the prison censor before he is allowed to see them, and father and son are not allowed to speak of such 'political' matters when they meet. On 6 January, *The Daily Express* published a feature article by Wolf Rüdiger Hess in which he wrote:

> I have had considerable help in my efforts and 100,000 people from all over the world have signed a petition supporting his release . . . I believe there are prominent Russians who have second thoughts, but I suppose there must be considerable problems for them in changing protocol.
>
> Now that my father is in hospital and there is cause for grave concern about his health, I believe he should be released on medical grounds immediately . . . In these circumstances I hope that the British Government will not accept a situation that would offend the conscience of the British people.

On 8 January the British press quoted from an article on Hess which had appeared the day before in *Pravda*, outlet for the Russian viewpoint. The article was quoted as referring to the campaign for Hess's release as a:

> . . . cunning propaganda move by forces which would like to perpetuate racism, Nazism and apartheid, turn back the course of history, disarm the peoples morally and dissipate their watchfulness against the intrigues of the forces of aggression and war . . . Why are bourgeois ideologists cynically speculating on people's humane sentiments and coming out zealously in defence of 'shades of the

past' like Hess ? . . . Imperialism is merciful . . . to criminals, be they fascists or racists, because its own policy of international brigandage and aggression, neo-colonialism and racial intolerance is itself criminal.

Herr Hess, who had returned to Germany, commented that he thought such a statement from Russia made it plain that the western allies should agree to release his father, 'despite Russian objections'.

The centre of discussion in the British press moved over to *The Guardian*. After some correspondence in favour of Hess's release, Terence Prittie, *The Guardian*'s diplomatic correspondent and author of an excellent book on the German resistance, *Germans against Hitler*, wrote an article which *The Guardian* published. Although in favour of the release, Mr Prittie declared this should not be undertaken without full Russian consent, since it might jeopardize the position of the millions of West Berliners. The article, which contained certain errors of historical fact, emphasized Hess's responsibility up to 1941 for all that the régime represented, and laid particular stress on Frau Hess's involvement in Nazism in the early days and her post-war publications which, he claimed, still favoured Nazism. Herr Hess was quick to reply to this, in a letter published in *The Guardian* on 5 February. He pointed out the errors of fact in Terence Prittie's article, and replied to the allegations against his mother. Terence Prittie qualified his argument to some extent in a letter published on 12 February, and asserted again that he believed Hess should be released.

Meanwhile on 2 February questions were put in the House of Commons to Mr Thomson, who was shortly to visit Germany, and a motion was tabled calling for the release of Hess on compassionate grounds. There was all-party support for the motion, which finally gained more than four-hundred signatures. Mr Neave made his own position quite clear when he stated publicly:

He was a leading Nazi and responsible for setting up the Nazi régime of repression in Germany and Austria, and also for the so-called Nuremberg laws restricting the rights of Jews. For this, in my opinion, he deserved the sentence he received . . .

But when the sentence was announced I think the three western powers had in mind a review of the sentence after some years. On the other hand, we have to remember that there are many countries where a life sentence means 'life' and the Russians look at it in that light.

On 13 March it was announced in the press that Hess had been returned to Spandau, with a slight easing of his living conditions. Editorials protesting against his return appeared in a number of British newspapers, including *The Guardian* and *The Daily Express* (on both 14 and 25 March). On 26 March Lord Chalfont, Minister of State at the Foreign Office, stated in the House of Lords that an appeal had been made to the Russians by the British Ambassador in Moscow. Lord Chalfont added that 'it would be fruitless to engage in a new appeal which would clearly meet the fate of all previous ones.' He explained that to release Hess unilaterally, without Russian consent, 'would mean breaking solemn international obligations, and we would not contemplate this.'[20] The doctors of the four Powers had agreed he would be better placed to recover in Spandau during his convalescence than in the British military hospital. The House of Lords were united in their opinion that Hess should be freed, and Lord Chalfont agreed that the Government 'would continue to seek his release.' The fact that four military contingents continued to guard in turn one sick old man, was referred to by Lord Amory as a 'ridiculous ritual'. When on 24 April, the eve of Hess's seventy-sixth birthday, Ilse Hess and her son visited him for the first time in Spandau, the guards refused to let them leave him a bunch of flowers. All she could give him was a book and a gramophone record. He was not allowed to give her any gift in return. The meeting took place in the presence of the four Wardens representing the four Powers.

In May 1971 the British Foreign Secretary made a further request for Hess's release to the Soviet Foreign Minister, while Mr Neave proposed a compromise scheme to secure Hess's periodic release to stay with his family during the months the Western Allies controlled Spandau.

Hess lives now as the sole inhabitant of the cell block which once housed the other six prisoners of Spandau. He has been given the former chapel in the block, consisting of two cells opened up to make a single, small room, and he is permitted to have the door open. He reads his four daily newspapers, with any political news thought unsuitable for him still blacked out. He shaves himself with an electric razor, and he is allowed to make coffee when he likes, using an electric water-heater. He listens to classical music on his record-player, and visits the prison garden, where he is allowed to feed the birds with bread-crumbs. And he waits for the visits of his wife, now aged seventy, and his son, with both of whom he maintains such correspondence as he may.

NOTES AND BIBLIOGRAPHY

NOTES

The primary published sources on which we have drawn include the past biographies of Hess, especially *The Uninvited Envoy* by James Leasor (1962), which contains much useful evidence, and *The Case of Rudolf Hess*, by J. R. Rees (1947), which presents the medical evidence resulting from the prolonged study of Hess by international teams of doctors and psychiatrists. We have also drawn continually on the transcript of the Trial of the Major War Criminals in Nuremberg; the edition of the latter referred to below as IMT is that published by HMSO in London in twenty-two volumes. We have also drawn extensively on the German edition, published in Nuremberg: and on the American edition *Nazi Conspiracy and Aggression*, referred to in this book as NCA for documents used in evidence at the trial.

We have expressed our gratitude elsewhere to Frau Ilse Hess and to Wolf Rüdiger Hess for tirelessly answering our enquiries, and for their permission to draw freely upon the published letters of Rudolf Hess, written while in captivity in England and Germany, the English translation of which appeared under the title *Prisoner of Peace* (1954), edited by George Pile. We have also been permitted to draw on certain unpublished letters.

Throughout this book we have drawn on material held in the German Federal Archives in Koblenz (referred to below as Koblenz) and the Institut für Zeitgeschichte in Munich (referred to as Munich), as well as in the Wiener Library in London.

In these Notes, the authors are referred to individually by their initials, R.M. and H.F.

CHAPTER I: *Hitler's Shadow*

1. Hess's grandfather, Christian Hess, was born in Wunsiedel, Northern Bavaria, in 1836. He left home in 1849, crossing the Alps by coach, staying with relatives in Livorno, and then taking a job with the Swiss merchant, Johannes Bühler in Trieste. He married one of Bühler's daughters in 1862. In 1865 he founded his own business in Alexandria, the export-import firm of Hess, later to be managed by his sons, Fritz and Adolf. Friedrich (Fritz), Rudolf Hess's father, returned to Germany to find himself a wife, and so married Clara Muench.

2. There were only three children. Rees, op. cit., states there were four, two of them girls. This is followed by J. Bernard Hutton in *Hess: the Man and his Mission*. Other branches of the family lived in Trieste and in Switzerland. The Hess family in Alexandria went on frequent excursions to Germany by sea via the Mediterranean.

3. See *Prisoner of Peace*, pp. 132, 145-46.

4. See *Prisoner of Peace*, p. 132.

5. The official file of Hess's war record (1916-18) is preserved at Koblenz.

6. In *Der Fuehrer* (1944), p. 68, Konrad Heiden claims that on one occasion 'they looked one another in the eye' in Lieutenant-Colonel Tubeuf's presence.

7. In a letter written from Spandau prison to his brother Alfred, Hess admits that his study of economics was undertaken only after pressure from his father. Writing on 24.11.54, he said, 'But for that I would never have thought of economics but am now glad of it. As for father, it was sad for him . . . since neither of his sons showed any inclination to follow in his footsteps.'

8. See Koblenz file NS 26/707 for correspondence referring to Hess's Freikorps activities. Ex-soldiers were excused qualifying entry examinations for the German universities after the war.

9. The Thule Society, in which Alfred Rosenberg was a strong influence. *The Protocols of the Elders of Zion* had recently appeared in German, and excited wide speculation as to Jewish aspirations for world domination. The Thule Society was disguised as a body founded for the study of German antiquity.

10. Heiden, op. cit., p. 110.

11. Hess joined the Party in 1920; though various other dates, some as late as 1923, have been given elsewhere.

12. See *Göring*, Manvell and Fraenkel, p. 25. See also Rees, *The Case of Rudolf Hess*, p. 10 for a reference to Hess's own testimony to the effect of Hitler's speeches upon him.

13. Heiden, op. cit., pp. 84-85. In another passage in his essay Hess effectively describes Hitler without giving his name: '. . . the power of his speech leads the workers to ruthless nationalism, destroying the international-socialist-marxist ideology. In its place he puts national-social [*national-sozialen*] thought . . . the commonweal to come before personal interests; first the nation, then the individual.'

14. The letter has been preserved in the files of the Bavarian Government, and is quoted in *Die Hitler-Bewegung—der Ursprung 1919-22* by G. F. Willing, Hamburg, 1962, p. 208.

15. See *Mein Kampf*, English edition of 1939, London, p. 417. Emile Maurice was later to become Hitler's chauffeur.

16. Lüdecke, *I Knew Hitler*, p. 58.

17. According to Bullock, *Hitler*, 1964 edition, p. 106, Hitler was in the hall all the time; according to Heiden, Hitler came in with Göring and Hess. See also *Der Hitler-Prozess*, Munich, 1924. The story is also told in the form of a novel by Richard Hughes (*The Fox in the Attic*, 1961).

18. See also Hanfstaengl: *The Missing Years*, p. 114: 'He and Hess had not so much cells as a small suite of rooms forming an apartment. The place looked like a delicatessen store. You could have opened up a flower and fruit and a wine shop with all the stuff stacked there.' He adds that Hitler refused to take any part in the prison sport and exercises because 'a leader cannot afford to be beaten at games.' He also claims that during

the composition of *Mein Kampf* Hess soon ousted Emile Maurice as Hitler's secretary, 'picking out the pages on a decrepit Remington type-writer.' (See Note 21 below.) 'What really worried me was the way in which Hess had succeeded in pumping his head full of the Haushofer thesis of getting the Russians to be knocked out a second time by the Japanese, who were Germany's only possible ally in the world, and so on. America had simply been banished from his mind. He . . . merely regarded America as part of the Jewish problem.' For Ilse's weekly visits, see *Prisoner of Peace*, p. 122. Writing from Spandau in 1949, Hess said of Landsberg and its director: 'I know that the director "Mufti" did not appeal to you, with his cool and unsympathetic ways, when you had to go to him for your "ticket of admission" on your weekly visits to the prison. . . . What would I not give today for another "Mufti" '. For Professor Haushofer's visits, see a letter by his son quoted in Rainer Hildebrandt's *Wir Sind die Letzten*, p. 35: 'Father went to see Hess only. He did not really like Hitler . . ., but he brought Hess books which Hitler wanted, such as Ribaut, Ranke's *German History*, Le Bon's *Psychology of the Masses*, etc. Father did not know at the time that this helped Hitler in writing his egocentric *Mein Kampf.'*

19. Lüdecke, op. cit., pp. 215-16.

20. Heiden claims, op. cit., p. 169, that Hitler began the actual manu-script of *Mein Kampf* in 1922.

21. The origin of the story that Hess took dictation from Hitler probably originates from Otto Strasser's *Hitler and I* (translation, 1940), p. 68. 'In July he started dictating to Rudolf Hess . . . Hess was completely and utterly devoted to him.' Heiden followed this, and so later did Bullock in his *Hitler*, and then others. Heiden maintains the dictation went on after Hitler's and Hess's release, at Berchtesgaden, and that Geli Raubal, Hitler's neice, also helped. See Heiden, op. cit., p. 226. We are assured by Wolf Rüdiger Hess that his father neither took dictation of the script nor typed it, but that he helped considerably at the proof stage.

22. See Rees, *The Case of Rudolf Hess*, p. 10. The quotation which follows from Hanfstaengl, op. cit., comes on page 115.

23. The letter is preserved at Koblenz. H.F. received confirmation of this contact between Heim and Hess at a personal meeting with Heim.

24. See Leasor, op. cit., p. 43. Haushofer was to remain a lifelong champion of Germany's friendship with Japan; he regarded the Japanese as the Asian equivalent of the Prussians. Haushofer was also an admirer of Kitchener, whom he had met in India, and whose biography he had written.

25. Heiden, op. cit., p. 254.

26. See Manvell and Fraenkel, *Himmler*, pp. 20-22.

27. Hans-Adolf Jacobson in *Nationalsozialistische Aussenpolitik 1933-38*, p. 3, refers to a letter written by Hess and preserved in Munich (PS-3753) in which Hess, writing on 8.12.28, echoes Hitler in stating it would take a long and enervating struggle to create the conditions required for the 'expansion by conquest' required to safeguard the life of the nation.

28. Heiden, op. cit., pp. 285-86. Hanfstaengl's suggestion in *The*

Missing Years, pp. 123-24, that there was some kind of latent homosexual attraction between Hitler and Hess can, we are sure, be completely discounted.

29. An entertaining letter from Hess to the Reichsleitung NSDAP is preserved at Koblenz; it is dated 20.9.29, and complains bitterly of lack of co-operation and efficiency on the part of Hitler's favourite photographer, Heinrich Hoffmann, who had failed to deliver in good time for publicity in the Italian press certain important photographs he took at the Nuremberg Party rally earlier that month.

30. Koblenz, Haushofer file 253/56 HC 937 E.

31. The letters are preserved by Ilse Hess.

32. See *The Early Goebbels Diaries*, pp. 77-78, 102 et seq.

33. In conversation with H.F., Hans Streck confirmed Hess's reticence, and also his 'gentlemanly' qualities. It was for this, as much as his toughness, that he had been chosen to handle the confinement of the ministers during the Munich Putsch of 1923.

34. Thyssen, *I Paid Hitler*, p. 129, claims that, in spite of the financial help he had given the Party, both Hess and Goebbels were later to work against him because they belonged to the Left in the Party and 'were suspicious of me as the representative of heavy industry' (p. 134). At no time could Hess be even remotely regarded as 'Left' in outlook. According to Hanfstaengl, op. cit., p. 148, Hitler met Emil Kirdorf through Otto Dietrich, who had family connections in the Ruhr. Kirdorf, along with Thyssen, 'started paying the Nazis quite large subsidies.'

35. See Hans Frank, *Im Angesicht des Galgens*, pp. 62, 90. According to Hanfstaengl in his second book, *Zwischen Weissem und Braunem Haus*, Munich, 1970, p. 238, it was Hess who, after Geli Raubal's suicide, telephoned the Nuremberg Hotel, which Hitler had just left with a motorcade in which he was to travel to Berlin. Hess immediately arranged for a fast car to be sent after Hitler in order that the news should be conveyed to him. Hitler immediately returned to Munich.

36. This letter written by Hess to Gregor Strasser is preserved at Koblenz. Hanfstaengl has an amusing passage in *The Missing Years* in which he describes how Hitler after the 1930 elections came to his house, accompanied by Hess, in order formally to offer him the post of foreign press chief of the Party. Hanfstaengl accepted the position in a voluntary capacity.

37. Thyssen, op. cit., p. 138. Thyssen, it would seem, did not have all the facts about the Schleicher-Leipart-Strasser axis, which can be considered one of the more interesting 'might-have-beens' of modern history. Schleicher shrewdly considered Gregor Strasser to be the most 'sensible' man among the leading Nazis. The 'faction' which would have been prepared to follow him in a division against Hitler was some ninety Nazi members of the Reichstag, that is, about one third of the Party's representation in the House. Schleicher's theory was that Strasser and the more moderate Nazis (such as Karl Kaufmann, the Gauleiter for Hamburg) could retain the more acceptable tenets of the Nazi 'ideology' in a more democratic form, and join some kind of coalition which would include

the trade union chief Theodor Leipart, and so gain the support of the Social Democrats. Hitler realized that any such coalition would be the end of him, and threatened to commit suicide if it should ever take place. To meet the threat, Hitler called a special meeting of the entire Parliamentary Party, and staged a spectacular attack on Strasser. This was in December 1932. It was personality against personality, and Hitler won. Strasser left the meeting, and sent Hitler a letter in which he resigned from all the posts he held in the Party. Hitler was never to forget this defection, or potential defection. Gregor Strasser was to be murdered during the Roehm purge of 30 June 1934. See Bullock, op. cit., pp. 237-40.

38. See Papen, *Memoirs*, p. 227.

39. Goebbels, *My Part in Germany's Fight*, p. 207.

CHAPTER 2: *'Conscience of the Party'*

1. In the Federal Archives at Koblenz a remarkable file of correspondence is preserved which starts on 7 June 1938 and continues until 22 June 1941. It begins with a letter from Hans Heinrich Lammers, Chief of the Reich Chancellery, concerning Hess's title *Stellvertreter* (Deputy) of the Führer, which Lammers thought applicable only in Party matters, and inaccurate when it came to the Führer's position as Reich Chancellor and Head of State. Hess was invited to think of some alternative to submit to Hitler. Thereafter the file is built up of submission and resubmission of correspondence on this subject, with Hess either evading answer, or promising to make suggestions. The last entry in the file, on 22.6.41, must have been a mere formality, sent after six months as a reminder. It came almost six weeks after Hess's flight to Scotland. See Lammers' evidence, IMT XI, p. 115.

2. IMT, VI, pp. 148-49.

3. See Bullock, op. cit., p. 547. For text of speech, see Hitler, *My New Order*, pp. 683-90.

4. Dietrich, *The Hitler I Knew*, p. 189.

5. IMT VI, p. 150.

6. IMT VI, p. 150.

7. Hanfstaengl, *The Missing Years*, pp. 230-31.

8. The title of Reichsleiter was a title with a national scope; the title of Gauleiter referred to an individual *Gau*, or district in Germany, following the Party's boundary demarcation for the purposes of organization.

9. Hitler's official headquarters in Berlin were at the Chancellery. His private residence remained in Munich, on the second floor of No. 1, Prinzregentenplatz. The place he loved most was, of course, the Berghof at Berchtesgaden on the Obersalzberg, the property developed for him largely by Martin Bormann.

10. Lüdecke, op. cit., pp. 519-20.

11. H.F. in interviews with both Klopfer and Heim was told that the legislation which passed through Hess's Ministry for scrutiny was concerned with everything except matters belonging properly to the Army,

the Police, or the Foreign Office. But there is no sign of this limitation in the official files. Frank in *Im Angesicht des Galgens*, pp. 157–60, shows how Hess's Ministry grew and how its influence permeated the legislature, interfering, for example, with the proceedings of his own Reichsrechtsrat (Reich Legal Council), the Party's equivalent of the Reich Ministry of Justice. He thought Hess acted weakly in letting Bormann steal so much of his place with Hitler. See also Appendix I.

12. Bormann also administered the royalties Hitler received from the sale of *Mein Kampf*, which in 1933 came to some $300,000. See McGovern, *Martin Bormann*, 1968, p. 32.

13. IMT, VI, p. 152.

14. Dietrich, op. cit., pp. 172-73, 196-97.

15. Hanfstaengl in *Zwischen Weissem und Braunem Haus*, p. 351, emphasizes that there could have been no homosexual orgy during the night before Hitler's dramatic arrival, as is commonly alleged. Dr Ketterer, who was treating Roehm for a neuralgic complaint, was present at the sanatorium, and had given Roehm an injection late on 29 June, and was himself staying at the hotel with Roehm's small company of aides. His current favourite, however, was there also, which gave rise to the story which has featured ever since in most accounts of this extraordinary 'raid' by the Führer on his old friend's privacy.

16. Both Hutton, op. cit., p. 19, and Rees, op. cit., p. 11, both claim that Hess was one of the prime instigators in the movement against Roehm, even implying that he could have been among the executioners. There is no proof of this, to our knowledge, though he would certainly have supported Hitler in his action. Gisevius, in his new edition of *Bis Zum Bitteren Ende* 1944, refers on p. 150 to a broadcast Hess made during the last week in June; he condemned those who sought to stir up revolution against Hitler's Reich. Gisevius claims him as one of the 'tough-liners'. On 3 January 1935 it was Hess who was made responsible for announcing that Generals von Schleicher and von Bredow had been murdered 'in error' during the Night of the Long Knives.

17. Lüdecke, op. cit., pp. 679-80.

18. Frank, op. cit., pp. 142-43.

19. NCA, VII, pp. 883-90.

20. See Speer, *Inside the Third Reich* p. 62.

21. Shirer, *Berlin Diary*, pp. 18-19.

22. Henderson, *Failure of a Mission*, pp. 70-71; the following passage is on p. 72.

23. A selection of Hess's speeches appeared in book form in *Reden*, Eher Verlag, Munich, 1938.

24. See *Zeitgeschichte in Text and Quellen: Das Dritte Reich*, 1963, p. 107.

25. *Prisoner of Peace*, pp. 66-67.

26. Speer, *Erinnerungen*, p. 69. Cf. *Inside the Third Reich*, 119-20.

27. In conversation with H.F.

28. Speer, op. cit., p. 133. Cf. English edition, p. 119.

29. Kersten, *Memoirs*, p. 89.

30. Rees, op. cit., pp. 12-13.

31. *Prisoner of Peace*, pp. 106-7; the passage quoted above is on p. 43.

32. Leasor, op. cit., pp. 41-42. Cf. McGovern, op. cit., p. 35: 'Hess took to reading books dealing with visionary revelations and prophecies. Nostradamus was a particular favourite. Hess also enjoyed consulting old horoscopes, seeking in them knowledge of his own fate and that of Germany. Astrologers, seers, mediums and nature therapists were among the people he saw frequently.' Cf. *The Schellenberg Memoirs*, p. 203.

33. IMT X, pp. 18-19.

34. Alfred Hess, after distinguished war service, had joined the Party in Munich in 1920, but soon returned to Alexandria, founding the Party's *Ortsgruppe* (or Local Branch) in Cairo. See Jacobson, op. cit., p. 114.

35. See Jacobson, op. cit., p. 108.

36. Albrecht Haushofer's letter of thanks to Hess is preserved at Koblenz.

37. *Ambassador Dodd's Diary*, pp. 167, 179.

38. For further interesting background to this, see Lüdecke, op. cit., p. 506 et seq.

39. Frank, op. cit. p. 265 describes how he accompanied Hess to Rome in October 1937 to represent Hitler at an anniversary celebration of the march on Rome.

40. We do not know of any evidence other than hearsay that Hess was personally involved in making the suggestion that Papen be murdered in order to provide an excuse for invading Austria. (See Rees, op. cit., p. 11; Hutton, op. cit., p. 19). Papen in his memoirs, p. 404, claims that a memorandum to this effect originated in Austria from Dr Tavs, one of the leading Austrian Nazis, and was sent to Party headquarters in Germany. According to Shirer, *The Rise and Fall of the Third Reich*, p. 323, Austrian police discovered in a raid on Austrian Party headquarters on 25 January 1938 'documents initiated by Rudolf Hess ... which made it clear that the Austrian Nazis were to stage an open revolt in the spring of 1938 and that when Schuschnigg attempted to put it down, the German Army would enter Austria.' He first referred to this in his *Berlin Diary*, p. 91.

41. IMT I, pp. 219-20.

42. IMT VI, p. 157.

43. IMT VI, p. 157.

44. Ambassador Dodd of the United States, in his *Diary* entry for 9 April 1935, p. 239, describes Göring, Goebbels and Hess as attempting to 'terrorize all Danzig people into voting for Nazi Party control there last Sunday. Many violences were visited on the people who did not have Nazi flags over their houses.'

45. IMT VI, p. 159.

46. *Vierteljahrshefte für Zeitgeschichte*, January 1970, p. 116 et seq.

47. *Prisoner of Peace*, pp. 14-15.

48. Kersten, op. cit., p. 26.

3: *Quixotic Mission*

1. For the preservation of these letters, see Leasor, op. cit., p. 51, note 2, and p. 219. They were first published by HMSO in *Documents in German Foreign Policy* (1918-45). Series D, vol. XI: *The War Years*, 1 September 1940—31 January 1941.

2. General Sir Iain Hamilton had recalled his schooldays in Germany in his book, *When I was a Boy*. Hess had read this.

3. *Prisoner of Peace*, pp. 42-43.

4. We owe much to Professor Messerschmitt's evidence given in conversation with H.F. See also *Prisoner of Peace*, pp. 16-17.

5. See Hans Baur, *Ich Flog Mächtige der Erde*, for background. Baur had first met Hess in 1926. Baur claims that Hess, whom he liked, was 'a passionate flier and pilot . . . and on many flights with him I taught him the techniques of blind flying.' Baur from 1933 was in charge of the 'Governmental Squadron', which started with six Ju 52s, and gradually built up to some forty aircraft. Leaders who had their own aircraft included Göring, Goebbels, Hess, Himmler, Keitel and Raeder. See p. 191 for Hess's abortive mission to Hitler in 1940 with a request that he be allowed to visit the front line. Baur reveals how Hess chafed at being kept at a desk job in wartime. Hitler refused to let him take the risk of visiting the front line.

6. *Prisoner of Peace*, p. 44.

7. Leasor claims it was thirty flights, presumably on evidence given him verbally by Pintsch. Messerschmitt gave the figure of twenty to H.F.

8. The *Evening Standard* Londoner's Diary of 10 January 1970 quotes David Irving as having discovered a memo by Messerschmitt written on 2 May 1941, which reads: 'Reich Minister Hess has asked what radius curve his aeroplane will follow if the auto-pilot is switched right over, and also how accurate this radius will be and what influence winds may have on it. I have no idea what he is up to, as I forgot to ask what he plans.'

9. According to Baur, Hess had told Messerschmitt in the first place about this mission, about which he would not talk.

10. *Prisoner of Peace*, pp. 12-13, 18.

11. For Hess's own account of the generation of the idea of the flight see IMT X p. 13: 'At the conclusion of the French campaign came the Führer's offer to England. The offer, as is known, was refused. This made me all the more firm in my belief that under these circumstances I had to execute my plan.'

12. This and the following passage occur on p. 19 of *Prisoner of Peace*.

13. According to the Duke of Hamilton's report, Hess claimed to have made four separate attempts, the first in December 1940. See page 105. For the full account given by Pintsch, see Leasor, pp. 73 et seq. Hilde Fath kept weather reports for Hess. See IMT, IX, p. 363.

14. See Count Lutz Schwerin-Krosigk, *Es Geschah in Deutschland*, pp. 239-42. 'A few weeks before his flight,' writes Schwerin-Krosigk, 'we

had a private chat about the situation when I was having tea at his Berlin apartment. No one else was present and he didn't conceal his desperation about the two great "Germanic" nations destroying rather than supporting each other . . . If only one could talk to influential Englishmen personally, reminding them of the danger to occidental civilisation and convincing them that Germany and quite certainly Hitler had no desire to wrest anything from Britain.' They simply did not realize the menace represented by Bolshevism, Hess declared.

15. *Prisoner of Peace*, pp. 20-21.

16. *Prisoner of Peace*, pp. 31-36, 98, 112-13.

17. According to the official report, Hess's plane was plotted off the coast of Northumberland at 22.08 hours and made a landfall close to Farne Islands. It flew west and at 22.56 hours was plotted as flying northwest 3,000 feet over Ardrossen. The crash was observed by an A.A. site a few minutes after 23.07 hours, when the plots had faded. A Defiant fighter was some four miles away at the time. In *The Times* Diary for 7 January 1970 an interesting additional note appeared: 'An intriguing footnote to the tragic saga of Rudolf Hess: his unheralded arrival in Britain in May 1941 passed, I am told, almost unnoticed by Fighter Command when the news that Hess had force-landed (by parachute) near Glasgow was first flashed through to its headquarters, Bentley Priory. The senior Czech officer at Fighter Command at that time was also called Hess and on the same day as the Nazi leader's flight, was flying to Scotland in a Tiger Moth to visit Czech units there. The Duty Officer at Fighter Command not unnaturally assumed that it was the Czech Hess who had baled out. Only an hour or so later was it made clear that the message referred to the German Hess.'

18. *Prisoner of Peace*, p. 36.

19. *Prisoner of Peace*, pp. 36-37.

20. We are grateful to the Duke of Hamilton for his help in preparing this account. His official report appears in *Documents in German Foreign Policy* (*DGFP*), Series D, Vol. XII, pp. 38-40. It is Document M-116.

21. It is difficult to follow Leasor's time scheme. According to p. 100, Hitler received Pintsch with the letter shortly after ten o' clock. Yet shortly after this (p. 102) Eva Braun comes in to announce lunch, which was not usually taken at the Berghof before three o' clock, though it was earlier on 11 May because Admiral Darlan was expected for a conference during the afternoon. Göring, summoned from Nuremberg (some 150 miles from Berchtesgaden) after Hitler had read Hess's letter, is said to have arrived during lunch (p. 103). On p. 67, the lunch is said to have ended by 3.30. If Göring had set off immediately from Nuremberg, it is conceivable he might have reached Berchtesgaden by 3.30. According to Otto Dietrich, who was present, Pintsch did not see Hitler until around noon.

There are many discrepancies in this crucial story as it has been recorded by the participants. Speer claims that it was he, not Todt, who gave place to Pintsch before lunch; see the German edition of his memoirs, p. 189. Ilse Hess, in *Prisoner of Peace*, quotes Halder's diary entry for

Saturday (not Sunday). Halder claims that Hitler put the 'package' aside, and only examined it when Göring had arrived with Udet.

The most pronounced discrepancies are those of Galland and Baur. Baur in *Ich Flog Mächtige der Erde*, p. 262 et seq. claims that Hitler flew to Berlin at eight am on Sunday, and that the meeting of the Party leaders to discuss Hess took place in the Chancellery in Berlin. Most mysterious of all, Galland in *Die Ersten und die Letzten*, p. 124 et seq., claims that during the evening of 10 May Göring ordered him by phone to take a squadron of fighters into the air to intercept Hess who was on his way to England. This implies that Göring knew about the flight more than twelve hours before Hitler, and kept the matter to himself. Is there any possible link between this and the phone call that Pintsch made to the Air Ministry before leaving the aerodrome?

22. Ilse Hess records a copy of the letter Hess had left for Hitler was in her possession until 1945. She writes: 'I remember perfectly that it was the furtherance of Hitler's old idea of an alliance with England and the consequent pacification of Europe which occupied the central place in my husband's letter to him.' See *Prisoner of Peace*, p. 27. Dietrich also claims to have read the letter; op. cit. pp. 62-63. According to him, Hess went into the technical details of the flight and the courage it would require before emphasizing the need he felt to bring about a peaceful understanding between Germany and Britain. Dietrich makes no reference to the concluding sentence with its suggestion that Hitler could always say that Hess was insane. It is Frau Hess who claims to remember these words verbatim.

23. NCA Supplementary Volume B, pp. 1271-73.

24. Among the names suggested are Lord Dunglass (Parliamentary Private Secretary of the late Neville Chamberlain), Lord Stanley, Lord Derby, Lord Astor. Even R. A. Butler (now Lord Butler) is mentioned. There are a number of others, including Foreign Office staff.

25. *Prisoner of Peace*, p. 18.

26. Hans Fritzsche, at this time head of Goebbels' Press Division, told H.F. that Goebbels was completely knocked out by the news, and so much at a loss how to handle it he retired to his lakeside home at Lanke for three days on the pretext that he was ill.

27. The German monitoring service kept a record of the broadcasts put out by the German service of the BBC. This began by simply repeating the news that Hess was either dead or missing, put out at ten pm on 12 May. At eleven pm the news began to be interpreted. Why was Hess permitted to be the Führer's Deputy if he was insane? 'We think that Hess committed suicide. He was one of the few idealists . . . He knew that Hitler was leading the German nation to perdition.' At six am on 13 May, the hard fact that Hess was alive in Britain was announced. A reasonably full account of the crash landing followed. Far from being insane, said the broadcast, he wanted to escape the Gestapo. See references to Hess in Asa Briggs' *History of Broadcasting in the United Kingdom*, Vol. III (1970).

28. See *The Schellenberg Memoirs*, p. 199.

29. McAuslane received a cheque for £6 for his service in connection with the Hess story.

30. Ciano *Diaries*, p. 341.

31. *Prisoner of Peace*, pp. 21-23.

32. Kirkpatrick, *The Inner Circle*, pp. 175-77.

33. For the Report, see Document M-117, IMT XXXVIII, pp. 177 ff.

34. Ciano, *Diaries*, pp. 342-43. Paul Schmidt, Hitler's interpreter, in *Statist and Diplomatischer Bühne*, p. 537, states that he was hurriedly sent with Ribbentrop to Italy to explain away Hess's flight. He claims that the news had 'detonated in the Berghof like a bomb,' and he had heard Hitler say that he hoped Hess had fallen into the sea.

35. Churchill, *The Grand Alliance*, p. 45.

36. *Prisoner of Peace*, pp. 24-25.

37. Among the letters Hess left for his wife and friends was one for Himmler, appealing to him to spare his staff, none of whom, he said, had known of his plans. See *Prisoner of Peace*, p. 27, note. But Bormann was to see to it that sufficient vengeance was taken. He instructed that all those involved in the 'Hess affair' were to be dismissed, expelled from the Party, and placed under arrest. Among those arrested were Leitgen, and, of course, Pintsch. Many who might have expected to be arrested were not, including Ilse Hess and Messerschmitt.

38. Dietrich, op. cit., p. 64.

39. Frank, op. cit., pp. 371, 377, 401.

40. Kersten, op. cit., p. 89.

41. Rudolf Semmler, *Goebbels—the Man Next to Hitler*, pp. 32-34.

42. Based on the report made by Ivone Kirkpatrick, and his memoirs, *The Inner Circle*, p. 179.

43. See *Prisoner of Peace*, p. 100. Hess was proud of the trick he used to discover where he was. He asked for a piece of paper on which to write his autograph and was given a piece of headed notepaper which revealed at once the location of his new prison.

44. Churchill, *The Grand Alliance*, p. 47.

45. Rees, op. cit., pp. 2-3. There were, of course, no arrests.

46. Semmler, op. cit., p. 34. The passage which follows is on pp. 34-36.

47. Schellenberg, op. cit., p. 203.

48. Sir John Simon was by this time Lord Chancellor.

49. *Prisoner of Peace*, p. 14.

50. J. Bernard Hutton, *Hess, The Man and his Mission*, 1970. Mr Hutton was quoted in *The News of the World* (26.4.70) as saying that he had studied transcripts of recorded conversations between the Nazi leaders in which Hitler finally approved the plan. The recordings were found at Nazi headquarters in Munich after the war, it is claimed, and have been suppressed by the Allies for security reasons ever since, and the original records are now at the West German Ministry of Interior Affairs. We have found no one among the many survivors who were in touch with Hitler at the time who believes that he had any knowledge of the flight. They report only Hitler's profound and lasting shock at the flight, a

reaction which, they declare went far beyond anything which could have been assumed for show.

51. *Prisoner of Peace*, p. 25.

52. Todt, Hitler's Minister of Armaments before Speer's appointment, died in a plane crash. Everything was done to suppress the memory of Hess in Germany. According to a decree by the Propaganda Ministry, his portrait was to be removed from all public places, and cut out of the revised editions of books in which it had appeared. His name, too, was to be eliminated from Nazi history. Bormann was also involved in this process of eradication. See Joseph Wulf, *Martin Bormann Hitlers Schatten*, p. 131 et seq.

CHAPTER 4: '*Dagger of the Mind*'

1. An unsubstantiated claim that there was an operation mounted in Germany to 'make contact with Hess' is put forward by J. Bernard Hutton in his book *Hess, the Man and His Mission*, p. 103 et seq. We believe the whole bias of the evidence is against this. Hitler did not want Hess back in Germany. Since he had not, as he hoped, drowned, he wanted only to dismiss him from his mind, and above all from the minds of the German people. There was no point either in contacting or rescuing him.

2. See above Chapter 3, p. 104.

3. *Prisoner of Peace*, pp. 100-101.

4. Rees, op. cit., p. ix. For Dr Gilbert, see below, p. 157.

5. Rees, op. cit., p. 21; the following passage is on pp. 24-25.

6. Rees, op. cit., pp. 28-29. But the eminent psychiatrist Professor Bürger-Prinz, who has made a special study of Hess, maintained in conversation with H.F. in Hamburg that Hess should not be considered a case of schizophrenia.

7. The Minister who finally came to look after his interests during his period in Britain was not the Swiss representative in London, but Dr Hans Fröhlicher. See Note 11 below.

8. Rees, op. cit., p. 44.

9. It is perhaps important to realize that the traditional code of behaviour for an officer in the German army demanded suicide after failure to carry out an important mission. Hence Hess put on his uniform before making this attempt on his life. H.F. is inclined to think this attempt is not to be taken too seriously, and was another of Hess's diversions. R.M. believes it to have been intended seriously because a jump of this kind down the well of a staircase was very dangerous.

10. Beaverbrook, during his farewell speech after his retirement dinner at the Savoy. Cf. Churchill, *The Grand Alliance*, p. 49. Churchill describes his meeting with Stalin, who still shows his resentment at the presence of Hess alive in Britain three years later. For the Hess-Beaverbrook meeting see Appendix 3.

11. Dr Fröhlicher was assigned to deal with Hess's case.

12. *Prisoner of Peace*, pp. 101-3.

13. Rees, op. cit., p. 92.

14. See *Prisoner of Peace*, pp. 65 and 120.

15. *Prisoner of Peace*, pp. 44 and 45.

16. Ibid., p. 45.

17. Ibid., p. 46.

18. Ibid., p. 49.

19. *Prisoner of Peace*, p. 47. Cf. Rees, p. 79. He quotes this letter, but dates it 21.1.44.

20. Rees quotes letters to Frau Hess and others not given in *Prisoner of Peace* referring to his pleasure at the 'return' of his memory. See Rees, op. cit., p. 93.

21. *Prisoner of Peace*, pp. 65-66.

22. Ibid., p. 137.

Additional Note. Early in 1945. there was a rumour in Germany that certain right-wing British Members of Parliament were thinking of using Hess as a sort of puppet head of government in Germany after the occupation. Correspondence preserved at Koblenz (photocopies of which are in the possession of the authors) passed between Schellenberg and Brandt, who was on Himmler's staff. They realized that the plan had been abandoned (if, indeed, it was ever to be taken seriously), but it was believed, in any case, that Hess had rejected the idea.

Meanwhile in Germany, Ilse Hess suffered some persecution by Bormann. On the files at Koblenz are letters appealing to Himmler for help in her negotiations to have her large house at Harlaching (which she had no means of keeping up) adapted as an officers' hospital or nursing-home. Himmler promised her that if anything should happen to her, he would personally see that Wolf Rüdiger was cared for. She also tried to care for certain individual children who were in difficulties through the war. Himmler appears to have acted with great consideration throughout this difficult time when Frau Hess was under nobody's protection.

CHAPTER 5: *Nuremberg*

1. C.f. English edition of Speer, *Inside the Third Reich*, p. 509.

2. Kelley, *22 Cells in Nuremberg*, pp. 26-27.

3. Hess was to make reference to this confrontation with Hildegard Fath in a cryptic remark the censor let pass in one of his letters home. He asked for his apologies to be conveyed to 'Freiburg' (the domestic nickname for Fräulein Fath, who came from this city) for his seemingly 'idiotic' behaviour in front of her. He had to keep up his mask of lost memory.

4. Rees, op. cit., pp. 134-35.

5. IMT I, pp. 31-32.

6. R. W. Cooper, *The Nuremberg Trial*, p. 267.

7. IMT I, pp. 302-4.

8. IMT I, pp. 305-6.

9. Gilbert, *Nuremberg Diary*, p. 67.

10. Ibid., p. 59.

11. *Prisoner of Peace*, p. 52.

12. Ibid., pp. 51-52.

13. IMT VI, p. 161; the passage following is on pp. 162-63.

14. See Heydecker and Leeb, *The Nuremberg Trials*, pp. 170-71. Cooper, op. cit., p. 269 calls Seidl 'the enfant terrible of Nuremberg.'

15. See IMT X, p. 15 et seq. Cf. Heydecker and Leeb, *The Nuremberg Trials*, p. 170 et seq. For background to this document used by Seidl, see Hutton, op. cit., pp. 197 et seq. As for Hess's habit of removing his earphones during the trial (when indeed he bothered to wear them), he made a practice of doing this ostentatiously whenever a Russian spoke.

16. See IMT XIV, pp. 273-74.

17. H.F. notes: 'My one day visit to Nuremberg was during the spring of 1946. Hess, as usual, was sitting next to Göring. One could see clearly from his gestures that Göring was remonstrating with Hess because he was reading a book. It was like a silent film, all gesture and no speech. Hess was resisting, in effect saying, "Leave me alone"!'

18. *Prisoner of Peace*, pp. 54-55. The letter to his son which follows is on p. 55.

19. IMT XIX, p. 367.

20. IMT XIX, p. 375.

21. IMT XIX, pp. 378 and 380.

22. IMT XXII pp. 384-85.

23. *Prisoner of Peace*, p. 56. Karli was Professor Haushofer.

24. Idem, p. 57. Hess's fears that there would be no reference to his speech in the Allied reports on the trial were groundless. The English-language broadcasting station gave the 'final sentences in full' according to Ilse Hess. See *Prisoner of Peace*, p. 58.

25. IMT XXII, pp. 487-88. The quotation following occurs on pages 488-89. For Hess's lip-service to peace and international cooperation, see IMT XXXVIII, pp. 177 et seq.

26. For Gilbert's comments, see *Nuremberg Diary*, p. 271. Hess was very angry that a plea for clemency was submitted without his knowledge and consent. See *Prisoner of Peace*, p. 62. The sentences were as follows for those tried alongside Hess:

Guilty on all four counts and sentenced to death—Göring, Ribbentrop, Keitel, Rosenberg, Jodl.

Guilty on counts III and IV and sentenced to death—Kaltenbrunner, Frank, Saukel, Bormann (*in absentia*).

Guilty on counts II, III and IV and sentenced to death—Frick, Seyss-Inquart.

Guilty on count IV and sentenced to death—Streicher.

Guilty on counts II, III, and IV and sentenced to life imprisonment—Funk.

Guilty on counts I, II and III and sentenced to life imprisonment—Raeder.

Guilty on counts III and IV and sentenced to twenty years' imprisonment—Speer.

Guilty on count IV and sentenced to twenty years' imprisonment—von Schirach.

Guilty on all four counts and sentenced to fifteen years' imprisonment—von Neurath.

Guilty on counts II and III and sentenced to ten years' imprisonment—Dönitz.

Acquitted—Schacht. von Papen, Fritzsche.

27. *Prisoner of Peace*, pp. 59-60. The letter following is on pp. 61-62.

28. The son of the American official who having obtained Hess's forty-nine page typescript tried to sell it for a high sum to Anthony Terry, the Bonn and Paris correspondent of *The Sunday Times*. It was finally acquired for a comparatively modest sum.

29. See Note 6 to Chapter 4.

CHAPTER 6: *Spandau*

1. Göring's suicide a couple of hours before his execution was due to take place was finally explained by Colonel Burton C. Andrus, the US Army Governor of the Nuremberg Prison when, in September 1967, he released the text of a suicide letter addressed to him by Göring and dated 11 October—five days before Göring's death. In this he explained that he had always managed to retain possession of two capsules, having permitted a third to be discovered and taken from him. The capsules contained cyanide poisoning, and were of the kind possessed by most of the Nazi leaders in case of difficulty. He committed suicide because the Control Board refused his request that the method of execution should be changed to shooting.

2. *Prisoner of Peace*, p. 82. The passage following is on pp. 86-87.

3. Ibid., p. 91.

4. Speer gave us the dimensions of his cell as three metres by two.

5. *Prisoner of Peace*. p. 92. The passage quoted below is on p. 93.

6. *Prisoner of Peace*, pp. 99-100. The passages which follow are on pp. 94, 107-8, 109, and 114 respectively.

7. Speer in conversation with H.F.

8. See Hutton, op. cit., on the staffing of the prison and its guards, pp. 215 et seq.

9. See Speer, *Inside the Third Reich*, p. 525, on the composition of his book, which was begun in prison.

10. *Prisoner of Peace*, pp. 126-27. The passages following are on pp. 128-29 and 126.

11. For an account of the various appeals launched for the release of the other prisoners from Spandau, see Fishman, *The Seven Men of Spandau*, chapter 16.

12. The costs to the West German Government of keeping Spandau open were estimated at this time to have risen to £90,000 a year.

13. See IMT XVIII, p. 80 et seq.

14. See *The Scottish Sunday Express* and *The Sunday Express* of 18 June

1967. See *The Times*, 1 October 1968 for the Berlin press conference.

15. We are very grateful to Dr Epstein for the information which follows and the texts of the letters quoted.

16. The article quoted appeared in *The Arizona Republic*, 15 March 1969. Other articles kindly sent us by Dr Epstein include those published in *Truth Forum* (March 1969), *The Telegram* of Toronto (8 April 1969), *The Stars and Stripes* (9 April 1969), and, in German, in the *Frankfurter Allgemeine Zeitung* (21 June 1968).

17. There had been earlier pleas for Hess's release, notably by Professor A. J. P. Taylor in *The Sunday Express*, Christmas 1963 (repeated in 1969) and by Bernard Levin in *The Daily Mail*, 2 May 1965.

18. Reported in *The Daily Express*, 29 December 1969. In 1968 Frau Hess had brought a case in Kassel in an endeavour to claim a pension due to her (she considered) as the wife of a prisoner-of-war. This gave rise to a legal query which left unresolved the question whether Hess's status was indeed that of a prisoner-of-war.

19. Mr Neave had ended the war as a Lieutenant-Colonel, and was awarded the DSO, MC and Croix de Guerre. He is now a barrister and Member of Parliament. A prisoner of war, he had escaped from Colditz Prison in 1942. Later he was assigned to MI9, which was concerned with developing escape routes behind the Nazi lines. After the war he became an officer of the British War Crimes Executive.

20. Lord Chalfont emphasized this in conversation with H.F. at the Foreign Office; so did Major-General Bowes-Lyon, Senior British Officer in Berlin, early in 1970. See Fraenkel, 'The Hess Quandary' in *Question 4* (Rationalist Press, 1971).

BIBLIOGRAPHY

BAUR, HANS. *Ich Flog Mächtige der Erde*. Kempton, Pröpster, 1956. Translated as *Hitler's Pilot*. London, 1958.

BULLOCK, ALAN. *Hitler: a Study in Tyranny*. London, Odhams, 1952. Revised, 1964.

CHURCHILL, WINSTON. *The Grand Alliance*. London, Cassell, 1948.

Ciano's Diary 1939-1943. Edited by Malcolm Muggeridge. London, Heinemann, 1947.

COOPER, R. W. *The Nuremberg Trial*. London, Penguin Books, 1947.

DIETRICH, OTTO. *The Hitler I Knew*. London, Methuen, 1955.

DODD, WILLIAM E. *Ambassador Dodd's Diary*. London, Gollancz, 1941.

DOMARUS, MAX. *Der Reichstag und die Macht*. Würzburg, 1968.

DOUGLAS-HAMILTON, JAMES. *Motive for a Mission*. London, Macmillan, 1971.

FISHMAN, J. *The Seven Men of Spandau*. London, W. H. Allen, 1954.

FRAENKEL, HEINRICH. *The Hess Quandary* in *Question 4*. London, The Rationalist Press, 1971.

FRANK, HANS. *Im Angesicht des Galgens*. Munich, Beck Verlag, 1953.

GALLAND, ADOLF. *Die Ersten und die Letzten*. Darmstadt, 1953. Translated as *The First and the Last*. London, Methuen, 1955.

GILBERT, G. M. *Nuremberg Diary*. London, Eyre and Spottiswoode, 1948.

GISEVIUS, H. B. *Bis Zum Bitteren Ende*. Revised 1960. Original edition translated as *To the Bitter End*, London, Cape, 1948.

GOEBBELS, JOSEPH. *My Part in Germany's Fight*. London, Paternoster Library, 1938.
The Early Goebbels Diaries. Edited by Helmut Heiber. London, Weidenfeld and Nicolson, 1962.

HANFSTAENGL, ERNST. *Hitler—the Missing Years*. London, Eyre and Spottiswoode, 1957.
Zwischen Weissem und Braunem Haus. Munich, 1970.

HEIBER, HELMUT. *Walter Frank und Sein Reichsinstitut für Geschichte des neuen Deutschlands*. Stuttgart, 1966.

HEIDEN, KONRAD. *Der Führer*. London, Gollancz, 1944.

HENDERSON, SIR NEVILE. *Failure of a Mission*. London, Hodder and Stoughton, 1940.

HESS, RUDOLF. *Reden*. Munich, Eher Verlag, 1938.

HESS, ILSE. *England-Nürnberg-Spandau*. Druffel Verlag, Starnberg Leoni, 1952.
Gefangener des Friedens. Druffel Verlag, Leoni, 1965.
Antwort aus Zelle Sieben. Druffel Verlag, Leoni, 1968.
Selection of family correspondence translated as:
Prisoner of Peace. London, Britons Publishing Co., 1954.

HEYDECKER, JOE and LEEB, JOHANNES. *The Nuremberg Trials*. London, Heinemann, 1962.

HILDEBRANDT, RAINER. *Wir Sind Die Letzten*. Neuwied/Berlin, Michael Verlag, n.d.

HITLER, ADOLF. *Mein Kampf*. London, Hurst and Blackett, 1939.

HUTTON, J. BERNARD. *Hess, the Man and his Mission*. London, David Bruce and Watson, 1970.

JACOBSEN, HANS-ADOLF. *Nationalsozialistische Aussenpolitik 1933-38*. Frankfurt/Berlin, A. Metzner Verlag, 1968.

KELLEY, DOUGLAS M. *22 Cells in Nuremberg*. New York, Greenberg, 1947.

KERSTEN, FELIX. *The Kersten Memoirs*. London, Hutchinson, 1956.

KIRKPATRICK, SIR IVONE. *The Inner Circle*. London, Macmillan, 1959.

KNIGHT-PATTERSON, W. M. *Germany from Defeat to Conquest*. London, Allen and Unwin, 1945.

LEASOR, JAMES. *The Uninvited Envoy*. London, Allen and Unwin, 1962.

LÜDECKE, KURT G. W. *I Knew Hitler*. London, Jarrolds, 1938.

MANVELL, ROGER and FRAENKEL, HEINRICH. *Doctor Goebbels*. London, Heinemann, 1960.

Göring. London, Heinemann, 1962.

MCGOVERN, JAMES. *Martin Bormann*. London, Arthur Barker, 1968.

PAPEN, FRANZ von. *Memoirs*. London, Deutsch, 1952.

REES, J. R. *The Case of Rudolf Hess*. London, Heinemann, 1947.

SCHACHT, HJALMAR. *Account Settled*. London, Weidenfeld and Nicolson, 1948.

My First Seventy-Six Years. London, Wingate, 1955.

The Schellenberg Memoirs. London, Deutsch, 1956.

SCHMIDT, PAUL. *Hitler's Interpreter*. London, Heinemann, 1951.

SCHWERIN-KROSIGK, COUNT LUTZ. *Es Geschah in Deutschland*. Tübingen, 1951.

SEMMLER, RUDOLF. *Goebbels, the Man Next to Hitler*. London, Westhouse, 1947.

SHIRER, WILLIAM A. *Berlin Diary*. New York, Knopf, 1941.

The Rise and Fall of the Third Reich. New York, Simon and Schuster, 1960.

SPEER, ALBERT. *Erinnerungen*. Berlin, Ullstein, 1969. English translation: *Inside the Third Reich*. Weidenfeld and Nicolson, 1970.

STRASSER, OTTO. *Hitler and I*. London, Cape, 1940.

STUBBE, WALTER. 'In Memoriam Albrecht Haushofer' (*Vierteljahreshefte für Zeitgeschichte*, Stuttgart, 1960, No. 3, pp. 236-56).

THYSSEN, FRITZ. *I Paid Hitler*. London, Hodder and Stoughton, 1941.

The Trial of the Major War Criminals before the International Military Tribunal. Proceedings, volumes I-XXIII; Documents in Evidence, volumes XXIV-XLII, Nuremberg 1947-49. The Proceedings were also published by HMSO in London in twenty-two parts (the edition referred to in this book). Translations into English of many of the documents used in evidence were published by the US Government Printing Office under the title *Nazi Conspiracy and Aggression* in eight main and two supplementary volumes.

WULF, JOSEPH. *Martin Bormann Hitlers Schatten*. Gütersloh, Sigbert Mohn Verlag, 1962.

APPENDICES

APPENDIX 1

THE HESS MINISTRY AND THE LEGISLATURE

APART from Hess's own inevitable task as a sort of Ombudsman in Party matters, the most important regular work of his Ministry was its involvement in the legislature. The Ministry was not properly established until the second year of the regime, some six months after Hess had been created a Reich-Minister without portfolio. To some extent he had his 'portfolio' after the *Führerbefehl* of 27 July 1934, addressed to all Reich-Ministers:

I herewith decree that the Deputy Führer, Reich-Minister Hess, is to hold the position of a Reich-Minister personally involved in the amendments and passing of laws drafted in all Reich-Ministries. He is to be acquainted with all impending legislature at the same time as the Reich-Ministers concerned. This applies even when only one Reich-Minister is concerned. Reich-Minister Hess is to be given the opportunity of passing an opinion on all draft laws.

This applies equally to the drafts of decrees and ordinances. In his capacity as Reich-Minister, the Deputy Führer can be represented by a member of his staff duly instructed by him. Such representatives are entitled, on behalf of their Minister, to make statements to the Reich-Ministers.

(signed) Adolf Hitler

This decree, issued while Hindenburg was still alive, was signed by Hitler in his capacity as Reich-Chancellor. Just over five months later, after President Hindenburg's death, Hess was included in another significant decree regulating the succession:

By dint of paragraph 1, section 1, sentence 2 of the law of 1.8.34 regarding the Head of State in the German Reich, I herewith decree:

Should I be incapacitated in the performance of my duties in the offices of Reich-President and Reich-Chancellor, united in my person, I am to be represented by:

The Prussian Minister-President and Reich-Luftwaffe Minister, Hermann Göring,
The Reich Defence Minister, Colonel General von Blomberg,
The Deputy Führer of the NSDAP Reich-Minister Rudolf Hess.

Reich Defence Minister von Blomberg is to be responsible for all matters concerning the Armed Forces and the defence of the Reich,
Reich-Minister Hess for all matters concerning the National Socialist German Workers' Party and its relations to the State,
Minister-President Göring in all other matters of State government.

I take it for granted that in all important matters differences of opinion would be resolved in such a way as to produce unanimous decisions from the representatives appointed by me.

Berlin, 7 December 1934
The Führer and Reich-Chancellor
(signed) Adolf Hitler

On the eve of the war, in his Reichstag speech of 1 September 1939, Hitler reverted to that early document on the succession, omitting, of course, Blomberg (by then dismissed in disgrace) and adding this significant rider: '. . . in the event of the incapacitation of Party-member Hess (as potential successor to Göring), a legally constituted Senate will be set up to select the most worthy, that is to say the bravest of its members.'

This is significant in that the notion of a Senate had been in Hitler's mind as early as 1931 when a Senatorial Hall was included in Munich's new Brown House. After the Reichstag speech of 1 September 1939 it might have been assumed that the Senate was to be set up forthwith. In point of fact, even though its composition—some 40 to 60 including all Reichsleiters, Reich-Ministers and Gauleiters—was never in doubt and had been decreed in some considerable detail, the Senate was never created; the reason obviously being that Hitler was loath to restrict his own powers during his lifetime through such a body, comparable to the Grand Fascist Council in Italy. * What actually happened was that a few weeks after Hitler's Reichstag announcement of the Senate, Frick, the Home Secretary, on 19 September 1939, sent a long letter to the Deputy Führer's office outlining the detailed suggestions

---

* Most of the documentary evidence surviving on the abortive scheme for the Senate—some of it in the Koblenz Federal Archives—is dealt with by Max Domarus on p. 142 of *Der Reichstag und die Macht* (Würzburg 1968).

already accepted. It was not even addressed to Hess personally, but to one of his senior officials, Ministerial-Director Sommer. But no further action was taken.

As for his Ministry's prerogative of being involved during the drafting stages of all civil laws, Hess (or Bormann, acting for him) watched jealously to see that these regulations were strictly adhered to, and frequently complained to Lammers, the Chief of the Reich-Chancellery office, if they were infringed. On 27 October 1934, acting on one such complaint, Lammers wrote to all Reich-Ministers stressing that the Deputy-Führer must obtain drafts in time to have his say; and on 2 March 1935, circularizing all Reich-Ministers, Lammers again voiced a complaint from Hess about delays in acquainting him with impending legislation. Henceforth it was to be a rule for Hess's Ministry to be informed on the first of every month concerning whatever new legislation was in immediate preparation. Moreover, Hess never failed to insist on his Ministry's right to initiate new legislation, apart from having a say in drafts prepared by the Ministries concerned. On 13 April 1938, acting on yet another complaint from the Hess Ministry, Lammers sent this reminder to all Reich-Ministers:

'The Führer has given special instruction that all legislative suggestions on the part of the NSDAP are to be forwarded to the Ministry concerned through the Deputy Führer's office.'

As for Hess's constant insistence on the privileges of his personal position and on due respect for the prerogatives of his Ministry, ample documentary evidence has survived, such as his letter to Lammers (signed by Bormann on Hess's behalf) of 23 December 1937. In it he complains that the Party generally and the Deputy Führer in particular are not invariably given the high priority due to them in official correspondence: '. . . I must insist on being named immediately after the Führer, no one else preceding me except possibly the Reich-Minister in charge of the legislation concerned.'

In the last few months before his flight to Scotland Hess was much concerned with the *Reichsbürgergesetz* legalizing the expropriation of Jews and the 'Aryanization' of Jewish firms and business concerns. Among Hess's last performances of official duties was a letter dated 24 March 1941, addressed to Frick, the Home Secretary. Upon the problems of confiscation of Jewish property Hess's principal comment is that, however much public opinion might be opposed to continuing the payment of pensions and other monies legally due to certain Jews it would make no sense simply to cut off all their financial resources; after all,

H

what with their own charity funds nearly exhausted, it would ultimately be up to the State to keep them from starvation; moreover, to deal with masses of special applications claiming extreme hardship would cause much clerical work which could and should be avoided. Hence, it would be common sense to keep them at subsistence level by continuing their own pensions on just such a scale.

Nothing could be more significant for the pedantic (and frequently repetitious) insistence of the Ministry on claiming and guarding its prerogatives than a statement issued in the *Reichsverfügüngsblatt* of 9 May 1940 signed by Bormann and marked 'Not for publication'. In it (on the pretext that various inquiries would seem to demand precise clarification once and for all) Bormann details the unique position as well as the unique rights and duties of the Deputy Führer and his Ministry. It should be added that Bormann was rather more eager than his chief in his insistence on the Ministry's unique prerogatives. Here is the text of that fully comprehensive document (which survives in the Federal Archives at Koblenz).

1. The office of the Deputy Führer is an office of the Führer. By the Führer's decree of 21.4.33 the Deputy Führer is authorised 'to make decisions on the Führer's behalf in all Party matters.' In all matters concerning the Party the Deputy Führer holds supreme authority, subject only to the Führer himself.

2. As for the relation of the Party to the institutions of the State, it is the Deputy Führer's *unique* task to represent the Party vis-à-vis the supreme organs of the State. Paragraph 2 of the law of 1.12.33 for safeguarding the unity of Party and State provided for the Deputy Führer to be the sole representative of the Party as a member of the Reich-Government. According to the Führer's decrees of 27.3.34 and 6.4.35 the Deputy Führer is to be involved in the legislature of all Reich-Ministries. It is his task in the drafting stages of legislature to acquaint the Reich-Ministers concerned with the Party's viewpoints. On 17.3.38 the Führer gave explicit instructions on legislative suggestions by the Party to be conveyed to the Reich-Ministers concerned through the Deputy-Führer and no one else. Being the sole representative of the Party the Deputy Führer has also been appointed a member of the Ministerial Council for the defence of the Reich.

3. By decree of the 10.7.37 on the appointment of civil servants the Führer gave the Deputy Führer sole authority to be consulted

by Reich-Ministers about the appointment of senior civil servants.

4. No other Party office or department is concerned with the above-mentioned matters coming under the sole responsibility of the Deputy Führer.

5. In naming his office the Deputy-Führer did not indicate that it is, in fact, an office of the Führer, because he wished to avoid his comments and suggestions relating to the supreme organs of the state being misunderstood as personal utterances of the Führer. Anyway there is no doubt that a final decision, should he wish to make one, is left to the Führer himself, either in his capacity of leader of the NSDAP, or as supreme chief of the State administration, or as supreme chief of the armed forces. The Deputy Führer wished to avoid the risk that any decision taken by him on behalf of the Führer or any letter or instruction by one of his departmental chiefs might be misconstrued as a personal opinion voiced by the Führer.

Munich 9.5.40   Chief of Staff of the Deputy Führer
(signed) M. Bormann

Among the significant decrees* signed by Hess (or by Bormann on his behalf, as his Chief of Staff), many of which were cited in the case for the prosecution at the International Military Tribunal, were:

9 June 1934
Security Service of the Reichsführer SS established as the sole political news and defence service of the Party.

> IMT, Vol. VI, p. 152, Jacobsen op. cit., p. 58. Doc. No. 3385–PS, quoted in Trial.

18 July 1934
Nazi League of German Students subordinate to Hess.

> IMT, Vol. VI, p. 152, 5.

20 December 1934
Law giving same protection to Party institutions and uniforms as enjoyed by State and Service equivalents.

> IMT, Vol. IV, p. 298; Vol. VI, p. 152.

---

* The decrees and instructions issued from Hess's office were so numerous that they were published officially in volume form.

14 February 1935
Instructions giving official support to the SD.
>   IMT, Vol. IV, p. 297, 1. Doc. No. 3237–PS.

16 March 1935
Hess signs decree for compulsory military service.
>   IMT, Vol. VI, p. 156, 10.

3 September 1935
Order to Party agencies to report to Gestapo all persons who criticize Nazi institutions or the Party.
>   IMT, Vol. IV, p. 297, 2. Doc. No. 3239–PS.

15 September 1935
Law for Protection of Blood and Honour (Nuremberg Racial Law).
>   IMT, Vol. VI, p. 153. Doc. No. 3179–PS, Hilberg 46, 107.
>   Signed by Hitler as well.
Same date: Reich Citizenship Law.

24 September 1935
Consultation with Hess required in appointment of Reich civil servants.
>   IMT, Vol. VI, p. 152.

10 July 1937
This reinforced in respect of minor civil servants.
>   IMT, Vol. VI, p. 152.

7 January 1936
Roman Catholic priests hostile to State or Party to be reported to Gestapo.
>   IMT, Vol. IV, p. 304, 8. Doc. No. 3246–PS.

3 April 1936
Consultation with Hess required on appointment of Labour Service officials.
>   IMT, Vol. VI, p. 152, 3.

8 January 1937
Refusal of financial assistance to patients of Jewish physicians.
See McGovern, *Martin Bormann*, p. 26.

8 January 1937
Financial assistance to government employees withdrawn if they employed Jewish doctors, lawyers, etc.
IMT, Vol. IV, p. 305. Doc. No. 3240–PS.

13 March 1938
Signs Law for reunion of Austria with German Reich.
IMT, Vol. VI, p. 156.

20 May 1938
Nuremberg Law extended to Austria.
IMT, Vol. VI, p. 153, 9. Doc. No. 2124–PS.

20 May 1938
Deprives Jews of right to vote or hold office.
IMT, Vol. VI, p. 153.

14 June 1938
Decree defining Jewish enterprise.
Hilberg, op. cit., p. 82.

17 June 1938
Reich Labour Service excluded from religious worship.
IMT, Vol. IV, p. 300–301. Doc. No. 107–PS.

25 July 1938
Licence withdrawn from Jewish physicians (except for Jewish patients).
Hildberg, op. cit., p. 84.

27 July 1938
Party Members should not join German-British Association.
>Federal Archives, Koblenz.

27 July 1938
Clergy prohibited from holding Party office.
>IMT, Vol. IV, p. 299, 4. Doc. No. 113–PS.

11 August 1938
Detailed instructions for employing children over twelve for holiday harvesting.
>Federal Archives, Koblenz.

16 August 1938
No victimization of people failing to subscribe to Party press.
>Federal Archives, Koblenz.

1 September 1938
Secret Order concerning relations with Brazil after banning of Overseas Organization of National Socialists.
>Federal Archives, Koblenz.

2 September 1938
Status of *Mischlinge*.
>Federal Archives, Koblenz.

27 September 1938
Elimination of Jewish lawyers.
>Hilberg, op. cit., p. 84.

8 October 1938
Strict prohibition from throwing flowers at the Führer.
>Federal Archives, Koblenz, decree No. 150/38 (signed by Bormann).

12 November 1938
Decree excluding Jews from economic life.
>   IMT, Vol. IV, p. 305.

21 November 1938
(Secret) Gas-mask deliveries.
>   Federal Archives, Koblenz, decree No. 191/38.

14 December 1938
SD taken off establishment of the Party and put directly under the SS.
>   Doc. No. 3385–PS.

14 December 1938
(Confidential) Concerning cooperation between Party and Gestapo.
>   Federal Archives, Koblenz.

17 December 1938
Order to stop writing and mimeographing garrulous, self-praising reports 'which no one has time to read.'
>   Federal Archives, Koblenz.

18 March 1939
Decree: Jews of German nationality to have no legal claims in cases arising from pogroms.
>   Hilberg, op. cit., p. 28.

30 April 1939
Decree concerning eviction of Jews by German landlords.
>   Hilberg, op. cit., p. 116.

3 June 1939
Followers of Christian Science excluded from Party.
>   IMT, Vol. IV, p. 300. Doc. No. 838–PS.

14 July 1939
All Party members who became clergy or undertook study of
Theology expelled.

    IMT, Vol. IV, p. 300. Doc. No. 840–PS.

1 September 1939
Decree incorporating Danzig in Reich.

    IMT, Vol. VI, p. 158.

8 October 1939
Decree incorporating Polish territories into Reich.

    IMT, Vol. VI, p. 158.

APPENDIX 2

ALBRECHT HAUSHOFER

ALL through this book the obvious importance of the Haushofers in the life of Rudolf Hess is evident, but it should be remembered that so far as Karl was concerned ('Uncle Karli' as he is frequently called in the letters) Hess's position over the decades changed from that of the student sitting at the feet of the admired professor to that of a powerful man able and willing to give patronage to his friends.

Such patronage was vitally important with regard to Albrecht's 'blemish' as the son of a 'half-Aryan' mother; to have the shame of one Jewish grandfather overlooked by the relevant authorities in the Third Reich required all the influence of the Deputy Führer. (See p. 70 for Albrecht's gushing letter of thanks when Hess had procured him his Berlin professorship).

Albrecht's counsel concerning Hess's flight to Scotland has been frequently misunderstood or misinterpreted. It should be remembered (see the Duke's statements pp. 105, 237) that while the youthful Hamilton (while still Lord Clydesdale) had come to be on friendly terms with Albrecht he had never met Hess before he landed in Scotland, not even on such social occasions as might have occurred during the 1936 Olympic Games in Berlin.

Some documentary evidence should be mentioned with regard to the actual or illusory motivation of Hess's flight by Albrecht's assessment of the mood in Britain (or rather in the social circles he consorted with). He may have had hopes, but he certainly did not have many illusions. In the January issue of *Zeitschrift für Geopolitik* (his father's journal) he wrote (p. 43):

> . . . the whole of English history would have to be rewritten if one were to believe that British rearmament these days is bluff or that the Anglo-Saxon world is prepared to be bluffed for ever.

Soon after the Sudeten crisis Albrecht gives in the same journal a veiled hint about treaties taken for 'scraps of paper', alluding to Hitler without mentioning him and observing that 'Chamberlain seems to be cured of his Munich illusions'; and there is nothing at all veiled in yet another piece published in the *Zeitschrift für Geopolitik* in the June 1939 issue (p. 445):

> . . . For London, Paris, Washington and Moscow to secure the peace now means: not another step on the road that led to Munich, likely to satisfy further desires on the part of Germany, Italy, and Japan.

Albrecht was born in 1903, matriculated at the unusually early age of seventeen and got his doctorate (summa cum laude) at the even more remarkably early age of nineteen. He wrote much esoteric poetry and some historical verse dramas, frequently with highly topical allusions such as this one in *Sulla* (1939):

> . . . The statesman is victorious when his armies no longer need to win in battle. A long war, even if one wins it, means defeat because one needs a lifetime to rebuild what had so quickly been destroyed.

One of Albrecht's pupils and friends, Dr Walter Stubbe, relates a significant incident on 22 August 1939, the day on which the Soviet-German 'friendship pact' had been announced (*Vierteljahrshefte für Zeitgeschichte*, 1960, 3). Entering the room in which Albrecht was alone with a few trusted friends Stubbe heard him say:

> Now they've made a friendship pact, and in four weeks at the latest we'll be at war. Then the crazy man, in the first intoxication of victory, will overrun the West, and then even Alfred Rosenberg will get his bellyful in the conquered East, and in the end we shall have the destruction of Europe.

On 8 September 1940 Albrecht was sent for by Hess and talked to him alone for two hours, candidly explaining that 'in the Anglo-Saxon world Hitler is considered Satan's own deputy on earth who will have to be fought tooth and nail. The English would rather hand over their Empire to the Americans than sign a peace leaving Hitler the master of Europe.'

Hess then asked why the British, having 'a special relationship' with the Americans, couldn't be persuaded to have a similar relationship with Germany. Albrecht (according to his own notes of the discussion) answered that Roosevelt 'represents an ideology which the Englishman understands; certainly Churchill does, being himself half-American. But Hitler appears to the British as the incarnation of all they hate and have opposed for centuries: and that applies to the British working class no less than to the plutocrats, who if anything (knowing how much they have to lose) might be a little less reluctant to talk peace than the middle and lower classes.'

Asked then about possibly suitable middlemen, Albrecht mentioned Samuel Hoare whom he didn't claim to know very well; better might be Lord Lothian with whom he had had good contacts for years, and 'a final possibility might be the young Duke of Hamilton who has contact with all who matter, including Churchill and the King.'

A week or two later, on 19 September 1940, Albrecht wrote a long letter to 'sehr verehrter lieber Herr Hess.' In it he analysed the technicalities of conveying (through a mutual lady acquaintance) a letter to Hamilton which, without compromising him, would suggest the possibility of a meeting in Lisbon. The note would be quite brief, signed 'A' and impress on the Duke that there was something more serious behind this than a mere personal whim. In this very long-winded letter Albrecht added that 'like so many Englishmen Hamilton is a very reticent man tending to be standoffish before strangers.' This letter was, in fact, written and despatched, but unlike the letter quoted on p. 87 it never reached Hamilton.

At a time when Hess was far advanced in the preparations for his flight, near the end of April 1941, Hess sent Albrecht to Geneva to meet Dr Burckhardt, the Swiss diplomat who had represented the League of Nations at Danzig all through the uneasy period before the war. He had just returned from a visit to London, and Albrecht proudly quotes his Swiss friend's message: 'Ich bringe Ihnen Grüsse von Ihren englischen Freunden' (Regards from your English friends). But apart from conveying such personal pleasantries the Swiss diplomat was even more pessimistic than his German visitor with regard to a realistic chance of peace talks between Britain and Hitler's Reich.

Less than two weeks later Hess was airborne en route to Scotland; and on 12 May, two days after the flight, Albrecht Haushofer was among those arrested. It happened to be the very day on which a clandestine meeting with Sir Samuel Hoare in Madrid had been arranged and confirmed by mutual friends. Albrecht was to be kept in custody for eight weeks, but immediately after his arrest he was flown to Berchtesgaden and taken to the Obersalzberg where, after his first examination, he wrote a long memorandum requested by Hitler, headed 'English connections and the possibilities of using them.'

In this long piece he reported previous efforts such as the meeting with Carl Burckhardt in Geneva and his attempts to contact Hamilton with a view to a meeting in Lisbon. He dropped a good many names of prominent persons he was more or less well acquainted with, such as Dunglass (later Alec Douglas-Home), Lord Eustace Percy, Lord Derby, Oliver Stanley, Lord Astor, Sam Hoare and even R. A. Butler ('who, despite public utterances to the contrary, is really no adherent of Churchill and Eden.').

The memo ended on the pessimistic note that, the more Churchill fell under the influence of Roosevelt, the less possible it would be 'to talk sense to the British.' After all, he stressed, 'the masses of the British people consider the showdown with Hitlerism as a sort of religious war, being quite fanatical about it.'

After dictating his memo (on a *Führer-Maschine*, a typewriter with the outsize lettering Hitler could read without glasses) Albrecht was taken back to Berlin and held in the Gestapo prison in Prinz Albrecht Strasse for eight weeks: he was then released and allowed to resume his professorship.

As for his contacts with members of the resistance, foremost were Beck, Schulenburg, Popitz, Jessen and Planck. He happened to be in Popitz's study when the news of the attempt on Hitler's life on 20 July came through. Popitz, of course, was arrested a day or two later and subsequently hanged.

Albrecht escaped from Berlin on 20 July, the Gestapo being in search of him. He was kept in hiding by loyal friends in the Bavarian mountains while his father, his brother Heinz and one of his nephews were arrested. Early in December the Gestapo found him in a haystack and took him back to the Moabit prison in Berlin. On the night of 23 April 1945 he and fourteen others who had shared his captivity were taken out of their cells and shot near the prison without trial.

APPENDIX 3

LORD BEAVERBROOK'S INTERVIEW WITH HESS

WE ARE grateful to Dr A. J. P. Taylor for permission to consult the verbatim record of Lord Beaverbrook's interview with Hess on 9 September 1941 (which at the time we saw it was still a classified document under the thirty year rule), and to quote from it as well as from the document which Hess gave Beaverbrook, the contents of which they discussed during the meeting. In this record, Lord Beaverbrook was referred to as Dr Livingstone, and Hess simply as Jonathan. The whole interchange was extremely friendly and informal, almost a light-hearted gossip about world affairs.

After an introductory gambit, in which Beaverbrook congratulated Hess on his English, they expressed mutual regret that their countries were at war. Beaverbrook explained how he had become a member of the new Government in May 1940, first of all to develop aircraft manufacture, and later guns and ammunition. 'Now, what do you think of that', he said to Hess, 'Extraordinary change in a man's life, who begins by being a newspaper-man and ends up by making bullets.'

Hess complained no one was allowed to visit him, not even the Duke of Hamilton – 'the only man who is, so to speak, a friend of mine, even though I don't know him very well.'* Beaverbrook promised to 'have a word' with the Duke about this. Beaverbrook, talking with great zest, described how he had flown from Scotland to Newfoundland for a conference. Hess complained he had known nothing of what was happening – he had been kept for five weeks without newspapers or radio: 'It has been a terrible time for me, you know. Coming here from Germany as a German Minister and not to hear the news of the world.' However, he now had *The Times* every day and a radio receiver. In reply to enquiries, he assured Beaverbrook that the food he was getting was satisfactory. Then the conversation continued:

* Hess's acquaintance with the Duke was even more limited than Hess implies here. Commenting on Hess's statement, the Duke told us that he met Hess only on three occasions in Britain—once alone on 11 May 1941 (when he did not know beforehand who it was he would be interviewing), and twice subsequently when he accompanied Kirkpatrick on his visits to Hess. He had not met him in Germany.

237

> *J.*   It is very, very dangerous to play what England plays with Bolshevism . . .
>
> *Dr L.* I can't myself tell why the Germans attacked Russia. I can't see why.
>
> *J.*   Because we knew that one day the Russians will attack us. . . . It will be good not only for Germany and the whole of Europe. It will be good for England too if Russia will be defeated.

Later on they discussed the tonic effects of the air-raids on national morale:

> *Dr L.* The English have done pretty well. The war hasn't done them a great deal of harm.
>
> *J.*   No.
>
> *Dr L.* It's hardened them and we're all greatly strengthened . . .
>
> *J.*   Yes. Yes. But I can say the same about the German people.

As for the outcome of the war, Hess revealed grave pessimism. He was sure, he said, that even if Russia were beaten, she was so large that she would in the end recover her strength and emerge even more powerful than before.

Hess next produced his 4,000 word memorandum, which Beaverbrook glanced through as they talked. It was headed 'Germany–England from the viewpoint of War against the USSR.' The following is a summary of this memorandum, which Beaverbrook took away with him:

> Hess starts with the question, *What is England's war aim*? Eliminating the answer 'A Super-Versailles' as impracticable, he deals with the alternative, a *'reasonable' peace on the basis of an English victory*, explaining that Germany wishes a 'reasonable' peace and is prepared to conclude it 'without victory over England, i.e. on the basis of an understanding with England'. He adds that in trying to win Britain would have to make gigantic sacrifices and 'run the enormous risks that the sacrifices may be in vain, for it is not certain that England can eventually win'.
>
> He then comes to his second point. *I am convinced now as before of the victory of the Axis and their partners* and devotes seven closely typed foolscap pages to attempting to prove his point.
>
> He thinks that 'war against the Bolsheviks cannot at all bring a decision against the Allies' and that even if the Russians did not suffer an early decisive defeat Germany's military position was

infinitely stronger than in the first war, partly because there was not really a Western front and partly because of the very much safer position with regard to food and vital raw materials, particularly oil. On morale he says: '. . . it will hardly be doubted that the spirit of the troops is magnificent. The elements which in the world war eventually weakened the spirit of the German troops—the disruptive influences from home infected with Marxist-communism and hunger at home—are missing today.' He adds that 'the length of the lines of communication is hardly a problem,' and concludes that *'whether an Eastern front persists or not, Germany and her Allies are in the position to carry on the war until England collapses through lack of tonnage.'*

He then elaborates on the ever-growing power of the German submarine and airforce and its inevitably devastating effect on British tonnage, to say nothing of the destruction wrought by the Luftwaffe, with its ever-growing bombing raids on Britain. Reverting to morale he says that 'the tenacity of the German people in endurance is certainly no less than that of the English', and he adds that 'Versailles and its consequences have remained ineradicable in [German] memories . . . and since the war against the Bolsheviks the German population recognizes for certain that a defeat would bring with it into Germany all the horrible machinations of the Bolshevik horde. This prospect has uplifted the spirit of the resistance to the highest plane.'

The third part of this memorandum is headed, *Let us assume, nevertheless, that England actually can win.* His conclusion is that the real victor would be the USSR, and 'a Bolshevik victory would sooner or later mean their advance on Germany and the rest of Europe. England would be as incapable of hindering it as any other nation.' He then stresses the enormous resources of the USSR in manpower and materials, both large enough to offset even the gigantic losses inflicted by the Wehrmacht, and he concludes: '. . . should England's hopes of a German weakening be realized, the Soviet State, after the expansion of its armament capacity, would be the strongest military power in the world. Only a strong Germany as counter-balance, supported by all Europe and in trustful relationship with England, could hinder this. I believe that Germany, destined by fate, was compelled at a given moment to draw aside the curtain covering the secret of the Bolshevik army so that revelation of the danger might even yet make possible the defence of the civilised world.' The alternative he considers disastrous for all Europe, not least Britain. '. . . Consider what competition a fully industrialized Soviet Russia with her low wages and her wealth in earthly treasure would present to world markets in the future. Lack of markets means hunger for Europe, above all for England.

He then expresses his doubts that 'even English labour would be completely immune from Bolshevistic influences if the war lasts much longer and need and want have been imposed on them' (He means privations).

He then comes to his final part IV, *Under what conditions is Germany ready to conclude peace*? 'The only important condition, apart from the return of her colonies, is a genuine understanding between the Axis and Great Britain which would eliminate all causes of friction'. . . . 'England to refrain from interference in the affairs of the European continent, the Axis for their part to regard the British Empire as the sphere of interest of Great Britain alone. They to renounce all interference in her affairs.' He adds that these conditions 'are known to me through innumerable conversations with the Führer and often emphasized by him. They have remained the same since the outbreak of the war.'

He ends by repeating that 'in all circumstances the relations between Germany and England should be placed on a new basis of trust' and concludes: 'England might ask herself whether it pays her, at great sacrifice, to make the most precarious effort to conquer the Axis and, into the bargain, to strengthen with certainty Bolshevik Russia as an immensely more dangerous opponent to her Empire.'

The serious intent of this memorandum was offset by the comparative light-heartedness of the conversation with Beaverbrook, who joked about the fact that he was always made a Minister in time of war. He reminded Hess that he was Minister of Information and Propaganda during the First World War. Hess replied:

Yes, yes. I know it. (Laughs). We in Germany, we have learned very much of your propaganda of the last war. You must confess it.

Hess, trying now and then to keep the conversation serious, emphasized the point made in his memorandum that Britain's life line was being threatened by the actions of Germany's submarines. But Beaverbrook would not be inveigled into discussing such things – he preferred to discuss generalities, such as Hess's previous war record – and he asked simple questions about Hitler's policy in widening his front in the East, with campaigns in Yugoslavia, in Greece and Crete, where, he said, the Germans had fought with great shrewdness. They discussed the great value of the American Fortress bombers, in one of which Beaverbrook was to fly to Russia. Hess tried again to impress on Beaverbrook the danger of Britain and Germany weakening each other with bombing attacks. But Beaverbrook reminisced about his visits to Germany before the war:

Dr L. I used to go to Germany quite often before Hitler came to power and I was in Berlin the day of Hitler's election. Of course you may know, my newspapers always gave him a good hearing. . . .

J. (Laughs). Oh, I know he likes you very much. He is very sorry we must fight one against the other, very sorry.

Dr L. The whole thing is bloody.

J. Yes, the whole thing is bloody, but we can use our blood for better things; you can use your blood in your Colonies and for your Empire, and we can use our blood for the East. We need ground for our population. . . . I thought I can come here and find here a certain common sense. (Laughs) But I have been wrong, I know it.

Dr L. Very difficult you know, to find commonsense when war is on.

They went on to discuss the difficulties in stopping a war once it is started, and the conversation ended once again with Hess stating his conviction that Russia was innately strong, and that it would need all the forces of Europe and the British Empire to withstand the pressures of Bolshevism. The interview ended with a joke that, in spite of all that Hess had said, Beaverbrook was soon to leave for Moscow. He also promised to visit Hess again, which in point of fact he was never to do.

APPENDIX 4

THE SIGNIFICANCE OF HESS'S
LETTERS WRITTEN IN CAPTIVITY

OUR quotations throughout this book from letters written by Hess to his family from captivity in the UK, and later during the year or two at Nuremberg and the decades spent at Spandau, require some supplementation since there can be no doubt about the importance of the letters in assessing Hess's true state of mind.

In addition to the three volumes of published letters* we have read unpublished ones too up to 1970. The vast majority of them provide unquestionable evidence of the writer's sanity. In these hundreds of letters he appears as a devoted and affectionate family man with a considerable knowledge of and interest in music and literature as well as in various aspects of science and technology; moreover, he reveals an indomitable sense of humour, albeit of a somewhat quaint kind and often as 'old fashioned' and ponderous as his style of writing.

As for the son he refused to see for nearly thirty years, Hess took a lively interest in Wolf Rüdiger's education and progress from infancy through boyhood and adolescence right through university and his subsequent career as a civil engineer; and he sent him the sort of letters any intelligent and affectionate father would write to a small boy eager to become an engine driver (see p. 169) or, when congratulating him on his fifteenth birthday, reminding him that 'swotting up' is not the most commendable kind of diligence and that what matters is to do the job one wants to do as best one can, and for its own sake rather than to impress others. A few years earlier when the boy was not yet ten Hess wrote to his wife:

> ... Only one thing I would wish for my son: I want him to be 'obsessed' by something; never mind if it is the design of an engine, a notion of medical progress or an idea for a stage play; and never mind even if no one will build the engine, no one will stage the play,

* See Bibliography. The published letters have had relatively restricted circulation and attention, confined almost entirely to Germany. A small selection was published in London in 1954 under the title *Prisoner of Peace*.

and all the pundits in the medical profession consider the notion ludicrous. . . .

In August 1949, from Spandau, he writes to the boy:

> . . . Glad to hear about your prowess at football, but you'll realize before long, dear boy, that what matters is to supplement 'footwork' by brainwork, using your head not only for 'heading' the ball. I am pleased about your decision to do 'prep' more regularly. What matters is to stick to what you have considered to be right. A man's best victories are those gained in conquering one's own weakness. That's something to be proud of.

In December 1953 he sends his son a long letter about religion, explaining that it is easy enough to feel relatively happy and secure within this or that church, but that there is such a thing as being just *gottgläubig*,* which is as far from the orthodox churchman as from the atheist. He suggests the boy should read Goethe's famous letter answering a friend of his youth, the Countess Stollberg when (at a very advanced age) she tried to convert him to 'proper' Christianity; and he concludes:

> . . . But let me assure you of this, my dear boy: should you at any time come to the sincere conclusion that you wish to be a 'proper' Protestant, Catholic, Buddhist, Moslem or what have you, I wouldn't in the least try to stop you; even long before you are 'of age' . . . and whatever your own opinion or faith, do respect other people's sincere faith and never hurt them by scorn or irony; and whenever you happen to pass a church no matter of what persuasion and you hear lovely music coming out of it, go in and feel nearer to whoever your own God may be.

In 1962, the year his son graduated at the University and started his career as an engineer, Hess showed particular interest in what he thought might interest the young man; and having just read Caesar's *De Bello Gallico* in a new German translation he went on at considerable length and technical detail about the astonishing engineering feat of a 1,200-foot bridge over the Rhine built by the Romans in ten days.

Since he spent most of the day reading and listening to gramophone

---

* This is very much Nazi terminology, a term favoured by Himmler and others who wished to emphasize that their schism from the established Church did not impair their faith in what Hitler liked to call the 'Almighty' or 'Providence'. *Gottgläubig* came to be the official term entered in forms, biographical notes, obituaries and the like in place of 'religion'.

records many of his letters report on his fairly substantial and varied collection of books and records. In April 1950 he writes:

> . . . Easter was celebrated by new records brought in by the chaplain. Some Bach and a lovely Mozart piano concerto as well as Schubert's Trout Quintet—Enchanting! Beautiful music seems to me always like God himself speaking to men. . . .

Nearly ten years later, just after Christmas 1959, he admits to having been disappointed by Bach's Christmas oratorio and continues revealing significant 'progress' in his attitude to modern art:

> . . . I had much pleasure in looking through a volume of very good reproductions of French Impressionists, those in the Louvre at any rate, particularly Renoir, Degas, Cézanne. When I was much younger they were attacked for being too 'advanced', and I wonder whether in due time I might find abstract art equally comprehensible. I can hardly imagine it, though.

His favourite reading most of the time was history (particularly Ranke and Mommsen) and technology, and his favourite philosopher Schopenhauer. While in England he improved his English sufficiently to read Lloyd George's, Churchill's and Grey's memoirs, also Jellicoe's —'a book I had often meant to obtain back home to supplement my own books on the battle of Jutland.' He also read *Ivanhoe*, which interested him because of the location.

In February 1965, having read some of the literature on Napoleon at St Helena, he ruminates about Hudson Lowe—'after all, the prison governor'—and how he actually apologized when calling on his prisoner unannounced. No doubt he was thinking of his own 'prison governors', four of them, and he then goes on to wonder why Napoleon, despite his generous surroundings, 'developed real prison psychosis, and was unable to shake off persecution mania and the suspicion that Lowe had been sent out by the British to stab or poison him.' An interesting point when considering Hess's own occasional persecution mania, real as well as bogus, and suspicions that his food had been tampered with.

Very significant too are occasional passages indicating what Schirach called his 'deliberate oysterization'; it was this tendency to develop a 'shell' around him that made him forbid his wife's and son's visits for more than two decades. On Christmas eve 1965 he writes to them:

> . . . The bells start chiming outside. I can see your candles flickering,

and the glowing sprig exudes the smell of Christmas; and yet, there is no festive atmosphere. It is astonishing how firmly my mind is encased in its armoury; and a good thing too! Otherwise such an evening would be unbearable.

And on another wintry day, with Spandau covered by a blanket of snow, he writes:

. . . How I used to delight in fresh snow! But now it doesn't impress me a bit . . . Maybe I don't *want* to see it because I don't *want* anything beautiful to impress me. The horny skin round my soul gets thicker from year to year. Only he who has lost freedom knows what freedom means.

Looking through this massive bulk of correspondence for significant pointers to the man's character and state of mind there can be no doubt that he did not appreciably change his adherence to Nazi ideology and certainly not his admiration of Hitler. On 18 June 1945 (while still in England and writing his first letter after Hitler's death and the Nazi surrender) he has this to say to his wife:

. . . Supplementing the routine letter for all of you I want to add a few lines for you alone, even though, with regard to censorship, I cannot write all I would like to say.

You can imagine how often in the last few weeks and months my thoughts strayed back to the past—that quarter of a century of history which for us is linked with one name and also with sublime human adventure. The historical part is not finished, and the threads which now seem severed will be taken up again one day with the inexorable logic of history.

Few, though, have been favoured as much as the two of us by having a share in the growth of a unique personality from the very beginning; a share too in joy and suffering, in worries and hopes, in hate and love, in the expression of human greatness as well as in signs of human weakness, all of which combines to make a person wholly lovable. That's why my thoughts are much with you whenever I think of him. . . .

And he concludes with a Nietzsche quotation:

I love all those who are like heavy drops, singly falling out of the dark cloud that hangs over mankind. They proclaim lightning and as proclaimers they perish.

But what has been paramount in Hess's mind throughout his imprisonment has been what he has repeatedly called 'the flight of my life'; all the time he has been very conscious and, indeed, proud of that central event of his life, not only with regard to what he considered his 'mission', but also with regard to the aeronautical achievement; after all, he was a frustrated airman all his life, frustrated in both wars and in his ambition to emulate Lindbergh in the early 1920s. Albrecht Haushofer, in one of his more cynical moods, aptly called him 'a motorised Parsifal'. From the ample documentary evidence available, it will suffice to quote one letter which, just over a year after the flight (20 May 1942), he sent the elder Haushofer; it was a birthday letter, and while he used the familiar 'Thou' he addresses the Professor as, 'Much respected and dear friend'.

> . . . Well, it cannot be denied that I crashed, but it can't be denied either that I was in the pilot's seat. That way I have nothing to reproach myself for; anyway I *was* in the driver's seat! You know as well as I do that the compass that guides us is influenced by forces which are adamant even if we do not know them. I do hope they will be friendly to you in the forthcoming year of your life.

For about six months late in 1969 and early in 1970 Hess was under treatment in the military hospital of the British sector in Berlin. After his return to Spandau many of the letters reveal the writer's considerable interest in both the Russian and American space flights, and he obtained a good deal of literature on the subject, particularly the technical aspects. But two of the 1970 letters are not without some personal significance. One is addressed to his wife's sister, congratulating her on her seventieth brithday. It starts with the suggestion that someone ought to invent a sort of alarm clock reminding people of birthdays and other anniversaries, and he continues to elaborate this at great length, considerable technical detail, and with that peculiar and somewhat whimsical sense of humour so typical of his style of writing.

The other letter is more interesting; it is addressed to his son and, initially, deals with some new books on Wallenstein, Duke of Friedland, one of the most controversial generals of the Thirty Years' War. Hess, at that period, was particularly interested in the subject, presumably on account of the Duke's fame as an astrologer no less than as a soldier and statesman. Hess thanks his son for the books and notes that before despatching them he could not find the time to read them; he adds that while such omission is regrettable, the reason—professional preoccupation—is very pleasing, and he continues at great length and in considerable technical detail to outline some lucid ideas of his own on his son's professional interest in modern airport-design.

Certainly the voluminous evidence of hundreds of letters over a period of three decades disproves any suggestion that the writer was suffering from schizophrenia or any other form of insanity.

INDEX

249